Behavioural Treatment of Problem Children

A PRACTICE MANUAL

Martin Herbert

School of Social Work,
University of Leicester, England

1981

ACADEMIC PRESS   London   Toronto   Sydney

GRUNE & STRATTON   New York   San Francisco

ACADEMIC PRESS INC. (LONDON) LTD.
24/28 Oval Road,
London NW1

United States Edition published by
GRUNE & STRATTON INC.
111 Fifth Avenue
New York,New York 10003

British Library Cataloguing in Publication Data

Herbert, Martin
  Behavioural treatment of problem children.
  1. Problem children   2. Behaviour therapy
  I. Title
  618.92′89142   RJ506.P63   80-41966

  ISBN (Academic Press) 0-12-791971-6
  ISBN (Academic Press) 0-12-791973-2 Pbk

  ISBN (Grune & Stratton) 0-8089-1367-0
  ISBN (Grune & Stratton) 0-8089-1375-1 Pbk

Filmset by Asco Trade Typesetting Ltd., Hong Kong,
and printed and bound in Great Britain by William Clowes
(Beccles) Limited, Beccles and London

Preface

The manual is a practical guide to the behavioural assessment and treatment of emotional and conduct problems of childhood. And it is a guide only! The style of manual writing may well convey an unintended impression of dogmatic inflexibility. There is no one way of carrying out assessments and behavioural programmes. There is nothing preordained about the ordering of the steps suggested.

The practice ideas in this manual are based upon theoretical and conceptual themes developed in more detail (and taking due account of the evidence) in two books by the author: *Emotional Problems of Development in Children* and *Conduct Disorders of Childhood and Adolescence: A Behavioural Approach to Assessment and Treatment*. A problem-solving model informs many of the ideas to be found in the following pages; this is in keeping with my basic attitude to most problems of childhood. Senn (1959) expresses it more succinctly than I can:

> The problem child is invariably trying to solve a problem rather than be one. His methods are crude and his conception of his problem may be faulty, but until the physician has patiently sought, and in a sympathetic fashion found, what the child was trying to do ... he is in no position to offer advice.

The text is written with various student and professional groups in mind: psychologists, psychiatrists, probation officers, social workers, teachers and school counsellors. It is also intended for care and teaching staff in residential establishments such as community homes, assessment centres and schools for the maladjusted. Although there is a bias (for reasons that are given) towards work in the natural environment of the child, the manual should prove helpful to the clinic-based therapist.

The reader will soon perceive that I run into difficulties over two issues of terminology or semantics. The first involves the question: who is being helped? Patient or client? Children have been referred to the Child Treatment Research Unit, University of Leicester, as 'patients' by doctors and as 'clients' by social workers and others. I prefer the theoretically more neutral term 'client' but sometimes slip into using the term 'patient'. More serious is my unresolved conflict over the choice of gender terms. I have favoured (if that is an appropriate description as we are talking about problem children) the literary device of using the masculine pronoun 'he' rather than 'she' in most cases; and I have generally avoided the rather clumsy repetition of 'he or she', or 'boy/girl'. This choice was made simply as a literary device and not because boys are labelled as problematic far more frequently than girls; and certainly not out of any sexist sentiment! I have been very concerned (see Herbert, 1980) to counter some of the facile matricentric accounts of child-rearing, and the reflex tendency of society to blame the mother—to the exclusion of the father and indeed the child—for her youngster's behaviour problem. So I would regret very much if an insensitive bias in expression in this text adds in any way to this burden.

Given the constraints of being concise and practical I have attempted to provide only the briefest account of the basic assumptions about children's problems and the theories that inform the practice of behaviour modification (and therapy). The emphasis is very much on the 'nuts and bolts' of assessment and of designing and implementing treatment programmes for children. Illustrations of the methods in practice are provided in brief case analyses. A manual can only give a *general* set of guidelines; specific problems (such as bowel or bladder incontinence, school refusal and the like) require specific refinements and elaborations of the *basic* approach.

The book is organized into five sections which follow the stages of a problem-solving exercise. After all, as was suggested, the child is usually trying to solve a problem, and so are parents and teachers in trying to cope with the ensuing crisis. Our task then is to use problem-solving methods to identify the areas of difficulty (and they are not always necessarily his alone), and to find practical solutions to them.

The first section examines the basic assumptions underlying the concept of 'problem behaviour' in childhood, and goes on to list the major implications of a behavioural approach to such problems.

The second section is concerned with the initial screening (Steps 1 to 6) and the early definition and specification of the particular problem/s in the individual case.

The third section (Steps 7 to 15) deals with the collection of data and information which will allow you to help the clients (with their active participation) to solve a child's (or, indeed, it may really be the family's) problems. It contains an extended consideration of the factors which influence the therapist's decision to intervene—extended because it can be such a complex technical *and* ethical issue. This section is also concerned with the formulation of hypotheses to explain the clients' predicament and the planning of strategies to undo the harm and misery being generated in the child and/or his family.

The fourth section is concerned with the choice of alternative procedures, the theories of human behaviour and learning that lie behind them, and how to put them into effect.

The fifth section (Steps 16 to 20) deals with the therapeutic intervention and the evaluation and verification of the choices made (i.e. the testing of the clinical hypotheses upon which the programme is based). This section also explains how to fade out and terminate the problem solving exercise.

The manual should be used in conjunction with further reading. The reader who wishes to look at the specialized literature should refer to the bibliographies in Bandura, 1977; Gambrill, 1977; Graziano *et al.*, 1979; Herbert, 1978; Kazdin, 1980; McAuley and McAuley, 1980; O'Leary and O'Leary, 1972; Rose, 1972; Turner, 1973; Van Hasselt *et al.*, 1978. Appendix III provides a brief introduction to basic learning principles, and to further reading on the subject. It might provide a logical starting point for the student with limited knowledge of learning principles.

Those who are not experienced in behaviour modification or in working with children in distress should only carry out therapeutic work in this field with the guidance of an experienced supervisor or consultant. The manual is intended to act as a guide to those who are experienced in behaviour modification, but who have not focused particularly on work with children. It is also designed as a training manual for personnel in the helping professions and students on clinical and educational courses, who are taking special option courses in the area of behaviour therapy and behaviour modification.

December 1980   Martin Herbert

Acknowledgements

It is impossible to acknowledge by name all those to whom I am indebted for ideas, research findings and case material which appear in this manual.

However I would like to express my appreciation to colleagues and students at the Child Treatment Research Unit for their support and stimulating influence. I am particularly indebted to Anndrea Reavill, Brenda Froggatt and Mary Harris for their help in the production of the text. I also owe a special debt to Joanna Reid for the skill and imagination she brought to me.

Contents

SECTION 1
Basic Assumptions

A consistent theoretical framework is necessary in order to set about altering children's problematic behaviour. Such consistency demands a clear conceptualization of what constitutes a psychological problem and how it comes about. This is no easy task.

In this manual it is assumed that:

1. Childhood behaviour problems, by and large, are exaggerations, deficits, or handicapping combinations of behaviours common to all children.

After all, we are talking about phenomena such as aggression, disobedience, fear, depression, school refusal, shyness, stealing. The evidence suggests that there is no absolute distinction between the attributes of those who come to be labelled 'problem children' and other unselected children. Most problematic conditions differ quantitatively from the normal in terms of severity and of accompanying impairment—the sort of difference there is between an assertive youngster and a bully. Minor variations of behavioural problems can be identified in most essentially 'well-adjusted' children. A majority of children have tantrums (to take an example) at one time or another. Some, however, display incessant and extreme explosions of temper. In other words normality and abnormality are viewed as the extremes of a continuum; normality merges almost imperceptibly into abnormality so that any child may be more or less problematic—but only with regard to particular characteristics. He is *not* all problem. It's a matter of degree!

But if it is a matter of degree, who draws the line?

2. The criteria are social ones and therefore relative.

The word 'norm' means a standard—in the Latin from which it derives. To be abnormal implies (the prefix 'ab' means 'away from') a deviation from a standard. People, as individuals or as members of groups (families, neighbourhoods, religious communities, societies), make the rules and set the standards of behaviour. For this reason, the therapist must beware of his personal and social biases, not to mention prejudices in making judgements.

3. Not only is problematic (abnormal) behaviour in children on a continuum with non-problematic (normal) behaviour, but it does not differ, by and large, from normal behaviour in its development, its persistence, and the way in which it can be modified.

It is hypothesized that a major proportion of a child's behaviour is learned, maintained, and regulated by its effects upon the natural environment and the feedback it receives with regard to these consequences. Behaviour does not occur in a vacuum. It is a result of a complex transaction between the individual, with his inborn strengths and weaknesses, acting and reacting with an environment which sometimes encourages and sometimes discourages his actions.

The theoretical position adopted in this manual, while not underestimating the contribution of biological determining factors, is summarized in the proposition that many behaviour problems are the consequences of failures of learning. The laws of learning which apply to the acquisition and changing of normal socially approved behaviour are assumed to be relevant to the understanding of socially disapproved (problem) actions.

4. *A social learning approach is particularly relevant.*

Learning occurs within a social nexus: rewards, punishments and other events are mediated by human agents and within attachment and social systems, and are not simply the impersonal consequences of behaviour. Unfortunately—and it is the case with all forms of learning—the very processes which help the child adjust to life can, under certain circumstances, contribute to maladjustment. An immature child who learns by imitating an adult is not necessarily to comprehend when it is undesirable (deviant) behaviour that is being modelled. The youngster who learns (adaptively) on the basis of classical and instrumental conditioning processes to avoid dangerous situations can also learn in the same way (maladaptively) to avoid school or social gatherings. A mother may unwittingly reinforce immature behaviour by attending to it.

5. *The behavioural approach has crucial implications not only for the way in which the therapist works, but also where he works. It affects the manner in which he listens to the caregiver's complaints about her child's behaviour, and the methods by which he later explores the specific details of the problems.*

If it is accepted that problematic behaviours of childhood are acquired, largely as a function of faulty learning processes, then there is a case for arguing that problems can most effectively be modified where they occur, by changing the 'social lessons' the child receives and the reinforcing contingencies supplied by the social agents. The so-called 'triadic model' or 'triadic approach' recognizes the profound influence that parents and other significant caregivers have on children's development and mental health, an influence far greater than that which any professional could exert even with extensive and intensive intervention. Several lines of reasoning converge to reinforce the logic of the triadic approach of involving parents (and others in the natural environment) in the work with psychological problems of childhood. First, prevention is better than cure! As parents and teachers exert a significant formative influence during the impressionable years of early childhood, they are usually in a strong position to enhance satisfactory adjustment and moderate the genesis of behaviour problems. Secondly, they are on hand and therefore in a good position to extend the beneficial changes (brought about in therapy) over time, and to generalize them across various life-situations.

6. The triadic approach gets around the problem of generalizing change from clinic-based sessions to the child's real world.

This is by way of emphasizing the last point. Home-based therapy is geared to the only people—parents and teachers or substitute caregivers—who can intervene often enough and long enough to produce the long-term changes in what are often (especially in the case of the more serious problems of childhood) matters of faulty socialization. After all the parents are 'on the spot' most of the time to initiate and consolidate social learning experiences.

7. All this presupposes a cooperative working alliance between the parent and the helping professional, both of whom are interested in the welfare of the child.

8. The assumptions (mentioned above) about behaviour development lead inexorably to the proposition that maladaptive behaviour can most effectively be changed by the therapeutic application of principles of learning.

Inappropriate behaviour that has been learned can be unlearned or modified directly (often in relatively brief periods of treatment) on the basis of applied learning principles. Behaviour that has not been learned (and where the deficit constitutes a problem) may be acquired by training.

9. To simplify: here are two basic learning tasks that are commonly encountered in child therapy:

(a) the acquisition (i.e. learning) of a desired behaviour in which the individual is deficient (e.g. compliance, self-control, bladder and bowel control, fluent speech, social or academic skills);
(b) the renunciation (i.e. unlearning) of an undesired response in the child's behavioural repertoire (e.g. aggression, temper tantrums, stealing, facial tics, phobic anxiety, compulsive eating) or the exchange of one response for another (e.g. self-assertion in place of tearful withdrawal).

10. Each of these tasks may be served by one or a combination of four major types of learning:

(a) classical conditioning;
(b) operant conditioning;
(c) observational learning; and
(d) cognitive learning.

11. Behaviour modification (or behaviour therapy, as it is often called) provides us with the practice 'know-how' for using these learning (and other psychological) principles for therapeutic (or, some might prefer to say) educative purposes.

12. All parents are informal learning theorists and all are in the business of behaviour modification (i.e. changing behaviour).

They use various techniques to teach, influence and change the child in their care. Among those used are material and psychological rewards, praise and encouragement, giving or withholding love, reproof, corporal and psychological punishment, approval and dis-approval, as well as direct instruction, setting an example and providing explanations of rules.

There are wide variations, in terms of type and extent of parental involvement in therapeutic work in the natural environment, ranging from carrying out simple instruc-tions in contingency management to a full involvement as co-therapists in all aspects of observation, recording, programme planning and implementation. The didactic element might range from basic behavioural theory and practice to the mastery of general learning principles.

13. Behavioural work starts from a clear objective of producing change.

The assessment in which the child and his parents (or teachers) are closely involved attempts to identify precisely what behaviours are to be changed. What can be said about these behaviours—the subject of this manual—is that they bring disadvantage and disablement to a multitude of troubled and troublesome children.

14. Behaviour modification, however, is not only about changing the undesirable behaviour of 'problem children'.

We have already stressed the fact that learning occurs in a social context; the child is interacting with, and learning from, people who have meaning and value for him. He is attached to some, feels antipathetic to others; he may perceive a gesture of affection from the former as 'rewarding', but from the latter as 'aversive'. The child is not simply a passive reactor to events; he initiates actions and tries to make things happen. Not surprisingly, behaviour modification does not concentrate only on the 'unacceptable' behaviour of the child. It is also about altering the behaviour of the persons—parents, teachers and others—who form a significant part of the child's social world.

Here is a crucial source of human variety—the susceptibility of people to many different types of environment. It provides their source of strength and (of course) weakness. The human ability to learn afresh new ways of living or to unlearn self-defeating means of coping with existence makes behaviour modification an exciting venture.

15. Behaviour modification is not simply a matter of conditioning, as some critics seem to think; nor is it a quasi-mechanical exercise in bribery and coercion. The approach is based upon the assumption—in this guide—that cognitive processes are critical in human learning; therapy can (and must) have a 'human face' and be an ethical endeavour.

Certainly, a behavioural approach emphasizes, indeed depends upon, an explicit under-standing by the client of procedures and goals, responsibilities and risks. It is assumed—at the 'micro-level' of teaching new responses and strategies—that learning and con-ditioning in humans is produced most often—perhaps invariably in adults—through the operation of higher mental processes. Awareness on the part of the child is particularly encouraged.

Behaviour modification, like all other therapies, is open to abuse. However, it constitutes a compassionate and moral response to the need for help of children and families in acute distress. The moral and ethical issues will be dealt with in the context of all the decisions which have to be made in the course of doing the assessment and treatment.

It is perhaps a back-handed compliment to the effectiveness of behaviour modification, that its many critics become anxious about the ethics and purposes of this kind of intervention—because they suspect that it really works. Behaviourism is thought to be demeaning because it allegedly fails to get at the 'real' person, ignoring his thoughts, fantasies and feelings—in sum, his experiences. The behavioural analysis is accused of being unfeeling, deterministic and superficial.

Other commentators warn that behaviour modification is downright dangerous because its practitioners are out to 'control' human behaviour. Therapies are not always quite how they are seen by the uninitiated. It is hoped that the treatment philosophy and methods described in this manual will indicate that such warnings and fears are misplaced.

16. *Behaviour modification is a craft; that is to say it is, or should be, a subtle amalgam of art and applied science; as such it requires careful study and apprenticeship—which in turn imply supervised practice experience.*

The latter is not always available. The trouble with a manual as a guide is the author's inability to pre-empt all the essential questions the reader would like answers to, let alone those important supplementaries—points of clarification or elaboration, and those unexpected, unplanned for, exigencies of practice. The manual cannot legislate for those times when one should be flexible in the approach; it cannot indicate when it is appropriate to take 'short cuts' (i.e. to 'concertina' or, indeed, leave out certain steps), or when extra information not mentioned in these pages is required. Certainly, the writing of this manual as a training and practice guide does not imply a slavish conformity to the sequence of work set out in the flow charts, nor an over-inclusive search for every bit of data mentioned. But, most of all, it fails if it leads to some facile and amateurish 'cookbook' application of techniques, or a mechanical insistence on numbers and measurement. The virtues of operationism can turn into quantiphrenia which acts to the detriment of warm empathic interactions with parents and children. The emphasis on rigorous thinking and scientific assessment in this book is not meant to be at the expense of clinical art and sensitivity. 'Scientism', a Pharasaical adherence to the *letter* rather than the *spirit* of scientific method (see Nottcutt, 1953), is to be avoided at all costs.

No manual can replace supervised practice experience. The complexity of behavioural interventions requires intensive study, structured sequential learning experiences and many opportunities for imaginative but informed practical application—with regular guidance and feedback from an expert.

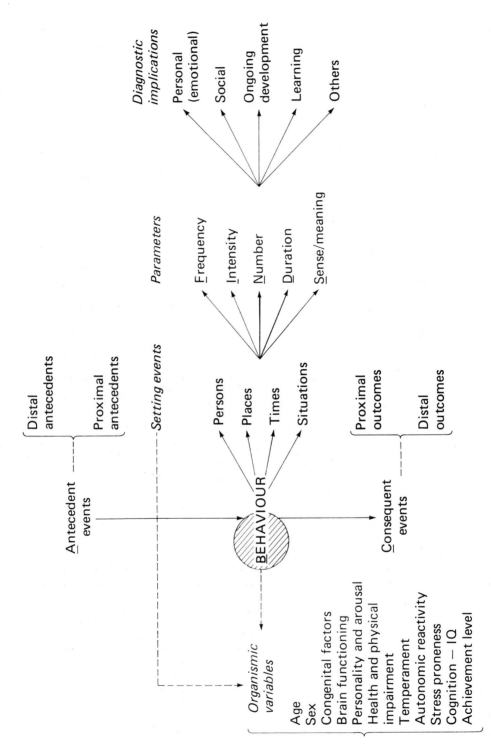

FIG. 1 General assessment guidelines: this provides you with an overview or groundplan to assessment, the first stage being an initial screening of your clients.

SECTION 2

Initial Screening

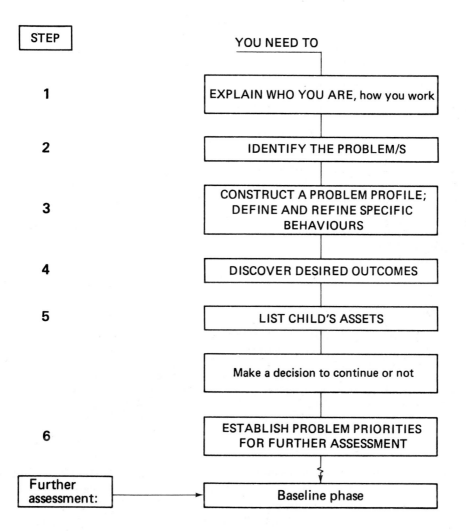

STEP	YOU NEED TO
1	EXPLAIN WHO YOU ARE, how you work
2	IDENTIFY THE PROBLEM/S
3	CONSTRUCT A PROBLEM PROFILE; DEFINE AND REFINE SPECIFIC BEHAVIOURS
4	DISCOVER DESIRED OUTCOMES
5	LIST CHILD'S ASSETS
	Make a decision to continue or not
6	ESTABLISH PROBLEM PRIORITIES FOR FURTHER ASSESSMENT
Further assessment:	Baseline phase

FLOW CHART 1   Assessment steps for the initial screening interviews.

Step 1 EXPLAIN YOURSELF: Who you are and how you work

Without being patronizing, use simple language, i.e. don't use jargon; communicate in plain English.

During the initial interview with (preferably) both parents (or other caregivers), give a brief account (with down-to-earth examples) of the theoretical rationale and practical strategies of behaviour modification; point out how problem behaviour, like normal behaviour, can be acquired through failures or anomalies of learning and how such problems might be alleviated by practical strategies based on theories of learning and development. You will be concentrating on 'common sense' and familiar aspects of child management.

You might find it helpful to provide the parents with a concise explanatory handout. Build up your own store of examples and metaphors in order to illuminate your explanations. Two of the formats for explaining the Child Treatment Research Unit approach and treatment principles (in this case bed-wetting) are to be found in Appendices IV and V.

Emphasize that if (after assessment) a behavioural treatment is felt to be appropriate, then it is likely to involve altering the consequences of the child's problem behaviour. But the child will not be the only focus of attention; family interactions are important and parents should be prepared not only to change their present *responses* to the child's supposedly maladaptive behaviours, but also to initiate new behaviours provided that they are not required to do anything distasteful or contrary to their values as parents.

There is evidence that sharing information with clients reduces the likelihood of their dropping out from treatment. An 'open agenda' and one which prepares the client for change (never a painless process) should pay a dividend in client motivation and cooperation. An accurate perception of what will ensue in the course of treatment can facilitate the therapeutic process.

Step 2 IDENTIFY THE PROBLEM/S Keep asking 'What ...'

Obtain information about all aspects of a child's behaviour which are considered to be problematic by his parents, by any other persons (e.g. teachers), agencies (e.g. medical or educational) or the child himself.

Avoid: For the moment, the more fascinating 'riddle' question, 'Why?', and interpretations and speculations ... at this stage, anyway. Be careful not to focus prematurely on specific problems at the expense of an initially open-ended and reasonably full exploration of the range of difficulties being expressed. It is critical that the first interview is sensitive to what the real problem might be.

Method: It is useful to begin with an open-ended question: 'Tell me in your own words about what is worrying you about X's behaviour? Do take your time.'
Later: 'Are there any other matters you'd like to go into?'

Prepare yourself to spend a fair bit of time on the 'What?' question before attempting the 'How?' or 'Why?' questions.

In order to get a good intellectual grasp of what a child is doing and why, it is necessary to have detailed and specific information (whenever possible, by direct observation) about the child's behaviour in his various life situations. The so-called behavioural assessment method or ecological interview are aids to obtaining the kind of evidence on which painstaking assessment (and thereby sound treatment) is based.

Remember: *Rigorous assessment leads to effective treatment.*

Method: The parent is encouraged to give descriptive examples of the problem, in other words to define what she means in specific and observable terms when she uses a particular label. If the informant says: 'Lorna is very aggressive', ask: 'In what way is she aggressive? Tell me what she says and does that makes you describe her as aggressive.' Also: 'Give me some examples (preferably recent ones) of what happens when she behaves like this.'

Avoid: Inferential language (at this stage) such as 'She is insecure ... has low self-esteem', by sticking to observable behaviour.

The preliminary information about a child's problem often comes from his mother. Parents often report their children's problems in terms of rather global labels such as 'tantrums', 'disobedience', 'rebelliousness' or 'aggressiveness'. These woolly concepts may be used to refer to very different kinds of behaviour by different parents, and, indeed, by the same parent on various occasions.

It is crucial to specify the problem in terms of observable responses which are accessible to other people (e.g. parents) as well as the child; 'public events' such as his striking, pinching or swearing at another person make for a more precise and consistent definition of the problem behaviour than a global statement that she is aggressive or filled with hostility. They can be verified by other observers.

Find out: While specifying what the problems are and what the desired outcomes might be, the steps taken to date to eliminate the former and bring about the latter. What methods have (say) the parents tried, and with what consequences? Such information is important in influencing your own treatment decisions and choices. Have other agencies been consulted? If so, will they give you permission to contact them?

Difficulties and indeed failures in the treatment of children's behaviour problems can frequently be traced back to a lack of precision during the crucial assessment (or diagnostic) phase of a therapeutic contact. The analysis of a problem situation and the planning of a treatment programme probably require more knowledge and skill than any other aspect of the behavioural approach. Sadly, what happens all too often in diagnostic conferences is an unwitting 'distancing' of the problem. This comes about, first of all, because of a tendency to describe the problem in global terms which are too fuzzy or vague to allow for the rigorous formulation of clinical hypotheses which can be put to the test. The serious pitfall of using diagnostic labels is the illusory impression it gives the user of having explained the behaviour. What it usually represents is merely a *renaming* process. Particular 'villains' are words like 'minimal brain damage', 'hyperactivity', 'psychopathy', 'disruptive'.

Avoid: Being trapped into premature 'explanations' or 'prescriptions' by anxious clients. Also avoid letting parents or teachers focus exclusively on what the child *is* and *has* ('he is immoral; he has no conscience'); steer them towards describing what he *does* and *says*.

> ## Step 3a   CONSTRUCT A PROBLEM PROFILE
>
> *Draw up a problem profile to take account of the problems of the child, and in addition those ascribed to others in the family. In this way you will have a record of perceptions of all members of the family.*

You are beginning (in a preliminary way) to find out:

(a) who is complaining about particular problems;

(b) who desires a given outcome;

(c) the level of agreement/disagreement between (for example) parents and child, or parents, as to how they would like things to be different;

(d) the implications of change in the direction of the desired outcome. Who benefits? Does anyone lose? Your overriding concern is that a programme should benefit your client in the short-term *and* the long-term. When your clients are a young child *and* his parents you may have to adopt a role of advocacy on the part of the child. Be on your guard against designing programmes that make life easier for staff (e.g. institutional staff) to the detriment of the client.

Problem profile

Problem as defined	Who complains	Who manifests the problem	Examples of problem	Settings	Desired Outcomes

Having (hopefully) narrowed your focus for a more detailed problem definition, move on to Step 3b.

Remember: You may have to back-track as you collect more information. You may find that you have chosen an inappropriate behaviour (or indeed person/s) on which to concentrate.

Step 3b   DEFINE AND REFINE SPECIFIC TARGET BEHAVIOURS

Begin with the behaviour.

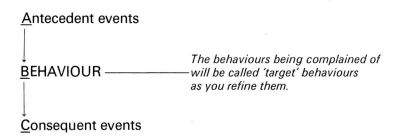

Antecedent events

BEHAVIOUR —————— *The behaviours being complained of will be called 'target' behaviours as you refine them.*

Consequent events

Remember: The key word in this phase of assessment is 'what'. The behaviour therapist asks: 'What is the person doing? Under what conditions are these behaviours emitted?'

You are beginning to teach parents (or teachers) the basic learning equation: the ABC analysis.

The analysis is functional in that it provides a description of the elements of a situation and their interrelationships. Thus diverse attributes (for example, actions such as hitting, kicking, pinching, swearing) would be considered to be members of the same response class ('aggression') because it could be shown that they enter into the same functional relationships: antecedent, concurrent and consequent stimulus conditions. Speaking more figuratively:

(a) The child is not simply a 'small volcano' erupting with 'bad' behaviour at the most inconvenient times. In other words, the 'problem' (in this case, aggression) does not reside within him like some figurative equivalent of molten lava: seemingly out of touch with surface events, but emanating from subterranean sources alone.

(b) His behaviour occurs in a social context.

(c) It is a *function* of the sort of person he is, and the situations he finds himself in.

In a functional analysis the importance of genetic predispositions and biological differences is recognized but the focus is on learned behaviour. It is based on the concept of a functional relationship with the environment in which changes in individual behaviour produce changes in the environment and vice versa.

All this can be said in the following shorthand:

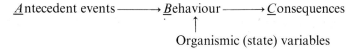

Antecedent events ——————→ Behaviour ——————→ Consequences

Organismic (state) variables

Method: You will have to ask (over a period of interviews/observations):

(a) What events precede, lead up to, set the stage for   Antecedent events

(b) the behaviour that is being complained of? (*What*   ↓
is it?)   Behaviour

(c) And what are the social (or other) consequences/   ↓
outcomes that flow from a display of problematic   Consequent events
behaviour?

In the jargon: the ABC sequence is referred to as the 'three-term contingency'. The child's behaviour is linked to *contingencies* in the environment, as well as *states* of mind, mood and health (etc.) within the child—the so-called organismic variables.

Remember: His behaviour may act as an antecedent to, and 'shaper' of (say) his sister's behaviour.

Here is a fairly typical sequence of behaviour—referred to by Patterson and Reid (1970) as 'the coercion process':

(a) John annoys Sally by grabbing her toy.

(b) Sally reacts by hitting John.

(c) John then stops annoying Sally, thus negatively reinforcing (see Section 4, Procedure 2) Sally's hitting response.

Sally has coerced John into terminating his annoying behaviour. A vicious circle is quite likely to be set in motion, an escalation of attack and counter-attack. To continue the sequence:

(d) John may, of course, react to Sally's hitting, not by desisting from his grabbing at Sally's toy, but by hitting back in an attempt to terminate Sally's aggression.

(e) Sally now responds to John's aggression with more intense counter-aggression.

This exchange would continue until it is interrupted by an adult or until one of the antagonists is negatively reinforced by the cessation of warfare on the part of the other child. We can see how it carries within it the seeds for a perpetuation of aggressive behaviour in the child's repertoire.

Method: Pause at suitable intervals to summarize what the clients have told you. Say: 'I would like to stop for a moment to see whether I have understood properly the points you have made.' Don't give the impression that the clients cannot express themselves clearly, but rather that what they say is worthy of being treated with due concern and seriousness. Indicate that the subtleties and complexities of behaviour problems are difficult to put into words, and for this and other (diagnostic) reasons you will have to ask many questions and a number of supplementaries. Try to avoid a manner which implies that the clients are being cross-examined; they already feel, more likely than not, embarrassed, guilty and apprehensive.

Step 4	DISCOVER THE DESIRED OUTCOMES

Step 4   DISCOVER THE DESIRED OUTCOMES
While collecting early statements of 'problems' also tease out statements about 'desired outcomes'

Parents express their concern about their child's shortcomings in different ways; they may make statements about:
(a) problems: 'He is so thoughtless' and/or
(b) desired outcomes: 'I wish he could be more helpful and cooperative'.

Remember: *Initial comments about desired outcomes provide the raw material for the formulation (later) of more specific goals and objectives.*

Goals are the behavioural changes to be sought; they define how the target behaviour is to be changed.

There are, broadly speaking, three classes of problematic behaviour:

BEHAVIOUR

that is *excessive* (e.g. screaming; hitting). These kinds of behaviour are called 'behavioural excesses' or 'surplus' behaviours.

that is '*normal*' or 'appropriate' of itself but occurs in restricted or inappropriate contexts (e.g. compliant behaviour to delinquent gang values but not prosocial family norms).

that is absent from, or *poorly represented*, in the child's behavioural repertoire (e.g. incontinence, poor social skills, low self-esteem). These kinds of behaviour are called 'behavioural deficits'.

Remember: *Behavioural and emotional problems, signs of psychological abnormality are, by and large, exaggerations, deficits or handicapping combinations of behaviour patterns common to all children. It is crucial to be familiar with developmental norms (see, for example Table IV, p. 37).*

The evaluation of normality and abnormality within a developmental framework requires a familiarity with *general principles* of development, with particular reference to personality. It necessitates a comprehensive knowledge of children—how (in general terms) they look, think and talk, their skills and limitations at various ages, their typical repertoires of behaviour and the life-tasks and crises that they confront. Such a comparative or normative approach needs to be complemented by an idiographic analysis which takes into account biographical and other intrinsic influences which give the individual youngster this *unique* quality. (See distal antecedents and organismic factors in Fig. 1, p. 6.)

Goals are generally formulated in terms of increasing, decreasing, maintaining, establishing or expanding particular target behaviours. Having clarified the goals (Steps 4 to 14) you will eventually translate them (Step 14) into a set of *behavioural objectives*.

Interlude

We have suggested that there may be an advantage in compiling a problem profile which takes into account the family as a complex and dynamic system. After all the child has a point of view. Who is 'problematic' to her? She may not be a problem in the eyes of everyone! Who else is experiencing difficulties?

Let us take time off for the moment to look at a child (whom we shall call Lorna) and her family. They were referred to the Child Treatment Research Unit for (specifically) *Lorna's* problems. But it wasn't that simple!

Lorna, aged four, demanded an inordinate amount of individual attention, monopolizing her mother's time wherever she was and whatever she was doing. She clung to her and followed her everywhere (even to the toilet) refusing to let her out of her sight, even for a few moments. Lorna would not play with other children, including her sister and brother—who had no real problems. By the time she was referred to us, her behaviour problems (including aggression, self-centredness of an extreme kind and other antisocial actions) were rampant and having serious implications for herself and her family. The problems were real enough, but there were other issues which required attention (see Table I).

A glance at this problem profile tells us why those who call themselves systems theorists are agreed in focussing not on the individual but on the system of relationships in which he interacts. We are not describing family therapy in this manual, but there *is* some overlap between home-based behavioural work and family therapy. After all, the latter is not so much a school or system of therapy as a basic redefinition of the therapeutic task itself. Therapists attempt to conceptualize the problem in a more horizontal (rather than vertical–historical) manner, viewing the client as part of a complex network of interacting social systems, any aspect of which may have a bearing on his present predicament. Whereas the treatment model tended to identify the 'nominated patient' as the unit of attention (for example, the child referred to the child guidance clinic), diagnostic thinking has since been considerably influenced by interactional frames of reference (explicit in systems thinking).

Thus the unit of attention, particularly in relation to Lorna's family, is far more broadly conceived, and the focus of help not prejudged as the nominated client, or not the child (in this case) alone.

The unit of attention may now be defined as the family (or one of its subsystems) rather than the individual in the context of his family—the rather different earlier child guidance focus. Increased understanding of the effects of group influences on individual behaviour has also modified views of what should be taken into account in assessment, and it has become necessary to consider whether behaviour on the part of an individual is to be seen primarily in individual terms or is more readily explicable in terms of group processes. In a residential context, group processes assume

Table I Problem profile

Problem as defined	Who complains	Who manifests the problem/to whom	Examples of problem	Settings	Desired outcome
Defiance	Mother	Lorna/Mother	Lorna ignores Mother's requests or says 'No'.	Bedtime, home; supermarket; visiting.	More obedient.
Demanding	Mother	Lorna/Mother	Mother has to 'obey' Lorna's commands or there is a temper tantrum.	Home; supermarket.	More patient.
Self-centredness	Mother/Father	Lorna (whole family)	Lorna is aggressive.	Home and elsewhere.	More thoughtful and unselfish.
Aggression	Mother	Lorna/whole family	Lorna pulls mother's hair, pinches back of her knees, hits her (to a lesser extent father and sister).	Home; in the car.	Stop lashing out for nothing.
Attention-seeking	Mother	Lorna/Mother	Follows mother everywhere, hangs onto mother, demands mother's attention when attending to others.	Home.	Give mother some peace.
Rudeness	Father	Lorna/Father	Make contemptuous remarks to father, e.g. 'you're stupid.'	Home.	Learn politeness.
Opting-out	Mother	Father/Mother	Father rushes off to work as if glad to get out of the house.	Home.	F to help more.
Depression	Father	Mother	Mrs G. doesn't enjoy life: no energy for anything.	Everywhere.	Be her old self.
Inconsistency; reinforcement of deviant behaviour	Therapist	Mother and Father with regard to Lorna	Parents give in to Lorna if she is coercive; attend to her when her behaviour is deviant.	Most interactions.	—
Infantalizing	Lorna	Father/Mother	'They treat me like a baby.'	Playgroup/home. When I don't want to play with other children.	Treat me like my sister.
Rejection: spoiling tactics	Her sister	Lorna *vis-à-vis* Father and Mother	'They have no time for me. Lorna spoils everything.'	Home.	Treat us the same.

particular significance and may themselves, rather than the individual, constitute the unit of attention.

It is small wonder when we look at the history of Lorna that we had a complex case on our hands: a depressed mother, an unhappy wilful child, a discontented sister, a frustrated and confused father, and a generally miserable, tense family life.

Lorna, from early in life, had been a difficult and hyperactive child. From the day of her birth Lorna would cry day and night. The nights were particularly difficult. Mrs Green spent most of them nursing her to allow the rest of the family to have some sleep. There were also serious feeding problems. The parents were worried that Lorna would starve herself, so forced feeding was necessary for several months. It could take up to three hours to feed the baby. Indeed, Lorna was an unusual child in other ways. She was difficult to amuse, taking only the most fleeting interest in toys. She seldom smiled. Her moods were volatile. When she didn't appear to be depressed and withdrawn she was often screaming for attention. Her mother and father found it impossible to enjoy their youngest child as she was so difficult to rear—she hated any change in routine and was predictable only in her unpredictability. Mrs Green felt guilty for having had the child when she had been advised not to and any nasty remarks in that direction, from anyone, would turn her to the fierce protection of Lorna, even though she might secretly agree with the criticisms. Finally, because of the marital tension and lack of husband's support when dealing with Lorna's behaviour, Mrs Green reached a low point of depression, involving physical and nervous exhaustion; all this further minimized consistent and effective handling of the child.

We shall return to Lorna later on. Even she had her good points! And this brings us to the next phase of assessment.

Step 5 IDENTIFY THE CHILD'S ASSETS   Note
and record prosocial behaviour

Seek out the child's 'good points'. Parents may be surprised at how many 'virtues', strengths and resources the child possesses when you encourage them to think about them.

Method: Ask the parents to imagine a credit and debit balance sheet with two columns (see opposite). Make a list. You most probably will have to say: 'There's a long list of items on Peter's debit side; what can you think of to his credit?'

You might choose to do the same with the child with regard to (a) himself, and (b) his parents.

The author has found, on the basis of many assessment interviews at the Child Treatment Research Unit, Leicester, that parents usually come to a clinic with a mental set for discussing the negative aspects of their child's behaviour. There are advantages in asking them to talk about and observe (by monitoring at home) those areas in which his behaviour is socially appropriate. They may be surprised at how much prosocial behaviour they have overlooked. This may increase their own self-esteem as parents and

Balance sheet

	Credit	Debit
	He is generous. He is good at his schoolwork.	He's always fighting. He's disobedient.

also help them to establish a more balanced view of the child's behaviour. If parents focus their attention more on the positive behaviour, even if of rather poor quality, this behaviour is quite likely to increase and therefore leave less time for antisocial behaviour.

When carrying out treatment an emphasis on the positive is crucial in balancing out the efforts to reduce deviant behaviour. If the child acts in a silly or 'clownish' way to obtain attention and self-esteem, it would be short-sighted (not to say unethical) to 'extinguish' this inappropriate behaviour without providing him with skills and a behavioural repertoire which will earn him attention and esteem in more appropriate ways. In any event, failure to do this would not be very effective. The child might find other ways to seek these 'payoffs'. And we need not call this 'symptom substitution'.

A comprehensive, imaginative assessment is required in order to have the child in full, 'rounded' perspective.

Step 6   **ESTABLISH PROBLEM PRIORITIES**
Discuss with the family the priorities for further assessment

It is important to select (after negotiation with the family) the problems on which to concentrate—at least initially.
(a) Establish a hierarchy of problems/outcomes in order of their importance to the parents.
(b) Establish your own hierarchy of problems in terms of their implications as you perceive them.

Ask: (a) 'If I had a magic wand and could wave it so that things could change for the better in the situation you've been describing to me, what would you change first? . . . and after that? . . .' etc; or

(b) 'Which aspect is the greatest worry to you at the moment?'; or

(c) 'Which of the desired outcomes you've mentioned would you regard as your top priorities?'

Criteria

Carter (quoted by Gambrill, 1977) suggests the following criteria for choosing among alternative outcomes:

(1) Annoyance value of the current situation to the client.
(2) Danger value of the current situation.

(3) Interference of the current situation in the client's life.
(4) Likelihood that the outcome will be attained with intervention.
(5) Centrality of the problem in a complex of problems.
(6) Accessibility of the problem. (Can you get at it?)
(7) Potential for change. (Can you do something about it; do you have the resources and skills?)
(8) Probable cost of intervention (time, money, energy and resources).
(9) Relative frequency, duration or magnitude of the problem.
(10) Ethical acceptability of the outcome to the counsellor.
(11) Likelihood that new behaviours will be maintained in the post-intervention environment.

Avoid: Assessing too many problems. The effect of this would be to 'swamp' the parents with too much data-collection, making it unreliable and possibly engendering resistance to the programme.

The baseline

Begin to plan your baseline as part of, and flowing from, your assessment interview/s. You will be moving from the more static collection of data (interview) to the more active, dynamic form of information gathering: the *baseline*.

Remember: *Behaviour modification is about changing behaviour: the frequency with which the child (for example) displays the behaviour may have to decrease, or increase—depending upon its nature. On the other hand, it may not be a matter of doing something less or more often, but of manifesting an action with different intensity.*

In order to change behaviour from some level to another level, you need to be clear about the definition of the problem and to know how much there is of that problem. In this way you will know:
(a) whether the problem is as extensive as parents say it is;
(b) whether your therapeutic programme (when it gets going) is producing real change.

The period of careful and controlled data collection stemming from the early interview/s is called the baseline.

The baseline is discussed in some detail in Step 9. If the target behaviour is occurring with some degree of consistency a week may be sufficient for the collection of data; if it is highly irregular you may require two or more weeks so as to get a picture of the day-to-day variations in the occurrence of the problem.

You may have to dispense with (or keep brief) the baseline period, if you are dealing with a problem that is dangerous to the client himself or to others. If, for *good* reasons, you have to dispense with a baseline, an estimated retrospective 'baseline' (based on the verbal report of a responsible informant) is better than none. Accept it as the most tentative of estimates unless the target behaviour had a 100 % or zero rate of occurrence (e.g. a child bedwetting every night; no incidence of speech at all in an elective mute).

SECTION 3

From Data Collection
to Problem Formulation

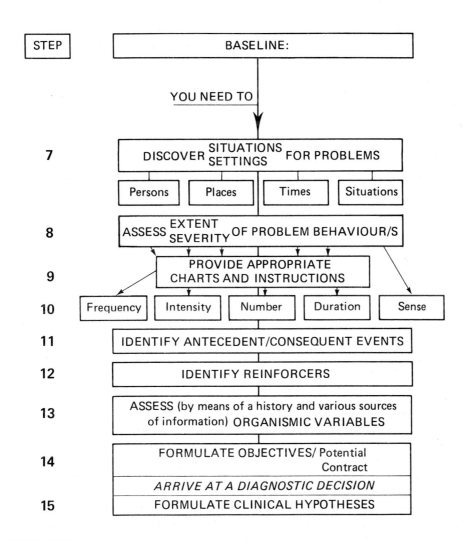

STEP	BASELINE:

YOU NEED TO

7 DISCOVER SITUATIONS SETTINGS FOR PROBLEMS

Persons	Places	Times	Situations

8 ASSESS EXTENT SEVERITY OF PROBLEM BEHAVIOUR/S

9 PROVIDE APPROPRIATE CHARTS AND INSTRUCTIONS

10 | Frequency | Intensity | Number | Duration | Sense |

11 IDENTIFY ANTECEDENT/CONSEQUENT EVENTS

12 IDENTIFY REINFORCERS

13 ASSESS (by means of a history and various sources of information) ORGANISMIC VARIABLES

14 FORMULATE OBJECTIVES/ Potential Contract

ARRIVE AT A DIAGNOSTIC DECISION

15 FORMULATE CLINICAL HYPOTHESES

FLOW CHART 2   Further assessment.

Step 7 SPECIFYING SITUATIONS (SITUATION SPECIFICITY) Discover the situations in which the problematic interactions/feelings/behaviours occur

Behaviour is not usually manifested on a random basis; the probability of a specific action occurring varies according to the surrounding environmental cues. If you are to understand, predict and prescribe, you need to find out how behaviour covaries with different environmental stimuli, i.e. how antecedent situations affect a particular action.

Setting Events:

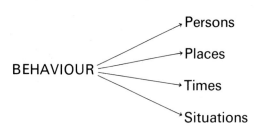

Find Out:

(1) whether there are particular persons with whom . . .
places at which . . .
times when . . .
and situations in which . . . the problem behaviours are displayed;

(2) whether there are particular persons with whom . . .
places at which . . .
times when . . .
and situations in which the problem behaviours are *not* manifested;

(3) the setting events for each problem separately. The problems may be related in the sense of occurring in the same settings.

You need to find out about the child and his responses to a variety of situations and environmental settings. A child referred for troublesome behaviour may display this kind of behaviour in his home, his school classroom, his playground, and perhaps on the streets of his neighbourhood. Furthermore, there may be refinements of such specific situations in which the problem behaviour occurs. For example, the child with severe temper tantrums solely at home, may show them only at bedtime and at mealtimes. He may be quite cooperative and pleasant at other times of the day when he is at home.

Note: *The best way to predict how a child is going to behave tomorrow in a particular situation is to observe how he behaves in that situation today.*

Parents, too, may behave in ways that vary more than the impression of consistency and generality that they convey in your interviews with them. This is where direct observation is so potentially revealing. For example, their handling of the 'target' child may be very different than that of their other offspring and they may be quite unaware of it.

So, while you may regard verbal report as a good predictor of real-life behaviour (see Mischel (1968) for the evidence), do not rely entirely on it (and that means the interview) for your data. Clients may not notice things, they may misperceive events, they may forget significant details and emphasize irrelevant points. Embarrassment or guilt may lead to errors of commission and omission in information-giving. If the crucial behaviour consists of overlearned responses, the client may be quite unaware ('unconscious') of his actions. So go and look for yourself and/or train the client to observe so that you can see things through his *informed* eyes.

Ask: The right sort of questions at interview: 'Does he do x or say y with everyone? No? Then tell me who ...' 'Can you think of anyone—a granny, teacher, friend—in whose presence he does not do x or say y?'

A technique used to tease out family interactions and behaviours is the so-called 'typical day' in the life of the child and family. It is worked through in minute (indeed, pedantic) behavioural detail, pinpointing those areas which cause confrontations and concern. It also provides the times and places at which, and the persons with whom, they occur. A 'blow-by-blow' account is sought of the events surrounding problem behaviours. The typical day (or days) makes for a reasonable sampling of the child's antisocial *and* prosocial behaviours. This (and other relevant information) is obtained from interviews with both parents or other significant adults (e.g. the child's schoolteacher). Don't neglect the child himself as a potential informant. His points of view, his perception of events are important sources of data in your assessment. Not all children are articulate. This is where behaviour itself, even more than usual, must be 'interpreted' for what it 'tells' you about the problem and its function.

Interlude

In trying to learn about the behaviour of other persons, the two principal ways are through questioning and observation. We 'ask them' and 'watch them'.

   (a) *Direct Observation:* Go and see for yourself at home, school, etc. what and where problematic behaviours are occurring.
   (b) *Record Keeping:* Ask the client to keep a diary and/or chart indicating when/ with whom/under what circumstances x occurs.
   (c) *Interviewing:* Interviewing (because of the opportunity it gives to question and observe a client) is one of the prime instruments of psychological assessment.

Interviewing

Interviewing involves the social interaction, in a face-to-face situation, between two or more persons organized for the purpose of obtaining information from, or making appraisals of, or modifying the behaviour of one or more of their number.

Interviews may vary from the *highly structured* (representing little more than an orally administered questionnaire) through what are termed *patterned* or *guided* interviews covering certain predetermined areas of the person's behaviour to *non-directive* and *depth* interviews in which the interviewer merely sets the stage and encourages the subject to talk as freely as possible. The guided (semi-structured) interview is the main vehicle for the *preliminary* assessment of the areas outlined in the diagnostic guide in Fig. 1. Such interviews provide chiefly two kinds of information:

(a) They afford an opportunity for direct observation of a rather limited sample of behaviour manifested during the interview situation itself (e.g. the individual's speech, language usage, thinking, competence, poise and manner in meeting a stranger).

(b) The interviewer seeks to secure directly as much information of a factual or personal nature from the subject as is relevant to the purpose of the interview (e.g. information, attitudes, beliefs, opinions, relationships, work record and experience). A particularly important function in a clinical or social work setting is to elicit life-history data. What the individual has done in the past is thought to be a good indicator of what he may do in the future, especially when interpreted in the light of concomitant circumstances, and of the subject's comments on his actions.

In practice, the interview is the most comprehensive of methods since it makes more or less use of various techniques (though usually in a haphazard manner).

Remember: *People, despite their generalized personality styles, still react to situations in highly idiosyncratic ways. Each situation requires an individual analysis. Bowers (1973) concludes that if the total variance in behaviour is 100 %, then an average of about 13 % of this variance is due to the person (personality traits), 10 % due to the situation and 21 % to the interaction between persons and situations. Although a detailed and specific assessment plan is de rigeur in behavioural work, it should not preclude opportunities for the 'person' as a personality and individual to express his feelings and attitudes.*

Step 8   ASSESS THE EXTENT AND SEVERITY OF THE PROBLEM   Explore the parameters of the problem behaviour

This is still part of the specification of the 'What' questions: the specification of the dimensions (and, indeed, the seriousness) of the problem.

The acronym FINDS refers to the specification of the target behaviours (problems) in terms of their frequency, intensity, number and duration, and the sense they make from the client's point of view. After an initial report from the clients, e.g. from parents (or teachers), you require careful and controlled observation of the behaviours you think are important, as they are presently occurring. Flow Chart 3 will help you get started.

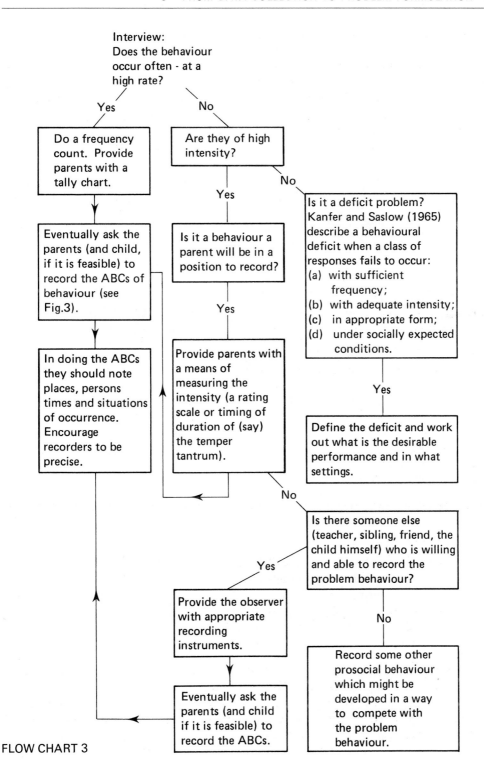

Interview:
Does the behaviour
occur often - at a
high rate?

Yes / No

Do a frequency count. Provide parents with a tally chart.

Are they of high intensity?

Yes / No

Eventually ask the parents (and child, if it is feasible) to record the ABCs of behaviour (see Fig.3).

Is it a behaviour a parent will be in a position to record?

Is it a deficit problem? Kanfer and Saslow (1965) describe a behavioural deficit when a class of responses fails to occur:
(a) with sufficient frequency;
(b) with adequate intensity;
(c) in appropriate form;
(d) under socially expected conditions.

Yes

In doing the ABCs they should note places, persons times and situations of occurrence. Encourage recorders to be precise.

Provide parents with a means of measuring the intensity (a rating scale or timing of duration of (say) the temper tantrum).

Yes

Define the deficit and work out what is the desirable performance and in what settings.

No

Is there someone else (teacher, sibling, friend, the child himself) who is willing and able to record the problem behaviour?

Yes / No

Provide the observer with appropriate recording instruments.

Record some other prosocial behaviour which might be developed in a way to compete with the problem behaviour.

Eventually ask the parents (and child if it is feasible) to record the ABCs.

FLOW CHART 3

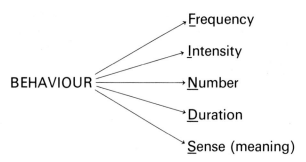

Note: *The dimensions (frequency, intensity, etc.) along which you quantify the behaviour depends upon the nature of the problem. (See Step 9 for aids to coding and recording.) Don't get bogged down by taking on too much at once. Record one or two target problems at first.*

Step 9 **PROVIDE CLIENT WITH APPROPRIATE MATERIAL (CHARTS, NOTEBOOKS) TO RECORD PROBLEM BEHAVIOURS, FEELINGS, INTERACTIONS** He thus '**FINDS**' out more about the parameters of the problem

This marks the beginning of the so-called baseline period.

The baseline period is not necessarily therapeutically inert as self-observation (or observations of a child)—especially when based upon more precise definitions of the behaviour —may produce 'insights' which predispose to beneficial effects. Some therapists claim that behaviours which can be quantified and counted are easiest to change; indeed that problem behaviours which cannot be observed and counted are not likely to be changed by the therapeutic agent.

Methods: (a) To do all this, you *train* the parents (and not infrequently, the child) to observe behaviour so that, in a sense, you can observe things through their eyes during the time you cannot be 'on the spot'. The very fact of the client being able to interpret behaviour sequences with greater accuracy and sophistication, seems conducive to change.

(b) Give the parents a tally-sheet (a chart) so as to keep a record themselves (Fig. 2).

(c) Write down the behaviour to be recorded (with symbols and definitions) as a reminder to the parent. You might simply ask them to keep a count in the first week (Fig. 2) and then a more detailed ABC diary the next week (Fig. 3).

(d) Go and record or observe for yourself—if possible. If you do, prepare the

Mandy's Chart   Date: Week:

	Mon.	Tues.	Wed.	Thurs.	Fri.	Sat.	Sun.
7-8	T, D	C	T, D	D/T	D, T	C	C
8-9	C		T	T	T, D		
9-10						T	
10-11							
11-12							
12-1						D, T	D
1-2							
2-3							
3-4							
4-5	D/T	D, T	D	D, T	D		
5-6	T, T	T, T	D, T	T	T	D, T	D
6-7		D	T (long one 25 mins)	T	C		C
7-8							C

Code: T = temper tantrum = mandy screams, lies on the floor, kicking, banging her head, banging her fists.

D = disobedience/defiance = M ignores request (ie after one repetition). M says 'no' / shakes head – refuses to obey.

C = cooperation behaviour = M helps mother (or others) as defined in contract.

FIG. 2 Daily counting chart to show how often a child does something within a given time period.

parents for this eventuality and explain why you wish to observe and how. Be as natural as possible and thereby unobtrusive as well. Keep your interactions to a polite minimum.

(e) Discuss your, and their record with them. Ask: 'Is this what it is usually like? . . . more? . . . less? . . . worse? . . . better?'

Parents who find their child's behaviour intolerable tend to overestimate the actual frequency of its occurrence. There are, on the other hand, parents who do not want to

CHART: *Mandy's*   DATE: 7/5 → 13/5   WEEK: 2

OBSERVER: *Mrs Sinclair*

BEHAVIOUR: 1 *temper tantrum* = *Mandy screams, lies on the floor,*   CODE: 1 'T'
2   *kicks, makes high pitched sounds,*   2
3   *bangs head / fists on floor.*   3
4 *Disobedience* = *Mandy ignores request (ie after one repetition)*   4 'D'
5   *Mandy says no / shakes head - refuses to*   5
6   *obey request / command (as defined in contract)*   6
7 *Cooperation* = *Mandy helps mother (or others) in ways*   7 'C'
8   *defined in contract.*   8

ANTECEDENT EVENTS (BEFORE)	BEHAVIOUR	CONSEQUENT EVENTS (AFTER)
7th May (10⁵⁰) I refused to buy Mandy a chocolate at the pay counter at the supermarket.	D, T	*She kept pestering me. I kept telling her 'no'; she could have an apple at home. She went on and on. I tried to coax her out of it. M. began to scream and stamp her feet. I felt awful, everyone looking. In the end I compromised. I brought her some chewing gum to keep her quiet.*
Eveng. (7⁰⁰) M helped me of her own own accord to wash the dishes.	C	*I praised her; scolded her a bit for being clumsy.*

FIG. 3   A detailed ABC diary.

admit that their child has problems. They deny the frequency (or intensity) with which a behaviour is occurring. Not surprisingly, the results of 'objective' observation and recording often differ markedly from the estimates of those involved. They also tend to underestimate the child's acceptable behaviour. Ask them to 'catch' the child out in good behaviour, and record it. Not all behaviours can be observed 'objectively' so as to reflect an accurate picture of their manifestations. Some are highly reactive to observation (e.g. fears, sexual problems). It might be impossible or unethical to observe them; or they may be distorted or inhibited by the process of observation. Questionnaires or interviews may have to serve.

From objective data, the therapist might refine the mother's complaint: 'He's always shouting and banging about', which is both inaccurate and vague, to 'This boy has temper tantrums, involving screaming, crying, hitting other children and throwing property, lasting an average of ten minutes on each occasion and occurring at an average of four times per day. They occur when he is thwarted, such as when he is made to …' etc., etc.

Equipment: Paper and pencils are much in evidence in busy day-to-day assessment. Other equipment includes stopwatches and counters to provide time samples and event recordings of behaviour. Audio and video tape-recorders can be most useful. The available literature suggests that quite satisfactory measures can be obtained without having to resort to complex and expensive equipment. However, where static (or better still, portable) video equipment is available, it can be quite revealing to show parents and children what their behaviour looks like. To see yourself as others see you is often the beginning of a decision to change.

Ways of measuring behaviour

One of the most direct ways of measuring behaviour is by observation of parent/child interactions. Fortunately, there has been considerable research into the measurement of behaviour by direct observation. Home (and, where necessary, school) observations are made prior to treatment and they contribute to the initial behavioural analysis. A painstakingly detailed interview about the child's typical day can produce reliable and valid data supplemented by parent and teacher observation records and diaries.

No one method of recording is suitable for all problems or situations. The dimensions (frequency, intensity, etc.) along which you quantify the behaviour depend upon the nature of the problem. There are many ways of monitoring behaviour—from the molar to the molecular—some of which (and the sheer amount of time given to which) are more suitable to laboratory-clinical research than to the work of a busy clinician. The following list gives an idea of the range of measures available.

Physiological measures

Electroencephalographs are used to measure brain waves (i.e. electrical activity).

A galvanic skin response apparatus is used to measure the electrical resistance of the skin.

Various apparatuses measure blood pressure, heart rate, muscular tension and so on.

Polygraphs are used to record several physiological measures simultaneously.

Behavioural measures

High speed cameras, tape-recorders, videotapes, event-recorders, stopwatches, etc. are used to record, measure, collate and time large segments or sequences of behaviour (molar behaviour).

Diary description

This, the oldest method used in the study of child development, employs the parent's (or therapist's) diary to draw up an account of the sequences and changes in the child's (and parents') behaviours and interactions.

Related to this is the use of written autobiographies or self-characterization with older children and adults. They may reveal all shades of attitude to self, other people, activities, and so on.

Time budgets

A record is made of the time the person devotes to his various daily pursuits. Such a record kept over many days is likely to betray significant interests and reinforcers as well as personal idiosyncracies (distractibility, procrastination, preoccupation and the like).

Time sampling

This procedure involves direct observation of the person's behaviour; the attention of observer and analyst is fixed upon selected aspects of the stream of behaviour as they occur within uniform and short time intervals. The duration, spacing and number of intervals are intended to obtain representative time samples of whatever is being investigated. Such 'field observations' may involve records of children at home, in nursery schools, boys in camp, patients in hospital, students at their studies, and so on. In other words, they represent a sampling of natural, everyday situations.

Many behaviours are not clearly discrete in nature. Some responses have no clear-cut beginning or ending. Time sampling provides the clearest analysis of such behaviours. For example, in the case of a student who makes many loud, disruptive noises, such as yelling out across the room, hitting his neighbour and pinching him, and shuffling his chair around, it might be difficult either to make a tally of the number of times such responses occur or to measure their duration. After all, when does one instance of chair shifting end and another begin? However, it is feasible to record the presence or absence of such responses within a short time-span at intervals during (say) a classroom lesson.

Event sampling

This is like the classical method of natural history research in biology. It begins with a plan to study events of a given kind, e.g., outbursts of temper tantrums in children or cooperative acts by adolescents doing some common task in the work situation. The investigator stations himself where the people involved can be seen and heard, waits for the events to happen and then describes them in great detail.

Trait rating

The observer goes, say, to a school playground and after several days of observation uses a rating scale to sum up what he has seen of the child's traits, e.g. friendliness, competitiveness, conformity, jealousy and so on, having defined them first in operational terms, i.e. in terms of observable behaviours.

Sociometry

This so-called 'nominating technique' is a procedure in which each member of a group (classroom, family, playgroup) is asked to name the members of the group with whom he would like to work, play or engage in other designated activities. Naming may not always be the method used. An observer may simply plot the interactions of a group of, say, children to see who is isolated, popular, gregarious, etc.

Situational tests

These tests place the client in a situation closely resembling or simulating a 'real-life' situation. An adolescent applicant for a position may be required to play a role as an interviewee or employer. Wahler *et al.* (1965) have demonstrated the value of structuring situations in which parent–child interactions of a problematic kind are likely to occur. The use of a one-way screen and a communication system with the parent allows the therapist to see certain confrontations and management sequences for himself. These situational techniques can be utilized for treatment as well as assessment purposes.

Remember: What you are particularly interested in is behaviour variability, i.e. the correlation or covariance between the rate of a target behaviour as displayed during one observation session, and the rate of the behaviour during previous or subsequent sessions (high correlation = low variability). Variability in observational data may be due to (i) variations in environmental influences (including your intervention), (ii) natural characteristics of the behaviour, or (iii) reactivity to the observation methods being employed. You have to take this variability into account when attributing change to your therapy (see Step 18).

Step 10a	**FIND OUT MORE ABOUT THE BEHAVIOUR** You can never know enough about the problem
	(a) Ask how often the problem occurs (interview).
	(b) Record how often the problem occurs (baseline).

BEHAVIOUR ⟶ Frequency

Method: Discover:
 (a) The frequency of the problem.
 (b) The overall rate at which the behaviour occurs—i.e. how often. The usual means of expressing this is frequency/time, e.g. confrontations per day, tantrums per day.
 (c) Whether there is a tendency for the problem to occur episodically.
 (d) Whether there is any evidence of a clustering of behavioural events.

The observation and recording of problem behaviour and its attendant circumstances by the therapist, the child or others, may be facilitated by suitable coding systems. Methods for coding behaviour in families (Patterson *et al.*, 1969, 1975) or at school (Ray *et al.*, 1970) have been developed.

In Table II we see one example of a system for coding observations of social interactions of disturbed children. (Normative base rates are also shown.) This sort of

Table II   Some noxious behaviours

Noxious behaviours	Base rate (From Patterson *et al.*, 1975)	Definitions
Disapproval	(0·1339)	Verbal or gestural disapproval of another person's behaviour or characteristics.
Negativism	(0·1153)	Making a statement with a neutral verbal message, but which is delivered in a negative tone of voice.
Non-compliance	(0·0918)	Not doing what is requested.
Tease	(0·0502)	Teasing another person in such a way that the other person is likely to show displeasure and disapproval or when the person being teased is trying to do some behaviour but is unable to because of the teasing.
High rate	(0·0439)	Behaviour that if carried on for a long period of time would be aversive, e.g. running back and forth in the living room, jumping up and down on the floor.
Physical negative	(0·0422)	Attacking or attempting to attack another person. The attack must be of sufficient intensity to potentially inflict pain, e.g. biting, kicking, slapping, hitting, spanking, and taking an object roughly from another person.
Yell	(0·0571)	Whenever the person shouts, yells, or talks loudly. If carried on for a sufficient time it would be extremely unpleasant.
Whine	(0·0360)	When a person states something in a slurring, nasal, high-pitched, falsetto voice.
Destructiveness	(0·0306)	Destroying, damaging, or trying to damage any object.
Humiliation	(0·0202)	Someone makes fun of, shames, or embarrasses another person intentionally.
Cry	(0·0193)	All forms of crying.
Command negative	(0·0083)	Command in which immediate compliance is demanded and aversive consequences are implicitly or actually threatened if compliance is not immediate. In addition, it is a kind of sarcasm or humiliation at the receiver.
Dependency	(0·0067)	Requesting assistance in doing a task that a person is capable of doing himself; for instance, a 16-year-old boy asks his mother to comb his hair.
Ignore	(0·0054)	When person A has directed behaviour at person B, and person B appears to have recognized that the behaviour was directed at him, but does not respond in an active fashion.

system may save observer and recording time. But keep it simple for parents. Perhaps the greatest merit of direct observation techniques is that they provide basic data about problems as conceptualized by the parents or teachers themselves. The child may also be involved in monitoring his own behaviour. It is always wise to check on the reliability of the client's observations by doing home or school visits and observing how they observe and record. Or, at the very least, check their recordings by discussing criteria with them.

	Monday						Tuesday						Wednesday						Thursday						Friday						Total
	1	2	3	4	5	6	1	2	3	4	5	6	1	2	3	4	5	6	1	2	3	4	5	6	1	2	3	4	5	6	
On-task	✓	✓		✓	✓								✓	✓	✓	✓			✓	✓	✓	✓	✓	✓						✓	15
Out of seat		✓								✓	✓				✓	✓			✓										✓		7
Inappropriate talking				✓				✓	✓																		✓	✓			5
Hitting				✓															✓						✓						3

FIG. 4   A classroom chart.

Quantifying frequency

It is important to determine the frequency of a problem in quantifiable terms. This should include not only the overall rate (i.e. how often it occurs on average—hourly, daily or weekly), but also any tendency of the problem to occur episodically (i.e. at particular times). Any evidence of clustering of behavioural events should lead to further investigation. A frequency recording procedure is the simplest type of data analysis. It is nothing more than a *tally* method. Figure 2, Step 9, provides an example of a tally chart. What the therapist does is to count the number of occurrences of the behaviour, as he has defined it. Recording the time at which the response occurred transforms the frequency data system into an even more useful instrument.

(a) *Interval method*
Break the observation period down into small *equal* intervals and record the chosen behaviour as occurring or not occurring during each interval up to one minute in duration, depending upon the rate of the response and the average duration of a single response.

(b) *Time sampling*
Record the presence or absence of the target responses during a short time period or interval. In order to obtain a representative sample of observations one might record the presence or absence of the behaviour within short, uniform time intervals, such as the first ten seconds in every five minutes of a half-hour classroom period. Just such a classroom chart is given in Fig. 4.

On one of your home visit observations you might record the interactions of a child and (say) her mother in ten second samples (on every minute) according to your own pre-coded categories (see Fig. 5).

	10	20	30	40	50
Sarah	T O S̆ H	T̆ O S H	T O S̆ H	T O S̆ H	T O S H
Mother	O V̆ N P	O V̆ N̆ P	O V̆ N̆ P	O V̆ N P	O V̆ N P
Sarah	T O S̆ H				
Mother	O V̆ N P				

FIG. 5   Interaction chart. Time sampling: Sarah and mother at home. *Code:* Sarah: T = throwing objects; O = no problem behaviour; S = shouting, screaming; H = hitting mother. Mother: O = no response; V = verbal interaction; N = near Sarah; P = punishment.

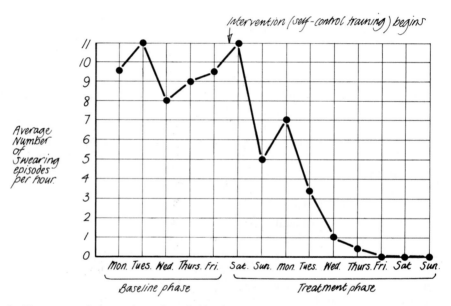

FIG. 6   Try to graph your data. See Gelfand and Hartmann (1975) for interpretation and construction of graphs. There are various methods (Glass *et al.*, 1973) for analysing slopes.

(c) *Use of graphs (see Fig. 6)*

Graphs basically tell you 'when' and 'how much' X, Y or Z occurred at a glance. Plotting behaviour rates across observation sessions may indicate trends (look for positive or negative slopes) in the frequency or intensity of the behaviour over time. A negative slope—in this case a reduction of target behaviour—is illustrated in Fig. 6.

It helps you to see what the data you have collected looks like, if you can bring it all together and summarize it in graphical form. Figure 7, for example, 'tells a story' about Andrew's progress with regard to his aggressive behaviour. (The scores represent ratings

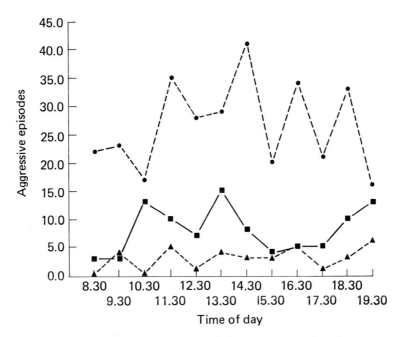

FIG. 7   Andrew's aggressiveness (weekly average) during: ●----● baseline; ▲----▲ termination week of treatment; ■———■ four-month follow-up.

of his behaviour at a certain time each day, i.e. the average number of aggressive episodes recorded at a particular hour over a period of a week.) We see a marked improvement during treatment which is maintained at a slightly more modest level on follow-up, after four months.

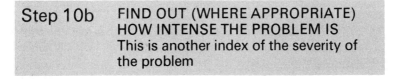

Step 10b   FIND OUT (WHERE APPROPRIATE) HOW INTENSE THE PROBLEM IS This is another index of the severity of the problem

BEHAVIOUR

Find out: How extreme the behaviour is. Expressions of emotional and behavioural acts have certain allowable intensity levels. Very 'high' intensities—behavioural responses of excessive magnitude—which have unpleasant consequences for other people (e.g. incessant screaming, overactivity, fidgety behaviour) are likely to be viewed as behavioural disorder. These problems are sometimes referred to as 'aversive behavioural repertoires'.

It may be appropriate to measure the level of the problem in terms of its intensity rather than its frequency. Intensity can be assessed by asking two questions: (1) How long does the behaviour last? (2) How severe is it?

(1) *Duration:* Some problems are most usefully described in terms of how long the behaviour lasts. A stopwatch is run continuously while the behaviour is occurring during an observation period of a specified length.

(2) *Severity:* This can be measured by constructing *ad hoc* severity rating scales of a graphical, numerical, or some other kind. Find out also when the problem is stronger in intensity, when it is less severe. Why are there these *contrasts* in expression ... with whom ... and in what circumstances?

Remember: *A child (and his environment) may suffer not only because he is (say) over aggressive (sadistic) but because he is under aggressive (not sufficiently self-assertive). Some appropriate responses may be entirely absent from his behavioural repertoire; let alone too weakly manifested (a knowledge of developmental norms is crucial). These problems are sometimes referred to as 'deficient behavioural repertoires'.*

Ask: Whether there are actions and skills which the parents would like the child to display, which he shows little or nothing of.

Methods: (a) *Rating Scale:* If the child is, say, anxious about making journeys and is old enough to rate himself, construct a simple *ad hoc* scale and put it on cards, so the child can assess his anxiety responses to different journeys he makes, in subjective units of anxiety (0 to 100).

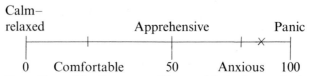

Calm–
relaxed   Apprehensive   Panic

0   Comfortable   50   Anxious   100
Date: Tues. 7th; Comment: Hemmed in in front of school bus.

(b) *Direct Observation:* Rate for yourself (or ask parents to rate) episodes of so-called deviant behaviour. The dimensions will be suggested by the nature of the problem.

Interlude

Rating methods

These come closest to the common, everyday practice by which one person arrives at conclusions about the traits of another person with whom he is acquainted. The judgement he makes is likely to be one of two extremes; the person is regarded ('mentally rated') as bright or dull, friendly or unfriendly, and so on.

Only when the observer begins to compare two or more individuals, or when he is *forced* by circumstances to make finer distinctions, is he likely to do so. Then he recognizes the appropriateness of speaking of *more or less* of some attribute. He is now on the way to making a judgement that has numerical properties.

There are several types of rating scales (5 point scales seem to be most efficient).

(a) *Numerical rating scales*

The rater assigns to each ratee a numerical value for each attribute. The numerical values may be defined in verbal terms. For example: a rating on serious-mindedness of 7 might mean 'takes everything as if it were a matter of life or death'; of 4 'neither serious nor unconcerned'; of 2 'ordinarily unconcerned and carefree'; of 1 'seems not to have a care in the world', etc. Such ratings would best be anchored in agreed and clearly observable behaviours.

(b) *Graphic rating scale*

This is a variant of the numerical scale. The judgement is made by marking a point on a line to define the client's position between two extremes

How depressed is the patient?

: × : : : : :
_____

Extremely Very Some Mildly Not at all

(c) *Personal concept tests*

There are a number of techniques available (e.g. the Q-sort technique, the Semantic Differential and the Repertory Grid), which allow for the direct expression of the personal conceptual system—the manner in which the individual 'sees' or conceptualizes himself, people and the world he lives in. They may reveal concepts, and relationships between concepts (constructs), that the person is barely aware of, or which function normally at the emotional rather than the verbally explicit level. For example, an individual may be construing her husband in much the same way as her father and a test like the Repertory Grid helps to point out such connections.

Step 10c	HOW MANY PROBLEMS ARE BEING MANIFESTED BY THE CHILD?
	List or check off (Table III) the number of problematic behaviours/emotions.

→Number

BEHAVIOUR

Remember: *There may be a tendency for parents to raise of their own accord only the more 'visible' and irksome problems. Without a full picture of the child's anti- and prosocial behaviours, the therapist's assessment will be partial and his treatment programme may run into trouble.*

Table III A checklist of problematic behaviours

Behaviour	Never	Sometimes	Often
Attention demanding			
Destructiveness			
Disobedience			
Disturbing dreams			
Enuresis (diurnal and nocturnal)			
Excessive modesty			
Excessive reserve			
Food finickiness			
Insufficient appetite			
Irritability			
Jealousy			
Lying			
Mood swings			
Nailbiting			
Negativism			
Overactivity			
Overdependence			
Oversensitiveness			
Physical timidity			
Reading difficulty			
Restless sleep			
School refusal			
Shyness			
Soiling			
Somberness			
Specific fears			
Speech			
Tempers			
Thumbsucking			
Wandering			
Whining			

Remember: *The number of deviant behaviours coexisting in the child is an index of maladjustment. The more problematic behaviours reported as such by parents, the greater the likelihood that the child will be found to have an emotional or behavioural disorder on clinical examination. Isolated 'symptoms' are very common and usually of little clinical significance.*

Table IV provides you with information about the problems of British school-going children, as manifested at different ages.

The point was made in the enumeration of the basic assumptions of this book, that no child is *all* problem. Indeed, there is relatively little overlap in the populations of children who show problems at home and those who display problems at school. This is why you should tend to 'sit up and take notice' when the child manifests behavioural disorders in both settings. And you would certainly do so when you note behavioural consistencies such that the child's typical behaviour pattern tends to be deviant across a wide variety of situational contexts.

Table IV   Percentages of children recorded as showing 'extreme' types of behaviour at each age from five to fifteen (from Shepherd *et al.*, 1971)

GIRLS	(age in years:) 5	6	7	8	9	10	11	12	13	14	15
Very destructive	2	—	1	—	*	*	—	*	—	1	—
Fear of animals	5	5	3	3	3	1	2	2	1	1	7
Fear of strangers	1	*	2	2	*	2	1	1	1	2	—
Fear of the dark	11	5	8	7	8	8	6	5	4	5	4
Lying	2	2	1	1	3	1	3	1	1	3	2
Dislike of school	1	3	2	4	3	2	3	3	5	7	4
Stealing	1	—	—	—	*	—	—	*	—	1	—
Irritability	10	9	9	10	12	10	12	10	11	16	11
Food fads	20	19	20	22	21	23	17	17	15	17	09
Fear of other children	—	*	1	1	*	1	*	1	*	1	—
Always hungry	5	6	6	10	9	10	10	13	15	11	16
Small appetite	21	17	21	18	13	12	12	8	7	8	5
Worrying	5	7	4	4	6	4	7	5	1	4	5
Whining	7	5	5	3	6	2	5	4	3	5	—
Restlessness	20	16	20	16	13	13	13	11	11	10	4
Underactivity	—	2	1	1	2	3	3	4	7	7	5
Jealousy	8	4	5	5	6	3	4	3	3	6	4
Wandering	*	*	—	1	1	*	1	2	1	2	4
Withdrawn	2	1	2	2	3	2	2	3	2	3	7
{ Disobedient	10	10	8	8	11	7	10	10	12	14	14
{ Always obeys	8	7	7	9	9	8	14	11	12	10	12
Truanting—at all	*	1	1	*	1	*	*	1	1	3	4
Tics	1	—	1	1	1	*	—	*	—	1	—
Mood change	5	2	4	3	5	3	5	5	7	7	14
Reading difficulty	5	7	14	14	10	13	10	11	5	7	4

BOYS	(age in years:) 5	6	7	8	9	10	11	12	13	14	15
Very destructive	3	2	2	—	2	1	1	1	2	1	2
Fear of animals	3	3	2	1	1	2	2	1	1	1	—
Fear of strangers	2	1	1	1	—	*	*	1	2	*	4
Fear of the dark	9	6	8	8	10	7	6	5	2	2	2
Lying	5	3	5	2	3	3	3	5	4	2	2
Dislike of school	4	5	5	3	5	5	5	6	7	10	4
Stealing	—	1	1	1	1	*	1	1	2	1	—
Irritability	10	7	13	11	12	14	11	14	11	9	16
Food fads	19	20	22	22	22	18	23	19	17	17	16
Fear of other children	1	*	—	—	*	1	1	1	1	*	—
Always hungry	11	10	10	14	16	13	16	19	15	23	39
Small appetite	11	13	17	14	11	10	13	9	7	5	—
Worrying	4	5	5	7	6	5	3	3	5	4	5
Complaining	7	6	8	5	4	3	4	4	3	2	2
Restlessness	23	19	25	21	22	19	20	18	15	17	20
Underactivity	1	2	1	1	1	2	2	4	3	6	2
Jealousy	6	2	4	4	4	5	3	4	2	3	2
Wandering	3	1	2	3	3	3	3	4	4	8	2
Withdrawn	2	2	4	3	3	3	2	3	3	2	7
{ Disobedient	17	11	14	12	12	13	13	14	11	12	9
{ Always obeys	8	7	7	8	7	6	7	7	9	9	16

BOYS	(age in years:) 5	6	7	8	9	10	11	12	13	14	15
Truanting—at all	1	—	1	—	*	2	—	2	1	4	16
Tics	*	1	1	2	1	2	1	2	2	1	2
Mood changes	4	3	3	2	5	3	4	4	2	2	2
Reading difficulty	7	18	21	27	25	17	21	22	13	13	9

Note: * = less than 0·5 %.

Also remember: *In checking for problematic behaviours look for 'interfering' behaviours, that is to say, actions which preclude or compete with the learning and performance of socially adaptive behaviours. These actions are sometimes manifested so often and intensely that they reduce dramatically the probability of alternative responses being made.*

Reliability

We referred briefly to this issue earlier on. There is little point in training caregivers to observe (itself a skill with a therapeutic pay-off) if the observations are not reliable. Methods for checking on observer reliability can be studied in Gelfand and Hartmann (1975); the more elaborate methods for calculating reliability will not be feasible for the busy therapist (although it may be a useful occasional team exercise—as a refresher or training task). However, it is a good idea (if you are an experienced observer) to record simultaneously with a parent, a sequence of behavioural events. Reliability for event recording can be calculated as follows:

$$\frac{\text{Number of agreed events}}{\text{Number of agreed events} + \text{number of disagreed events}} \times 100 = \% \text{ agreement}$$

A rather more precise assessment of agreement between observers can be obtained by use of an interaction matrix. You assess agreements and disagreements for each sampling interval rather than overall observer agreement on event totals over an observation session (as above). Both observers mark 1 for the first interval observation; 2 for the second; and so on—in the appropriate interactional cells (see Fig. 8). Agreement is defined as both observers marking the same cell during the same sampling interval. Percentage agreement is worked out as above (80 % or above is generally considered a satisfactory level).

The issues of reliability, internal consistency and interobserver agreement are important aspects of behavioural observation but are too complex to deal with in depth in a pragmatic guide like the present one. The question of validity—the degree to which measured differences represent true differences—cannot be taken for granted, simply because you have carried out direct observations of behaviour. As a busy therapist you may not be able to implement all the 'niceties' of quantification and checking used by the researcher, but this is no excuse for not being aware of the problems and pitfalls of attaining reliable and valid data. Chapters 5 and 6 in Haynes (1978) are recommended to the reader in pursuit of such an awareness.

PARENT

CHILD	No response	Positive verbal	Negative contact (eg reprimand)	Physical contact (positive)	Physical contact (negative)	TOTAL
Pester	8 MF, 20 MF [2]	[0]	3m; 9F, 10mF; 11m; 19m [5]	[0]	4m, 13m [2]	9
Hit	[0]	[0]	5m, 12m [2]	[0]	14m [1]	3
Play	1mF, 2mF; 7mF 16mF [4]	15F [1]	[0]	17F [1]	[0]	6
Whine	6 mF [1]	[0]	18m [1]	[0]	[0]	2
TOTAL	7	1	8	1	3	20

FIG. 8 Interaction matrix. M = mother; F = father. Numbers = the sampling interval in which the particular interaction occurred.

Step 10d **THERE ARE TWO 'DURATION OF PROBLEM' QUESTIONS:**

(a) Target behaviour duration: how long the behaviour lasts (say, a temper tantrum).
(b) Time-since-onset: the date of the onset of the problem/s.

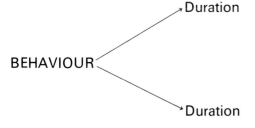

BEHAVIOUR

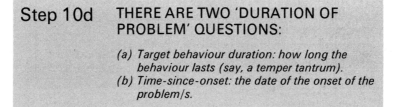

Duration — When Jenny has a fit of screaming, how long does it go on for?'
(a) Ask parents to time samples of the tantrums.
(b) This will provide baseline data as well as diagnostic information.

Duration — 'When did the problem begin?'

Note: *Many of the problems of childhood are the emotional equivalent of 'growing pains'; they are transitory. Problem behaviour is sometimes a 'normal' reaction to a difficult phase of life (see Table VI, Step 14a). They will 'grow out of it' given sensitive and sensible home and/or school management. The clinician refers to this phenomenon as 'spontaneous remission'.*

   Given that the persistence of behaviour problems is the exception rather than the rule, the duration of the problems should be estimated; it may serve as an index of the seriousness you ascribe to it.

		Mon	Tues	Wed	Thurs	Fri		Total (by subject/per week)

Name of Pupil: *John Simpson*

Date: *24/6*   **Stage:** *Baseline*

Recording/observation time: *2 x 3 minute sessions per subject*

		Mon	Tues	Wed	Thurs	Fri		Total (by subject/per week)
	1	1' 2"	1' 15"	2' 15"	1' 2"	40"	Maths	11' 34"
	2	50"	1' 2"	1' 18"	2' 5"	55"		
	1	10"	40"	55"	1' 10"	1' 10"	History	6' 56"
Week 1	2	1' 30"	30"	1' 13"	40"	38"		
	1	—	1' 10"	10"	—	1' 0"	English	3' 40"
	2	1' 10"	10"	—	—	—		
Total		4' 42"	4' 47"	5' 51"	4' 57"	4' 13"	Weekly percentage 27 %	

	1	50"					Maths	
	2	40"						
	1	42"					History	
Week 2	2	55"						
	1	1' 15"					English	
	2	5"						
Total (all subjects)		4' 27"					Weekly percentage %	

Problem definition: *Poor attention = off task behaviour*

= doing things / tasks not given

daydreaming

talking to others

looking out of window / at others

playing with objects (pencils, etc)

FIG. 9   An illustration of one way of collecting information (in this case, duration of 'off-task' behaviours) to answer the question, 'How much of the problematic behaviour does the child show?' Record the proportion of time spent on a particular set of actions out of the total possible time (i.e. the time available).

Ask: The parent, 'Has the problem gone on for so long that, on balance, there are more incidents of high tension, in which you are at odds with your child, than moments of relaxed enjoyment of him?' If the answer indicates that the balance has tilted badly in the direction of long-enduring aversion, your diagnostic 'mental alarm system' should start sounding.

Step 10e	WHAT *SENSE* OR MEANING IS THERE IN THE PROBLEM BEHAVIOUR?
	(a) From the child's point of view. (What are his perceptions of his behaviour and situation? Does the problematic behaviour have a pay-off? What function does it serve for him?)
	(b) From the family's point of view. (Is there a pay-off for them in his problematic status?)
	(c) From your professional point of view.

Sense

BEHAVIOUR

What a person tells himself about his experience affects his behaviour (see Meichenbaum (1977) on cognitive aspects of behaviour modification). Problems arise when he misperceives events and then bases his actions on his distorted conception of a situation.

An individual's behaviour is affected by much more than the particular nature of reinforcements (pay-offs) or goals. According to Rotter (1966), the effect of reinforcement depends on whether or not the person perceives a causal relationship between his own behaviour and the reward. This perception may vary in degree from individual to individual and even within the same individual over time and situations. A truly significant influence on behaviour is provided by the person's *anticipation* ('expectancy') that his goals will be achieved. Such expectations are determined by his previous experience.

Remember: A child's alleged 'problems' may serve as an 'admission ticket' for parents who may have other problems they need to discuss. The hidden agenda may be family problems, the child with the so-called 'symptoms' acting unwittingly as a diversion from the recognition of such problems (marital or other). It is not unknown for the 'successful' treatment of the child to change the family system in a way that exacerbates other areas of tension; conflicts between the parents may be laid bare.

Interlude 1

Insight

Insight is not rejected as a facilitative therapeutic agent; it often produces changes during the assessment phase. For behaviour therapists, it does not constitute a primary method of achieving therapeutic aims. It can argued that insight is a consequence rather than an agent of beneficial change. Cautela (1965) suggests that changes in verbalizations during psychotherapy, commonly called 'insight', frequently *follow* rather than precede behavioural changes. As relief from tension and difficulties proceed, insight as to their causation may develop. There are many instances of successful therapies without insight being invoked, and examples where insight, having apparently been obtained, has had little effect on behaviour.

Yellowly (1972, p. 147) makes what seems a fair comment on this vexed question:

> ... awareness may operate in a number of ways. The sheer provision of accurate information may correct a false and erroneous belief and bring about considerable change in behaviour; prejudice, for instance, may be diminished by new information which challenges the prejudiced belief. And in human beings (pre-eminently capable of rational and purposive action) comprehension of a situation, knowledge of cause and effect sequences, and of one's own behaviour and its consequences, may have a dramatic effect on manifest behaviour. Thus to ignore the role of insight is just as mistaken as to restrict attention wholly to it. It would seem that the relative neglect of insight by behaviour therapists until recently has occurred partly in reaction to the over-emphasis on it in traditional psychotherapy, and partly because of their pre-occupation with directly observable behaviour, particularly in laboratory studies of animals. As Bandura notes, the potential of symbolic factors for therapeutic change has not been fully exploited although classical behaviour therapy procedures rely heavily on cognitively-produced effects; for example, symbolic rehearsal of behaviour in imagination forms part of systematic desensitization and of some aversive techniques. Such imaginative rehearsal or fantasy is surely evidence of the powerful effects of symbolic arousal on manifest behaviour. Even so it would appear that the use made of higher-order processes in behaviour therapy is relatively unsophisticated by contrast with the wealth and richness of the human symbolic processes and inner mental experience portrayed in language and art.

Ask yourself: What are the implications of the child's particular problems? It is here that an analysis of the consequences that flow from the behaviour will help your understanding (Step 11). And at the stimulus end of the equation, the child's behaviour may indicate the presence of stress—frustration, threat, conflict or defensive attitudes—to which you should pay attention in your assessment. So it is a good idea to 'stand back' for a moment to look at the 'meaning' of the child's style of behaviour in the context of his life-situation and circumstances. What sense can you make of his behaviour? Look at it from his point of view.

The following interlude represents that figurative 'standing back' which allows for a broad (and admittedly speculative) view: a macro-analysis to complement your micro-analysis.

Interlude 2

'Intervening variables'

Concepts like the ones mentioned above (i.e. frustration, threat, etc.) and others such as 'drive', 'learning', 'self' and 'ego' which are invented in order to account for certain observed behavioural effects, are usually referred to as intervening variables. We can observe an animal searching for food and then consuming it. But we cannot see the 'drive' (as it is called) of hunger functioning within him. We can only put it forward as an abstract explanatory concept. Such notions are, by definition, unobservable in a direct sense.

Needs and motives usually manifest themselves in relation to particular kinds of stimulus situations. The stimulus situation (SS) is that part of the total environment to which the individual attends and reacts. Murray (1938) classifies the SS according to the effect—facilitating or obstructing—it exerts upon the individual. Such a tendency he calls a 'press'. The environment, as it appears in a psychological description, occurs not as a physical or chemical agent impinging on the body or sense organs, but in terms of its *meaning* for the individual. The way in which the child interprets or categorizes (labels) events is likely to colour his emotional response to them. The same stimulus may have many different meanings, and many different stimuli may have the same meaning. It is the meanings that are important and not the stimulus in its own nature as a physical or chemical process. It should be said (in fairness) that the use of such concepts as 'meaning', and the explication of other symbolic processes, is retrogressive—in the eyes of many clinical theorists. Yet within the field of contemporary experimental psychology, as Goldfried and Davison (1976) indicate,

> It is not at all unusual to find researchers and theorists conceptualizing learning in mediational and cognitive terms. By carefully anchoring their concepts operationally, they often appear considerably more willing to deal with such issues than are some more radical behaviour therapists. (p. 14)

It is important in doing diagnostic work to be aware of some of the psychological contexts which make sense of what would otherwise appear bizarre in a child's actions. For this reason we now look at some of the more clinically relevant intervening variables. Some of the concepts that follow may prove useful in formulating more clearly the issues which arise in complex problem situations.

Frustration

Frustration is a condition in which an objective, goal, or desired course of action cannot be fulfilled or brought to a conclusion. This may be due to some lack of personal resources, such as a lack of the necessary skills or an emotional or personality problem.

There are two broad types of frustration:

(a) *Objectless frustration.* The child cannot get what he wants because what he wants is simply not there; he has a particular need but is without the means of satisfying it. For example, he may be thirsty but there is no water available. He may be lonely, but he knows nobody in his new home town. The child may want to please his parents, but whatever he does their praise eludes him.

(b) *Barrier frustration.* What the youngster wants is available, but not to him, because a barrier prevents him from obtaining it. The word 'barrier' is used here in its most general sense to include physical or social barriers, mental or moral barriers, and barriers of distance and time. When frustration involves some external barrier, it could be:

(1) someone thwarting the child's wishes (e.g. the mother who won't let her teenage daughter go hitchhiking with friends);

(2) a lack of opportunity for using potential. The child is intelligent and eager to learn but he is gravely impaired by cerebral palsy. There is a resistance on the part of many people he meets to treat him as intellectually and emotionally normal.

Unlike environmental barriers, mental barriers—such as the degree of difficulty of a given task, or a moral barrier, such as taboo against premarital sex—are internal. Frustration is generated if the urge to act persists in spite of the difficulty or the moral restraint.

There is a very important difference between objectless and barrier frustration, corresponding to the difference between *privation* and *deprivation*. Privation implies that what we need is not to be had. In such circumstances our reaction tends (although by no means always) to be one of placid resignation and acceptance. In deprivation, however, there has been an adverse reversal of fortune, which we resent, and which may evoke in the individual an aggressive reaction. A child who was successful and powerful at his previous school, and loses this authority at high school, does not behave in the same way as a child who was an 'underdog', who consequently has never known any position of status, achievement or authority. The same applies to the loss of a 'good home' as against the total lack of experience of what it is like to live in a loving home of one's own.

Threat

This category of stress refers to the anticipation of harm. By harm is meant any circumstances which the individual concerned considers to be undesirable. This consequence may be physical, such as pain, injury, illness or death. It could be material deprivation, or psychological, as in the cases of loneliness, loss of self-esteem or social disapproval.

Conflict

Another kind of stressful situation consists of a conflict between two incompatible responses or goals. They are incompatible because the performance of the response necessary to accomplish one goal prevents the performance of the response required to accomplish the other one.

Thus conflict makes frustration or threat inevitable, since actions designed to satisfy one goal necessarily frustrate or threaten the other.

(a) *Approach–approach conflicts.* Some conflicts are between the different responses required to satisfy two goals each of which is attractive to the person concerned. They are called *approach–approach* conflicts.

A young child who is offered either an ice-cream or a lemonade may well attempt to get both. But generally a resolution of a conflict of this type is not difficult:

(1) one alternative can be made more attractive than the other, the child abandoning one goal in favour of the other; or

(2) the youngster could pursue each goal consecutively rather than concurrently.

(b) *Avoidance–avoidance conflicts.* A second type of conflict is between two courses of action each of which is unattractive to the person concerned, e.g. between incurring the unwelcome attentions of the headmaster, or doing the much-hated homework. The child is caught between the devil and the deep blue sea.

These *avoidance–avoidance* conflicts are likely to lead to two kinds of behaviour:

(1) Vacillation—as the child pursues one course of action it becomes increasingly unattractive to him, he therefore retreats into the alternative course which in turn increases in unattractiveness, so that he returns to his original course with the same outcome. Thus, the youngster may constantly vacillate between exposing himself to the headmaster and doing his homework.

(2) Secondly, such avoidance–avoidance conflicts are likely to precipitate the person into escaping from the stressful situation. For example, he may truant from school, or develop an 'illness' to keep him out of school.

(c) *Approach–avoidance conflicts.* A third type of conflict occurs when the same goal has both attractive and unattractive features for the person concerned, e.g. gaining a high-powered position in the school team may involve a tremendous gain in status plus privileges but it also places severe emotional demands on the child which he is ill-equipped to cope with.

The approach–avoidance conflicts are the most difficult to resolve.

There are many situations where we may want one thing and not want something else, at the same time. Here the individual caught in the conflict swings, like a pendulum, both towards and away from his decision.

An example of this sort of situation is that of the youth who is driven by his forceful and ambitious father to demand an appeal against his failure in his English examination. He leaves home for school full of bold intentions planning to confront his headmaster. However, as he approaches his office, his courage fails him. He fears he may get a hostile reception; 'If you think you are so expert, why don't you mark the paper yourself?' The distraught boy is caught between two forces: he dare not face his father empty-handed, but cannot pluck up enough courage for a showdown with his headmaster.

Resolution of such conflicts will depend on either strengthening the positive approach element or on weakening the negative or avoidance element. Better still would be a strengthening of the one *and* a weakening of the other. An alternative way of meeting frustration due to conflict, is to seek a compromise.

Biological defensive mechanisms
Fear is a natural response to events which are threatening to an individual's personal security; it is a vital adaptive (protective) reaction. Mothers make use of it in training

their children to avoid dangers. It also prepares the individual to cope with, or escape from, emergency situations. The function of fear (in its positive role) is to mobilize physical energy to overcome obstacles, to alert the individual mentally to unexpected and unexplained changes in the environment.

If the newly perceived situation or object turns out to be dangerous or threatening, there are (it is postulated) three basic types of self-protective response available: attack, flight and submission. The fearful person in these crisis situations experiences a variety of physical sensations, a pounding heart, shivering and trembling, butterflies in the stomach, dry mouth and perspiring hands. These reactions are due to the physiological mechanisms which will be described later; they have the express purpose of toning up the system for maximum fighting or fleeing capacity.

(a) *Attack.* Some strategies are designed to deal directly and actively with a problem. Attack and aggression are the most basic animal and human methods for removing or surmounting obstacles which stand in the way of the satisfaction of their needs. Some children characteristically act as if they invented the maxim: 'attack is the best means of defence'. They lash our physically or verbally if they feel threatened or if they can't get their way.

(b) *Flight.* Another basic method of coping in life is strategic withdrawal, or (not to put too fine a point on it) flight. It may not necessarily be physical withdrawal; it can take the form of psychological retreat such as escape or avoidance behaviour, inhibition or emotional insulation ('being switched off').

(c) *Submission.* Submission is yet another basic coping tactic or, indeed a long-term defensive strategy. A cat may 'freeze' when faced by a large dog. This can sometimes save it from the final disaster. A person may characteristically adopt a submissive stance (extreme timidity and shyness are examples) toward other people. This defensive strategy seems to say in effect: 'I am no threat. I am too weak to be worth attacking.' If the individual makes extensive use of self-abasement, the passive tactic of denigrating and humbling himself, he is likely to find out to his regret that people take advantage of him anyway. Some people characteristically take the blame on themselves when circumstances are frustrating.

Psychological defensive mechanisms
Psychological problems are very much bound up with the child's favourable or unfavourable perception of himself—his self-image—and his perception of, and relationship with, other people. Many of the difficulties which a child has to cope with are social ones—the problems of getting on with other children of the same age, with teachers, with his own parents, and also with himself. He needs to like himself, to rely on himself and to know himself. Positive self-attitudes are among the basic ingredients of positive mental health, and negative self-concepts among the critical predispositions to maladjustment (Coopersmith, 1967). From a very tender age, people discover and make use of complex defensive reactions (Lee and Herbert,

1970). Human beings old enough to have acquired even a rudimentary self-image demonstrate a need to perceive themselves in at least a moderately favourable light. A reasonable agreement between the self-concept ('myself as I am') and the concept of the ideal self ('myself as I would like to be') is one of the most important conditions for personal happiness and for satisfaction in life. Marked discrepancies arouse anxiety, and are associated with psychological problems. Such discrepancies are often a feature of so-called 'neurotic personalities'.

The construct self (or ego*) is seen by some theorists as the central integrating aspect of the person, and any threat to its valuation and function is a vital threat to the very being of the individual. As a result a variety of 'devices' are gradually accumulated by the self as part of the armamentarium so as to soften anxieties and failures and protect the integrity of the ego by increasing the feeling of personal worth. There is evidence (Lee and Herbert, 1970) that all of us learn to use strategies such as these. It is when we use them inappropriately or to excess, with too great intensity or too inflexibly, that they become maladaptive (and are called neurotic).

It is the frequency and extent to which we use defensive strategies which is the key to their maladaptiveness. The trouble is that they involve a certain amount of self-deception and distortion of reality and may prevent, by a sort of short-circuiting, the realistic and painstaking solution of problems.

To a very great extent we are unaware (unconscious) of our use of these strategies. One of the purposes of adopting particular strategies is to reduce tension. The minimizing of immediate discomfort reinforces their use! An individual makes choices and carries out actions which will reduce and if possible, avoid anxiety, pain or any other distress.

He is also concerned with the obverse—maximizing immediate comfort and pleasure. The self-indulgent hedonist takes this strategy to its extreme. Some critics of society comment on the pervasiveness of this principle in our culture. It has been called 'fun morality': 'What is fun is good; what is good is fun'. These critics note the worship of fun and play in our daily activities, including work. It is claimed that these strategies can lead, when taken too far, to a chaotic alienated existence lacking long-term purpose and meaning.

Let us look at some of our psychological strategies. They may aid us in understanding a child's behaviour.

(a) *Emotional insulation, isolation, dissociation.* In all these defensive strategies the individual reduces the tensions of need and anxiety by withdrawing into a shell of numbness and passivity. He may do this by lowering his expectations, by remaining emotionally uninvolved and detached. Apathy and defeated resignation may be the extreme reactions to stress and frustration of long duration. Cynicism is often adopted by adolescents (among others) as a means of protecting themselves from the pain of seeing idealistic hopes disillusioned.

---

*Bandura (1971) makes the point that accounts of personality theories frequently draw sharp distinctions between phenomenological approaches in which the self-concept is a central feature and behavioural approaches that supposedly reject self-evaluative phenomena. Behaviour therapies differ among themselves. However, self-evaluative and self-reinforcing functions assume a prominent role in social learning theory.

(b) *Rationalization.* Rationalization is a technique which helps us to justify what we do and to accept the disappointments arising from unattainable goals. The 'ego' uses rationalization to modify otherwise unacceptable impulses, needs, feelings and motives into ones which are consciously tolerable and acceptable.

Rationalization helps to reduce 'cognitive dissonance'. In simple terms this means that when there is a discrepancy between behaviours and thoughts (cognitions), psychological distress is caused. This distress will persist until the behaviours and cognitions are made harmonious again. The student who sees himself as brilliant but does badly on exams may say to himself that the entire examination system is unreliable and disadvantageous to someone with his highly strung temperament. By this rationalization the gap between his estimation of himself and his performance disappears. Thought and behaviour are made congruent. It tries to make the repugnant more acceptable and the incompatible compatible. So it involves thinking up logical, socially approved reasons for what we have done in the past, are doing now or intend to do in the future. It is largely an unconscious process through which we can have our cake and eat it.

Common rationalizations are called 'sour grapes' and 'sweet lemons' attitudes. In the former we justify failure to obtain something that is desirable on the grounds that it was not really worthwhile after all. In the 'sweet lemons' attitude we mollify ourselves for an undesirable outcome by saying that it was for our good in the long run anyway.

(c) *Escapism* (denial of reality). A child may evade disagreeable facts of life by refusing to see them. Escapism is the name given to one of the methods for denying unpleasant circumstances. He may simply withdraw from competitive situations if he feels he is at a disadvantage and may fail. He escapes by getting 'sick' at exam times or he may tend to be indecisive and procrastinate in times of stress, putting off the actions that have to be faced realistically.

(d) *Fantasy.* Fantasy is related to escapism and is one of the favourite tactics of children. In order to cope with stressful circumstances we not only deny unpleasant reality but we create the sort of world of fantasy we would like to inhabit. Incidentally, fantasy also provides children with the opportunity to rehearse in imagination the solutions to their problems without entailing the risks of the real situation. Fantasy can be productive in such cases. Non-productive fantasy is the too persistent indulgence in a wish-fulfilling kind of mental activity. It compensates for lack of achievement. The 'Walter Mitty' fantasies allow a person to be the conquering hero he would like to be. He may also explain away his failures and inadequacies by what are called 'suffering hero' fantasies—seeing himself as the misunderstood, 'put-upon', but nobly courageous victim. In this way the individual retains his self-esteem. Fantasy solutions gloss over unpleasant reality. Children who day-dream a lot are frequently trying to compensate for or escape from unacceptable environmental realities.

(e) *Reaction formation.* Reaction formation is a method of defence whereby the individual suppresses his desires and then adopts conscious attitudes and behaviour patterns which are quite opposed to the unconscious wishes. Reaction formation is extreme and intolerant in its manifestations. Those who devote all their time to the obsessive condemnation of sexual licence in others may well be having trouble in coping with their own sexual inclinations. In children a 'don't care' independent attitude may well mask a craving for nurturance and a need for dependency.

(f) *Displacement.* Displacement is a defensive strategy which involves a shift of emotion or an intended action from the person toward whom it was originally intended on to another person or object.

A more serious example would be a problem child who is a nuisance because he pinches, bites and scratches his playmates at school and harrasses the teacher in a variety of ingenious ways. Investigation might reveal that the fault lies not in the playground situation at school but rather in the home situation.

(g) *Projection.* When feelings arising from within ourselves are unjustifiably attributed to others, such behaviour is called projection. It helps us to avoid conflict over our own barely conscious or acknowledged feelings and impulses by finding scape-goats and ascribing these obnoxious, intolerable and therefore unacceptable ideas to them. By disowning these tendencies we protect ourselves from anxiety.

The individual who feels hateful jealousy and hostility to his colleague may deny these feelings to himself but complain bitterly that his colleague is unplea-sant to him and dislikes him.

The defensive strategies (or 'mechanisms' as the psychoanalysts call them) are not without experimental confirmation (Lee and Herbert, 1970). The mention of psy-choanalytic or psychodynamic theory is a reminder to us that its tenets are not wholly antagonistic to behavioural theory, although many would claim that they are. The psychodynamic approach to problem development stresses the 'understanding' and historical element more than does the behavioural approach, with its emphasis on explanations of behaviour in the here-and-now. Nevertheless, our next stage of analysis—the specification of reinforcers, the 'C' term in the ABC analysis—is one in which some theorists would see a potentially useful borrowing from Freudian ideas.

Whether or not you agree with that particular notion, the monitoring of the ABC sequence will provide you with information about the function (meaning, if you like) of the child's behaviour from his point of view, even when he is unaware of the reasons for behaving in this way, or cannot articulate them. At this stage we shall look at proximal (immediate) consequences and later, at the distal (more removed) outcomes (see Fig. 1, p. 6).

Step 11 ASSESS THE CONTINGENCIES; IDENTIFY THE ANTECEDENT, AND CONSEQUENT EVENTS (CONTINGENCIES)

Having gathered all the information you can about the problem and its settings, in order to put forward hypotheses about the conditions influencing the behaviour you need to identify the functional relationships between As and Bs and Cs.

(a) What happens just before the behaviour occurs; what sets it off?

(b) What happens immediately following the behaviour; what happens as a result of the behaviour?

Antecedent events (prior stimulation) are the antecedent stimulus events which reliably precede the (target) behaviour. They may be functionally related to the behaviour by:

(1) setting the stage for it (discriminative stimuli); or
(2) evoking it (eliciting stimuli).

What factors (situations, persons, etc.) can 'push' or 'pull'—make more or less severe—the level of the problematic behaviour? In other words, what sets off the behaviour; what moderates it?

Consequent events (outcomes) refer to the new conditions which the target behaviour was instrumental in bringing about. The effects of this behaviour on the person's internal and external environment are crucial determinants of whether or not the behaviour will recur. What conditions seem to be maintaining the problematic behaviour; what are the positively reinforcing and/or negatively reinforcing consequences of the troublesome actions?

Remember: *Parents are often conscious only of the child's problem behaviour; to them he seems to erupt unpredictably with 'bad' behaviour. They cannot always tell you of the events which precipitate (or indeed) ameliorate a sequence of troublesome behaviour. It is up to you to tease out the information by precise interviewing, or by observation (theirs and/or yours). They may be too bound up in the problem to see their own role in triggering or prolonging the events. Teach parents to observe so that with your help they can identify the conditions that elicit, cue, or promote deviant behaviour.*

You may attempt to measure or obtain an estimate of:

(1) the overall rate of antecedent events (e.g. commands per hour; affectionate overtures per day);
(2) the overall rate of consequent events (e.g. praises or punishments per hour; response costs per day);

(3) the ratios of antecedent/behaviour, behaviour consequents (e.g. what is the probability (rate) of obedience or disobedience following a command and what is the ratio of verbal reinforcement following these two behaviours).

A major difficulty for inexperienced behaviour analysts (not unlike the parents) is the 'I can't see the wood for the trees' problem. Paradoxically, the very richness of the data becomes an embarrassment. They don't know where to start. Work slowly and systematically. Take one target behaviour at a time. Write it down in ABC terms. Tease out all the implications you can.

Don't stop at one consequence; *follow* the chain of outcomes. For example:

Student: My client steals games and sweets from the supermarket.
Q: Then what happens?
A: He brings them home.
Q: And then ...?
A: He is punished.
Q: How and by whom?
A: His mother tells him off.

It might be tempting, apart from getting more detail, to leave the sequence there ... but what about the stolen items?

Q: What happens to the sweets and games?
A: In the evening the family eat the sweets and settle down with the child to play the games.

This *true* sequence, with its final sting in the tail, puts a different complexion on the episode as a learning experience about theft for the child.

Illustration

Here is an example of an ABC analysis (obviously a small illustrative fragment) for a child named John, aged six, and his 'demanding' behaviour.

A Antecedent events

Demanding occurs in and out of the house, but more frequently and intensively in public places like shops or friends' houses. At home it can happen any time, but more often when mother has got company or is very busy, cooking, washing, telephoning. Tea-times and mornings are particularly difficult. Demanding occurs seldom with his father and is less frequent when father is present. It never occurs with people he does not know well and never at school. Demanding is triggered off if mother doesn't respond immediately to his request or if she says 'no'.

B Behaviour

John will demand that mother give or buy him something, ask her to let him do something or go somewhere, things of which she does not approve, or demands she cannot fulfil immediately. He will go on and on repeating his 'request', getting very angry so that the request becomes a querulous command. He follows the mother, pulls her, eventually screams and shouts at her or becomes destructive throwing things about, etc. The frequency is seven times a day on average, each episode lasting up to 20 minutes at times, and is very intensive—depending on what he wants and where it happens.

C Consequences

Mother interacts a good deal with John during these episodes, she pleads with him, disputes with him, tries to distract him, getting angrier and more frustrated, threatens him (threats are seldom carried out), screams and shouts at him, and occasionally hits him. He obviously gains a lot of attention. Eventually she gets tired and just for peace and quiet she gives in. In a public place, e.g. shops, she gives in quickly to avoid embarrassment, criticisms from other people and scenes. She gets very upset and at times ends up in tears.

Recording adult behaviour

You may get a hunch that (say) the mother's moods are part of the stimulus configuration of antecedents leading up to problematic behaviour on the part of the child, or fraught interactions between parent and child. Try to quantify your hunch by getting the mother to keep a diary (see Fig. 10).

There is evidence that self-monitoring can be an accurate method of assessment. You must be cautious, however, as it is reactive to various factors (see Haynes, 1978). Intermittent monitoring and reinforcement of the process (by the therapist) can facilitate accuracy.

Stimulus control

Antecedent events or stimuli with potential stimulus-control properties are many and various; the concept of multiple or compound stimulus-control is thus useful in assessing the behaviour of children in the home or classroom. You might be looking at the parents' verbal messages (tone and content), physical gestures, eye-contact and so on. Other antecedents could be the particular persons or number of persons present, their age and sex; their relationship to the child. There are those stimuli which derive their behaviour-control potency through association with different contingency (reinforcement) probabilities. Others are, to an extent, non-contingent in their behaviour-control properties, e.g. states brought about by illness, drugs, alcohol, rejection, and so on.

Many problematic behaviours are the final events in a sequence of behavioural 'happenings' which may have been provoked in another place and at another time. A careful tracing of such behavioural chains is necessary because an early intervention in a chain may successfully pre-empt the problem behaviour.

DIARY RECORD: *Mrs Val Smith*   STAGE: *Baseline (1st week)*
(self-report)

MORNING	AFTERNOON
1 24/3 Am feeling irritable and low. Real 'blue Monday'. Have to shout a lot to get Pauline ready for school. P fractious defiant - refused to get dressed. We had a real set-to.	Feel a bit brighter. Still worried about the bills. But something will turn up. Did my relaxation exercises. No problem with P since coming from school. Thank Heavens!
2 Period pains!! Feel v. tense. Pauline annoyed me, not sure if she got out of the wrong side of the bed... or I did? P dawdled over breakfast. Argy bargy.	Nothing eventful — P. OK.
3 Feeling depressed. Had an argument with Frank over shouting at the children (Had to shout at P - fighting with Barbara I don't seem to be able to manage. But tearful)	More relaxed. Did relaxation exercises with tape recorder on. Pauline in good mood; amused herself.
4 P's defiance is really getting me down. It tires me out. She just won't listen. After a restless night my nerves are raw.	Feeling OK; Pauline a bit whiny but not bad. I'm so much better when she's behaving, or is it the other way round?!
5 No change. P horrible. I could have 'murdered' her this a.m. I nagged at her. Frank left for work in a mood.	Blessed peace P out with her gran Feel a bit guilty saying that.
6 Sat. Usual hell. P played up at the supermarket, wanted things. Ended up feeling embarrassed.	Feeling tired. P wouldn't eat her lunch. In the end left it to Frank. Threatened to leave them all.
7	

CHOSEN TOPICS: 1   My moodiness (getting irritable and depressed)
2   Pauline's behaviour (defiance and fighting)
3   Frank's attitude to me and the girls.
4   Any random thoughts and feelings
5   _____
6   _____
7   _____
8   _____

FIG. 10   A self-report diary.

Up to now we have been referring to proximal antecedents (see Fig. 1, p. 6)—antecedents which are close in time to the actual behaviour. The distal antecedents refer to the more distant (historical) events in the client's life. The child's past and present development is described in terms of the known medical history as well as parental reports of the child's early behaviour patterns, his growth and developmental milestones (see Herbert, 1974). Apart from information about his physical status at birth and subsequently, parents are also asked for details of the child's temperamental characteristics during infancy and early childhood. It is useful to know about evolving parent–child interactions and something of the parents' child-rearing philosophy.

An analysis of these factors is not necessarily a condition of successful interventions—distal antecedents, so-called, are more or less removed in time from the events of the client's current life-situation. An analysis of these factors is, however, a valuable exercise. Haynes (1978) lists four advantages:

(1) it may suggest conditions under which the behaviour problem may reappear after successful modification;
(2) it may provide clues concerning controlling variables;
(3) understanding of how behaviour problems begin is very instructive to clients; and
(4) the historical information may be relevant to behaviour theory and to the development of preventative programmes (see Step 20b).

Step 12   IDENTIFY REINFORCERS

In order to make therapeutic use of the law of reinforcement, find out what the child (and the parents) find rewarding.

(a) You need to identify reinforcers (rewards). Children find different things pleasurable or aversive. After all, they have different kinds of genetic constitution and reinforcement histories.
(b) You need to know something of the child's reinforcement history. The analysis of outcome controlling factors (consequent events) includes an assessment of why, when and how parents (and others) reward the child. This means finding out whether rewarding the child is contingent on his behaving in a certain way; whether rewards are applied indiscriminately or whether there is any consistency in the pattern of rewarding. Indeed, is he ever praised or encouraged for behaving well, or does he only receive attention when behaving 'badly'? Using praise as a source of reinforcement may be counterproductive with some children when they have received so little in the past that they have not learned to value it.
(c) Timing of the rewards is also crucial. There should be as little delay as possible between the child's behaviour and its consequences. Meacham and Wiesen (1969) remind us that human beings do have the ability to delay reinforcement or punishment because they have verbal means to mediate this delay. In fact, teaching a child to delay gratification is one of the major jobs of parents and society. We tend to think of adults who cannot do this as childish or immature. People do learn to work for

distant goals such as a professional diploma. However, a careful examination of the situation surrounding such long range activities would undoubtedly reveal many reinforcements along the way that tend to maintain the behaviour (see Appendix III).

(d) Do not underestimate the amount and frequency of reinforcement required when the child is learning new skills or tasks. (When the skill is acquired and has to be maintained the reinforcers are modified.)

(e) The reinforcing consequences should be very closely related to the desired 'terminal' behaviour (i.e. the particular and immediate treatment goal which is required) not the long-term objectives.

(f) Parents should be *clear* about what behaviours they are reinforcing and consistent (i.e. predictable in the consequences they apply to those behaviours).

(g) And they should make it plain to the child what it is they are reinforcing him for (cognitive structure).

The above assessments are made not only for the use of positive reinforcers but also for sanctions and punishments.

It is at this stage of the analysis (to take one example) that knowledge of the developmental literature is helpful (see Herbert, 1980). As the child matures, the way in which he cognitively structures (labels) a situation will determine whether or not anxiety about deviant acts is elicited or not. This has a bearing on whether he inhibits the 'immoral' act or not. What happens is that disapproved behaviours and the cues associated with the immediate antecedents of such behaviours ('impulses') come to elicit anxiety. Parents may have, in a sense, a choice of whether they bring out to lesser or greater degree one or other of the attributes of guilt and resistance to temptation, in their children. This will depend primarily on two things: the timing of the sanctions they administer for misconduct, and the nature of the explanations they provide when they do so. There is evidence that punishment which immediately precedes a forbidden act (i.e. as the intention to transgress is forming and becoming explicit) maximizes resistance to temptation. Punishment has undesirable side-effects when it is not modulated. Above a certain optimal level of intensity it produces a state of emotionality in the child which appears to interfere with learning. If discrimination of the punished choice is difficult, intense punishment is actually more likely to lead to transgression. A child must be able to distinguish what aspect of his behaviour is being punished if he is to be able to exercise control over the consequences of his actions.

Note: *Reinforcers and punishers (the C term in our ABC equation) are defined in terms of how they influence the child—the learner—and not how the therapist or parents think they might or should affect him. Reinforcers are individual to the particular child.*

You can identify reinforcers in the following ways:

(1) Observe the child's behaviour. What does he like doing most? What does he choose to do a lot of when he has the choice (high probability behaviours)?

(2) Ask the child . . . what he likes . . . likes doing . . . with whom.

(3) Ask those who know the child.

Table V   Some suggested reinforcers[a]

	Home	Classroom
Things	Crayons, plasticene, note pads, play-money, football cards, charms, pencils, marbles, ball-point pens, comics, records, favourite meals, small toys, book/record tokens, models, puzzles, stamps, magazines, sweets, crisps, fruit, stars.	Good report to take home, loan of books, magazines, records. Tokens. Use of stimulating rarity-value items/equipment. Special place in the classroom.
Activities and games	Pictures to fill in—in stages,[b] cutting out pictures, drawing/painting, stickers, watching TV, listening to records, playing monopoly, ludo, puzzles, etc. visits, helping mother/ father.	Finger painting, quiz, writing on the board, being read a story, helping teacher, clay modelling, looking at magazines, listening to records, using the tape-recorder, other favoured individual/group activities.
Privileges	Staying up late, choice of meal, extra pocket money, extra long story from parent, outing with father (football match, etc.), going to the cinema.	Longer recess, no homework, not having to take a test, outings, leaving school early.

[a] These items may be offered as part of a reinforcement menu (with a tariff) for older children, or put on display in a 'pretend shop' with its price list, for younger children.
[b] See page 100 for an imaginative example of a reinforcement picture drawn by a child's mother.

(4) Table V provides you with a few questionnaire/checklist items.

(5) Check on particular states of deprivation. Some children are deprived of so few of the 'goodies' in life that it is very difficult to find effective reinforcers.

(6) Premack's Principle: Therapists have made use of the principle that the opportunity, or privilege, to engage in preferred activities can reinforce activities or behaviours that are less popular. In other words, high probability behaviours can act as contingent reinforcers for low probability behaviours. The value to a child of reinforcing activities can be estimated by observing the frequency of behaviours in a free-choice situation. This principle is sometimes referred to as 'Grandma's rule'. It states that 'first you work, then you play' or 'you do what I want you to do before you are allowed to do what you want to do'. Clearly this notion, like so many other learning principles, has been known and practised by succeeding generations of child-rearers as simple common sense. However, it has been enshrined as a formal principle—the Premack principle—defining one type of reinforcer, following Premack's research into the problem of response probability and his search for an index that would predict between response preferences for a wide variety of topographically dissimilar behaviours.

Remember: *Attention is very rewarding! Especially for children; and parents can (unwittingly) support disruptive behaviour by attending to it (scolding, nagging, distracting). Don't forget to look for what is reinforcing in the maladaptive, self-defeating behaviours of parents or parent-substitutes.*

The popularity of physical punishment with some adults may to some extent be due to the fact that it is often rewarded by the immediate cessation of (say) the child's aggression. However, its longer-term and more general effects may not be so beneficial, because it is likely to be administered in ways that are excessive, ill-timed, inconsistent, retaliatory and without any accompanying promotion of alternative behaviour. (In the words of the cliché: 'punishment tells you what you can't do, not what you should do.') This sequence may provoke the child to more aggression, as well as providing him with adult demonstrations of aggressiveness that he may imitate. As Jehu (1975) points out, punishment may actually increase aggressive behaviour, especially towards people other than those who administer the penalties. Another possible disadvantage is that the child may learn to avoid or escape from punitive adults, which can create problems like truancy and absconding. Finally, punishment may produce excessive anxiety in the child, and some cases of school phobia are instances of this.

'Ventilationists', as they have been called, advocate the expression of anger and other emotions and their acting-out in therapeutic and other socially approved situations, so that they will be 'drained away' or 'purged'. In fact, most of the available evidence supports the contrary view that such ventilation will tend to lower inhibitions against aggression and to make it more rewarding to the child. Thus, it is likely to increase rather than to decrease aggressiveness outside the special therapeutic situation.

Because of the maturing child's capacity to anticipate events, conditions of reinforcement also have potent incentive and motivational effects. Although immediate reinforcement is (as we have said) particularly powerful, especially with children, most human behaviour is not controlled by immediate external reinforcement. As a result of prior experiences and through the capacity to represent actual outcomes *symbolically*, future consequences can be converted into current incentives/motivators that influence behaviour in much the same way as *actual* outcomes. Cognitive skills in the maturing child allow him to be foresightful.

The motivational function of reinforcement has implications for your assessment. Problems arise when the incentive system is faulty, for example when (1) social stimuli which are positively or negatively reinforcing for a majority of persons (praise, attention, encouragement, blame, criticism, disapproval) do not work for the client; (2) the potent reinforcers for the client are deviant or harmful (drugs, alcohol, glue-sniffing, fire-setting); (3) the environment (wittingly or unwittingly) is reinforcing maladaptive behaviour; (4) there is a relative absence of reinforcement in the individual's life-situation.

Motivational function of reinforcement

Reinforcement and its vicissitudes may play a part (see Goldfried and Davison, 1976) in the depressions manifested (fairly rarely) in children, and more frequently in adolescents. In the experience of the author, many parents (especially mothers) are reacting with depression and demoralization to the child and family problems they find themselves coping with so ineffectually. Depressive reactions may result from any one, or more, of the following situations:

1. The individual's perceptions of his ability to control his life is distorted; he feels helpless or hopeless because of a perceived absence of any contingency between the

person's own efforts and the reinforcing nature of the consequences that flow from them.

2. The individual's efforts to bring about reinforcement are inadequate.

3. His environment is providing him with scanty reinforcers.

> ## Step 13 ASSESS ORGANISMIC VARIABLES (or obtain information from other sources)
>
> *You are not dealing with an 'empty vessel'; there are all sorts of things going on within the organism. The child's behaviour does not occur in a vacuum. He is responding to an external and internal environment as he grows up. An assessment of organismic factors tells us something of the intrinsic child.*

The pre-treatment assessment

There are various quantitive indices of constructs such as intelligence, anxiety, depression, assertiveness, measured by tests and questionnaires. It is useful to have information about the child's own expectations or mental set about certain situations. The way in which a child labels or categorizes events can influence his emotional reactions in such situations (Ellis, 1962).

Although a person's beliefs, attitudes and expectations may often be modified by changes in overt behaviour, there are times when such organismic (inferred, mediating) variables should themselves be the target for direct modification. For example, there may be certain physiological and cognitive states of the youngster which might constitute the objective of a behavioural intervention. To take but one specific instance, phobic anxiety may involve avoidance or escape strategies, physiological signs of arousal, cognitive factors like faulty attribution or attitudes of helplessness, or combinations and permutations of all of them. Here then is a mixture of overt and covert events playing actiological, maintaining or mediational roles in the manifestation of the problem. Any of them might become the focus of an intervention.

Age and sex appropriateness

What is normal at one age in a child may not be normal at another age. Temper tantrums are extremely common at age two and, in that sense, fairly 'normal'. Frequent temper explosions at age 13 would seem rather problematic. Girls are much less likely to respond to frustration with a temper tantrum than boys at that age (see Table VI).

Congenital factors

Information about genetic or congenital factors aids the fuller understanding of problem behaviour. Interpretations of socialization in terms of social reinforcement have shared (in the past) a common view of the infant as an essentially passive organism whose character is moulded solely by the impact of environment upon genetic predispositions. There is evidence (see Herbert, 1974, 1980) that the direction of effects of socialization is not always downward—from parent to child—and parents are not the sole possessors of power and influence within the family. Children exert an influence on significant adults in their lives and, in a sense, socialize them into a parental role. What is obvious from recent studies is that important individual differences are manifested in early infancy, among them being autonomic response patterns, temperament, social responsiveness (cuddliness), regularity of sleeping, feeding and other biological patterns, and perceptual responses (Thomas *et al.*, 1968). These can influence the way in which parents respond to, and manage (or mismanage) their offspring.

Brain functioning and integrity

Damage to the brain is one of several main types of congenital abnormality in babies. Congenital, a word that means 'born with', is used in medicine to describe inborn diseases or defects. Congenital defects may, but need not, be inherited. As advances in medicine have brought infectious diseases under control, an increasingly large proportion of ill health in childhood has been caused by congenital defects.

The brain can be compared with an incredibly intricate machine. Like a machine, it can go wrong; but, unlike most machines, its standards of reliability are remarkably high and it goes wrong only rarely. This is just as well, considering that the brain and nervous system must always be on the alert, processing information which is crucial in the individual's ever-changing surroundings, and coordinating the many adjustments that are essential to survival. In each and every second of waking life, more than a hundred million electrical impulses flow into the brain. Even when we are asleep, more than fifty million neuronal 'messages' are being relayed, every second, to and from the brain and different parts of the body.

Even a sturdy organ like the brain can have its functions adversely affected by injuries (such as a blow, a fall or some penetrating wound), oxygen deprivation (for example, asphyxia at birth), infections, tumours, degenerative diseases, and mechanical trauma (brought about by difficulties during birth). Brain injuries or defective functioning of the central nervous system can have an influence on the emotional stability of the child, on his motor and sensory abilities. They may also impair the processes he relies on to interpret the messages from his environment and those which coordinate his reactions to such information. This can be very disabling as can be seen in autistic and spastic children—for differing reasons.

Apart from the adverse consequences for the child's emotional intensity and control which can follow directly from injuries to the brain, the physical difficulties (e.g. clumsiness and overactivity) so often associated with brain damage may provide another (if indirect) route to emotional maladjustment. There is evidence that babies born precipitately after a short, sharp labour, or born after their mothers have endured difficult pregnancies, or a protracted birth process, tend to be irritable, hyperactive and difficult as babies and as older children. These attributes may be due to transitory or longer lasting cerebral dysfunctioning. They can make for children who are extremely difficult and tiring to rear.

Some theorists describe a general condition called 'minimal brain-dysfunction' and talk about 'the brain-damaged child'. The cluster of symptoms which is supposed to describe the brain-damaged child includes overactivity, motor incoordination, distractibility, impulsiveness and perceptual disturbance. This notion of brain damage as a unitary problem is not consistent with the facts. The symptoms resulting from different types of brain injury are (not surprisingly) extremely varied, and the popular stereotype applies to only a very small proportion of the 5 % of cases of brain damage in the general child population. We cannot refer to the brain-damaged child as if there were only one type; what we get is a variety of children, with quite different problems (if any), whose conditions call for intensive individual analysis of a kind which some of the current generalizations do not provide.

So many children with school learning problems fail to show any positive evidence of neurological damage or dysfunction that a new diagnostic term has begun to make headway in the clinical world. This is 'learning disability', which reflects educational rather than medical criteria. The child with a learning disability exhibits a disorder in one or more of the basic psychological processes involved in understanding or using spoken or written language: listening, thinking, talking, reading, writing, spelling, arithmetic. Such disorders include conditions which have been referred to in the past as perceptual handicap, brain injury, minimal brain dysfunction, dyslexia, and developmental dysphasia.

Brain arousal and personality

There are nervous system properties which help determine the way in which we respond to situations. These are concerned with what is called the 'arousability' of the nervous system. This concept has blurred the distinction between motivation and emotion. Many theorists consider that both are aspects of the level of arousal of the individual.

The point is that this system—a more or less unitary system like a central switchboard—can alter the *excitability* of the nerve cells, increasing the level of arousal or alertness of the individual. Part of the system also has an inhibitory role. As one would expect of a 'switchboard' system, not all messages can be accepted; there is a selection process. This portion of the system can have a 'switching off' or 'dampening down' effect on selective stimuli.

Physiologists relate this system to the 'reticular formation' at the back of the brain, and centres connected with it. The brain, as we saw, regulates the individual's adjustments to the external environment. Within the brain the reticular formation determines his characteristic level of *cortical* arousal—the 'idling properties', so to speak, of his brain. These 'reaction tendencies' as they are called, of the central nervous system, are thought to have implications not only for normal emotional and personality development (e.g. introvert *vs* extravert patterns), but also for psychological problems. They are also thought to account for individual differences on a variety of vigilance and perceptual skills. Disorders of thought are related by some investigators to defects in the basic properties of neural activity; and individual differences in susceptibility to fatigue, sensory deprivation, isolation and tolerance of pain have been explained in terms of these nervous system tendencies.

Health and physical impairment

There is a variety of physical conditions, such as hunger, anaemia, mild infections and drug-effects, which can lead to lassitude—something often mistaken for laziness. If a child is to be successful at school, good health is vital; it provides the basis for the stamina demanded by long hours of concentration in the classroom. Regular attendance at school depends upon it, and effective learning, in turn, depends upon reasonably consistent presence at lessons. Some subjects (e.g. arithmetic, mathematics) are hierarchical in structure; that is, one step is logically preceded by, and dependent upon, another. So the child who misses a series of lessons (particularly the child who has chronic, recurrent illnesses) may experience great difficulty in catching up. Subjects like mathematics, which tend anyway to attract negative emotional attitudes, may (in the absence of an under-standing teacher) become the focus of intense anxiety for the vulnerable child. Even the regular attender may not be able to learn efficiently if he is tired or apathetic.

The clinician needs to be alert to physical and intellectual limitations such as short-sightedness, deafness, epilepsy, slow learning and low IQ and the referral services available for dealing with these disabilities.

Physical problems are not only responsible for undermining scholastic endeavours; they may themselves be the consequence of emotional disturbance. If a child shows physical lethargy and a lack of interest, he may be depressed. In its milder forms, depression may show itself as a lack of physical energy and well-being. In its more severe manifestations, the child tends to be irritable and bad-tempered, and, when it is at its worst, he sleeps poorly, lacks an appetite and is always dejected, apathetic and lifeless. The child who is (for whatever reason) depressed refuses to meet the challenges of life; he ceases to strive and to use his full effectiveness in whatever sphere of activity he finds himself. An essentially emotional problem like this is often mistaken for a physical one.

Temperament

Information about behaviour style aids the fuller understanding of problem behaviour. For example, it is clear that early differences in temperament set the stage for varying patterns of interaction with the environment, leading to the shaping of personality along lines which are not predictable from knowledge of the environment alone.

A group of research workers and clinicians have demonstrated just how important these inborn or constitutional aspects of personality—the temperamental qualities of the child—can be in the development of normal behaviour and behaviour problems (Thomas et al., 1968). An intensive study of 136 New York children measured temperament in terms of nine descriptive categories: activity level, rhythmicity, approach and withdrawal, adaptability, intensity of reaction, threshold of responsiveness, quality of mood, distractibility, attention span and persistence. They classified babies according to clusters of temperamental characteristics; these groupings were referred to as 'difficult', 'easy' and 'slow to warm up' babies. The difficult child showed irregularity in biological functioning, a predominance of negative response (withdrawal) to new stimuli, slowness in adapting to changes in the environment, frequent expression of negative moods and a predominance of intense reactions. The easy child, on the other hand, was positive in mood, highly regular, low or mild in the intensity of his reactions, readily adaptable and usually positive in his approach to new situations. In short, his temperamental organization was such that it usually made his early care seem easy and pleasant. The third temperamental type—the slow to warm up—combined negative responses of mild intensity to new stimuli with slow adaptability after repeated contact. An infant with such characteristics differed from the difficult child in that he would withdraw from new situations quietly rather than loudly. He did not usually exhibit the intense reactions, predominantly negative mood and biological irregularity of the difficult child.

Identical twins are more like each other in every one of the nine attributes than are the two children in a non-identical pair. In every aspect, there seems to be a genetic factor at work.

The authors found that 65 % of their original babies could be assigned to one of the general 'types' of temperament. Some 40 % of the children fell into the easy category, while 10 % were difficult. Another 15 % of the children were slow to warm up. That left about 35 % of children who showed a mixture of characteristics not fitting into any of the three main groups.

The significance of differences in temperament (or behavioural style) is underlined by research which demonstrates the releasing effect and initiating role exerted by the behaviour of the child on his parents (Bell, 1971). The reciprocal interactions of parent and child are in a state of constant adjustment as each reinforces the other positively or negatively. Rewardingness or punitiveness, for example, are not qualities inherent in the parent but are called out by a particular child and his behaviour. These are vital factors in the various learning situations encountered by the child.

There is evidence that even as early as the second year of life, and before the manifestation of symptoms, children who were later to develop behaviour problems showed particular temperamental attributes. Children with markedly irregular patterns of functioning, who were slow to adapt to new situations, whose emotional responses were usually at a high level of intensity, and whose predominant mood was negative were the ones who were most likely to come to psychiatric attention for later problem behaviour (70 % of this so-called 'difficult' category).

Activity level is a temperamental attribute which tends to be stable over time. A mother will react to a child with a high activity level in a different manner than to a child with a low activity level. High rates of activity and high intensities of emotional expression in the repertoire of children tend to be aversive to adults, and, indeed, are among the most frequent complaints made by adults in referring children to out-patient clinics.

Hyperactivity is the name for one of the most trying problems a mother or teacher has to cope with: the overactive child, who seldom sits still. Such a 'hyperactive' child faces severe impediments to achieving success at school, because his problems militate against efficient learning. First of all, he suffers intense and disorganized overactivity. This, in turn, is associated with distractivity, a very short span of attention, and impulsiveness. Also, more often than not, children with these problems do not get on very well with their peers, being aggressive and rather destructive. Their control over their emotions may be limited, and trivial setbacks may trigger sudden and violent outbursts of rage, while stressful situations may precipitate panic attacks. High rates of activity or restlessness may have automatically reinforcing effects because they enable the child to use up energy and escape the unpleasant properties of sitting still. In other cases these behaviours are reinforced by the attention of (say) the teacher.

Given the various caretaking and socializing tasks a mother has to undertake and which demand a degree of stillness, attention and cooperation from her offspring, *overactivity* is particularly tiring and sometimes disturbing, and leads willy nilly to excessive attention giving.

Autonomic response patterns

The control system responsible in large part for emotional reactions is the autonomic nervous system (ANS). It is also responsible for the more mundane day-to-day maintenance of the *internal* environment via the glands, blood vessels, smooth muscles and heart muscle. The activities of these effectors (as they are known) are controlled by the autonomic nervous system. Most of the motor impulses that control these internal organs (viscera) and keep us functioning efficiently operate below the level of consciousness.

This control system—a network of motor nerve cells—plays a large part, not only in maintaining the individual's internal environment and homeostasis, but also in determining his level of arousal, particularly his emotional state. It regulates the work of:

(a) the glands,
(b) the blood vessels,
(c) heart muscle,
(d) stomach muscles,
(e) intestines,
(f) bladder.

It has two components which often, but by no means always, work in opposition to each other:

(1) *The sympathetic system.* The sympathetic division of the ANS acts to adjust the body to states of alarm or emergency, i.e. when we are highly emotional. It has, among others, the following effects: it increases the heart rate, increases the blood pressure, and distributes blood to the exterior muscles. Broadly speaking the sympathetic division accelerates those bodily processes concerned with the mobilization and/or expenditure of energy.

(2) *The parasympathetic system.* This system tends to predominate when we are calm and relaxed. It does many things which, taken together, build up and conserve the body's stores of energy. It decreases heart rate, reduces blood pressure, and diverts blood to the digestive tract.

Emergency functions
Suppose that something frightens us. In such time of stress the sympathetic system predominates. How do we react physiologically?

(a) The pupils of the eyes dilate.
(b) The eyelids lift.
(c) The eyeball protrudes.

(d) The heart rate increases.

(e) Blood pressure is elevated.

(f) The volume of blood in internal organs increases and more blood is pumped to the extremities and muscles.

(g) Blood sugar is increased.

(h) Digestion ceases.

(i) The spleen pours out more blood cells to carry oxygen.

Thus some functions are halted by stimulation of the sympathetic branch, while others are accelerated. In times of emergency, the sympathetic nervous system produces nerve impulses which reach the adrenal glands, located on top of the kidneys, and cause the secretion of certain hormones which are vital in the person's adjustment to the crisis. These effects are analogous to the priorities typical of a national wartime economy. In emergency situations some functions are more vital than others to survival. Digestion can cease, for example, while the supply of blood is increased to muscles, for if the animal does not survive by means of flight or defence, it will make little difference whether the last meal is digested. On the other hand, the muscles are toned up for maximum performance.

Stress proneness

The autonomic nervous system, then, not only controls the day-to-day 'vegetative' functions of the body, but also operates to change the economy of the body when the animal (or person) is faced with stress. Disturbance of this latter function sometimes causes pathological conditions referred to as psychosomatic illnesses. Those individuals who are high on the dimension of personality named 'neuroticism' are thought to have inherited the properties of an excessively reactive ANS, one that is biased toward sympathetic predominance. The integrating processes which regulate the balance between the two divisions of the ANS are located in the master control system—the brain.

It is useful, when diagnosing a child's difficulties, to be aware of the concept of 'stress' and stress proneness and the part it plays in the disposition to problem development. The term 'stress' covers any state of *overload* when the child is being pushed to his limits, i.e. when he is beset by powerful pressures which tax his capacities to cope (adjust). It can refer to physical factors like injuries, infections or excessive cold, or to psychological situations involving *inter alia* frustration, threat or conflict.

There are many sources of stress for some youngsters in a modern industrial society: noise, overcrowding, a sense of powerlessness in a large impersonal world. There is the unremitting emphasis on success, achievement and efficiency in our competitive society. Some adolescents feel alienated from the education they are receiving. There is a lack of meaning or fulfilment in many of the jobs people have to perform—and for some that includes parenting. Role and identity confusion—the ambiguities in what is expected of modern children and adolescents—can also create tensions.

Stress is a difficult concept to pin down because individuals differ markedly in their reactions to similar situations. For example examinations may be stressful for some pupils but not for others.

Remember: *To consider both the situation and the individual's reactions to it, when you are identifying stresses in his life.*

Maladaptive fear

Although the words 'fear' and 'anxiety' are close in meaning, there are subtle differences in the way certain experts use the terms. According to some theorists, anxiety is a form of fear or apprehension without a focus. Whereas the word fear is attached to specific situations—like examinations or a physical assault—the word anxiety is taken to mean an unpleasant emotion that is not associated with anything that is directly threatening in this way. Anxiety has been described as 'fear spread out thin'. As they get older, the majority of children's fears are anxieties of an anticipatory, intangible kind rather than realistic and immediate fears of tangible situations and dangers. The same can be said of adults. A crossover in the source of most of our fears occurs roughly at the end of childhood and beginning of adolescence. There is a decline in those fears aroused by intense and novel stimulation and an increase in social fears.

Fear is a crucial factor in the development of neurotic (nervous) problems, yet it has the useful function of spurring on the individual. It can arouse him to more efficient performance in such situations as athletic competitions or examinations, just as the physical accompaniments of fear tone up the individual to deal most effectively with emergencies in which he must fight or flee for his life. Fear, however, primes the individual to more efficient performance up to a certain point only. Beyond that level, it has the effect of *over-arousing* the individual. Instead of enhancing his performance it disrupts it.

The development of fear is, of course, influenced by the child's history and the setting in which the fear-provoking situations occur. The tendency of a child to over-react with fear is closely related to the inherited degree of instability or sensitivity of the autonomic nervous system.

Cognition

There are many factors including maturational processes which predetermine the sequence and structure of developmental stages. Jean Piaget's theories of cognitive development indicate how intellectual processes change qualitatively as the child grows up. It is important for the child therapist to know about these processes if he is to understand what sense and meaning the child is able to make of the physical, social and moral world he inhabits—at different ages and stages of development (Piaget, 1932).

What children think may influence their performance of deviant behaviours. Thus knowledge of the way he perceives and structures events—say, a 'provocative' incident—may provide a clue to changing his behaviour, if it is self-defeating.

The guiding principles of cognitive-developmental theorists such as Piaget and Jerome Bruner are that children structure the environment by the route of internal experiencing and that cognitive structures and functions unfold in a regular developmental sequence. This is an interactional point of view in the sense that enduring and significant behavioural trends are the product of the interaction of certain structuring tendencies within the organism and the structures of the external environment.

Karoly (1977) describes some of the common dimensions in the varieties of cognitive growth associated with that important therapeutic concept 'self-mastery': an increased capacity to differentiate, store and represent experience, and the ability to act in accordance with an 'internal' frame of reference. He believes that some of the major components of behavioural self-management (decision-making, standard-setting, self-evaluation, symbolic self-reinforcement, self-labelling, planning and directive self-instruction) are built upon the gradually developing capacities of:

(a) selective attention;
(b) long-term memory;
(c) time perception;
(d) coordination of internal and external perspectives.

Level of achievement

The under-achieving child's academic performance is significantly below that predicted on the basis of a measure of his intelligence or scholastic aptitude. There is a highly significant correlation between maladjustment and under-achievement.

The home environment is a most potent factor in determining the child's attainment at school. A parent's early encouragement of independence promotes concern for intellectual competence in the child. The educational aspirations of the parents for their child, the literacy of the home, the interest of the parents in the child's work, the physical amenities of the home, the father's occupation, and the parents' own educational level, all have a bearing on the level of the child's achievement.

Chronic under-achievement in boys of above average aptitude may begin in the primary-school classes. It is not likely to show itself in girls until they reach secondary school.

Most under-achievers fail to find academic work rewarding, and, when they do work, they exert little effort. They tend to be distractible, seldom complete their work, and set themselves low standards of academic achievement. Under-achievers generally find school unsatisfying, and develop negative attitudes towards teachers.

Some parents set unrealistically high levels of aspiration for their children. Children are likely to 'internalize' these standards and they have a bearing on the way in which they reinforce themselves, i.e. the threshold at which they perceive their performance as adequate or inadequate. If the child's standards of competence are unrealistically high, he is unlikely to find himself in many situations in which his performance is worthy of self-reinforcement, regardless of the objective value of the actions.

Step 14a   ARRIVE AT A DIAGNOSTIC DECISION

Ask yourself:
(a) Is one of your objectives to intervene and bring about some change?
(b) If so, specify precisely what the areas of change are to be; why they need to be brought about; and how these alterations are likely to change not only the child but the whole (family/classroom) system.

There are essentially two issues to be resolved at this stage (and it must be emphasized that Steps 14 and 15 merge):

(a) *Diagnostic:* Is it a problem of sufficient seriousness to merit an intervention?
(b) *Ethical:*   Is it ethically right to intervene so as to produce changes in the direction of goals X, Y or Z?

Arriving at diagnostic criteria

One of the simplest ways to uncover a therapist's implicit or latent definition of mental health is to ask him about his criteria for successful termination of a therapeutic case. The other side of the coin, of course, is to ask him how he decides that treatment is actually required. As 'healthy' adjustment, in the opinion of the author, cannot be discussed meaningfully as an abstract quality of abstract children, and implies an inappropriate medical model of behaviour, we shall look at particular strategies and competencies developed by individual children to meet the specific needs and problems of their life situations. The framework for this examination is a psychosocial one.

Problems are so-called because they have a variety of unfavourable consequences; when they are not deficit problems (a failure to learn adaptive responses), they are conceptualized as strategies of adjustment which the child has learned to his own disadvantage (and often to the disadvantage of others) in the attempt to cope with the demands of life. They are therefore referred to as maladaptive strategies: they are inappropriate in terms of several criteria which are assessed by the clinician.

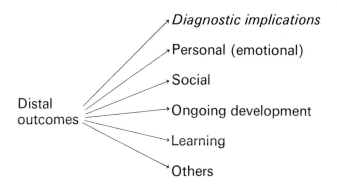

Distal outcomes →
- Diagnostic implications
- Personal (emotional)
- Social
- Ongoing development
- Learning
- Others

The diagnostic criteria are listed on the right of Fig. 1 (p. 6), with regard to (a) personal, (b) social, (c) developmental, and (d) learning factors. They arise from a consideration of the longer-term consequences (distal outcomes) of the problem behaviours. You should have arrived already at some reckoning of the probability that you are dealing with a problem meriting serious concern—in your working out of the FINDS parameters (Step 10).

Ultimately, the professional judgement of a child's mental/behavioural well-being is made in individual terms, taking into account the child's unique personality, his particular circumstances and the opportunities, privations and stresses associated with them. (On another level, similar questions can be asked of the family unit in which he resides.)

Ask yourself: What are the implications of the child's (and his family's) life style? More specifically, what are the consequences—favourable or unfavourable—that flow from the child's ways of behaving and his interactions with others?

You must establish what the implications of his behaviour are for the following factors.

(a) His personal well-being (his emotional state)

Ask yourself: Is he in a state of distress: anxious, discontented, unhappy, morbidly preoccupied, hostile, insecure, overly dependent, guilty?

(b) His social development

Ask yourself: Does he get on with other children, with adults? Can he go out and enjoy himself or is he socially restricted in some way? Can he make and keep friends?

Immature, self-centred children are not always able to manage the give-and-take of friendship. Exchange theory gives us pointers to why this should be so; it provides one method of evaluating friendships. Those theorists who employ 'exchange theory' in analysing aspects of social behaviour and friendship, view social interactions as a social exchange somewhat analogous to economic exchange; people are influenced (consciously and unconsciously) by the ratio of 'rewards' and the 'costs' incurred in the interaction.

In the assessment of the implications for social relationships, it is useful to draw up a balance sheet. On the debit side, the term 'cost' is applied to deterrents that may be incurred in contacts with another person—such as hostility, anxiety, embarrassment, and the like. For attraction to a potential friend to occur the reward–cost outcome must be above the 'comparison level', a standard against which satisfaction is judged.

Technique: *Do a cost-benefit analysis:* Gelfand and Hartmann (1975) suggest a cost–benefit analysis to evaluate the desirability of changing the target behaviour as it affects the child, the caregiver (parent/teacher) and oneself (or the agency).

Costs to the child might include being singled out (and embarrassed) as needing help; benefits anticipated might include happier relations with siblings, less failure at school.

Costs to the caregiver (say teacher) may involve distraction from teaching duties to other children in the classroom; benefits (in the longer term) might include more time for creative teaching in the absence of disruptive interjections by the target child.

Note: Ways should be worked out to minimize costs.

(c) His ongoing development and maturation

Ask yourself: Do the child's problems interfere with the forward momentum and course of normal development? Are they causing him to 'regress', or slowing him down? Do they represent a 'cul-de-sac', taking him in the direction of a self-defeating life-style?

Cameron (1955) suggests that it is the task of the therapist to ascertain where a child stands on the developmental scale, whether his progress and status—mental and physical—are appropriate to his age, retarded or advanced. It is obviously very useful to be familiar with physical and social norms and the norms of development when making a diagnosis. In the light of all the information the therapist decides whether the child requires help or not.

Ask yourself:

(1) Is the child's adaptive/adjustive behaviour appropriate to his age, intelligence and social situation?

(2) Is the environment making reasonable *demands* of the child?

(3) Is the environment satisfying the crucial *needs* of the child, i.e. the needs that are vital at his particular stage of development?

The family (or some other agent of socialization) may be dysfunctional. Thus, if the child's behaviour is abnormal (unusual), troublesome and self-defeating—and the answers to questions 2 and 3 are 'No'—then you are still faced with a problem. However, it is more of a 'problem situation' than a 'problem child'. In a sense this is always the case, and it is a matter of judgement as to where the emphasis in treatment will be.

A feature of much problem behaviour in childhood is its transitoriness. So mercurial are some of the changes of behaviour in response to the rapid growth and the successive challenges of childhood that it is difficult to pinpoint the beginning of really serious problems. A long-term study (MacFarlane *et al.*, 1954) of the development of 126 American 'run-of-the-mill' children provides us with information (see Table VI) about the incidents and shifts in their problem behaviours as manifested at different ages between 21 months and 14 years.

It would be helpful if we could identify the periods when a child is most vulnerable to emotional problems, and concentrate our efforts and resources so as to help him (and his parents) through such crises. Some theorists talk of 'developmental discontinuities'. One of the chief types of developmental discontinuity is brought about by significant and relatively rapid shifts in the individual's biosocial status. These periods in which qualitatively new and discontinuous (inter-stage) changes in personality organization are being formulated are referred to as transitional phases or developmental crises. During these transitional periods the individual is in the marginal position of having lost an established and accustomed status and of not yet having acquired the new status toward which the

Table VI   Behaviour problems shown by one-third or more of normal boys and girls aged 21 months to 14 years (behaviour problems shown by one-third or more of the boys and girls at each age level) (MacFarlane *et al.*, 1954)

		Age 1¾	3	3½	4	5	6	7	8	9	10	11	12	13	14
Enuresis	B	+													
(diurnal and nocturnal)	G	+													
Soiling	B														
	G														
Disturbing dreams	B										+				
	G						+				+	+			
Restless sleep	B	+													
	G														
Insufficient appetite	B														
	G						+								
Food finickiness	B		+												
	G	+	+	+			+								
Excessive modesty	B														
	G														
Nailbiting	B													+	+
	G									+		+			
Thumbsucking	B														
	G	+	+												
Overactivity	B		+	+	+	+		+	+	+					
	G		+	+	+	+									
Speech	B														
	G														
Lying	B			+	+	+	+		+						
	G			+	+	+	+								
Destructiveness	B														
	G														
Overdependence	B														
	G														
Attention demanding	B														
	G														
Oversensitiveness	B			+	+	+		+	+	+	+	+	+		
	G			+	+	+	+	+	+	+	+	+	+	+	+
Physical timidity	B														
	G			+		+									
Specific fears	B		+	+	+	+	+	+	+	+		+			
	G	+	+	+	+	+	+	+	+			+			
Mood swings	B							−	−	−	+	+		+	
	G											+			

		Age 1¾	3	3½	4	5	6	7	8	9	10	11	12	13	14
Shyness[a]	B	−	−	−	−	−	−	−							
	G											+			
Sombreness	B				+										
	G					+									
Negativism	B			+	+										
	G				+										
Irritability	B														
	G														
Tempers	B	+	+	+	+	+	+	+	+	+	+	+	+	+	
	G	+	+	+	+	+	+	+				+			
Jealousy	B					+			+	+	+	+	+	+	
	G			+		+		+			+				
Excessive reserve[a]	B	−	−	−	−	+	+					+	+		
	G					+	+	+	+	+	+	+	+		+

[a] Data not obtained

factors impelling developmental change are driving him. The superimposition of other problems on these sensitive periods may have a delaying effect on development.

Each stage of development is thought to correspond to a particular form of social demand; the child must deal with and master a central problem. Erikson (1965) is a major proponent of such a developmental timetable. At each stage a conflict between opposite poles in a pattern of reciprocity between the self and others has to be resolved. The crises are related to: trust *vs* mistrust; autonomy *vs* shame; initiative *vs* guilt; industry *vs* inferiority; identity *vs* identity diffusion; and so on (see Herbert, 1974).

(d) His learning skills, competence and self-esteem

Perhaps one of the most serious consequences of emotional and behavioural disorder is its deleterious effect on the child's learning in the classroom and hence, his achievement. Even highly intelligent, maladjusted pupils tend to have real difficulties in school performance. The greater the number of problems reported, the poorer, on the whole, is school performance.

Some children, for a wide variety of reasons, lack skills which are essential in order to cope with growing up in a satisfactory manner. Physically handicapped children, for example, are massively overrepresented in the population of youngsters with behaviour problems. If such children behave dysfunctionally in response to a variety of stresses, frustrations and humiliations, it is hardly surprising. They can be helped to become more competent and thus have less need of what proves to be counterproductive problem behaviour.

Seligman (1975) suggests that what produces self-esteem and a sense of competence in a child and thus immunizes him against depression and helplessness is not only the absolute quality of experience. He states that 'to the degree that uncontrollable events occur, either traumatic or positive, depression will be predisposed and ego strength undermined. To the degree that controllable events occur, a sense of mastery and resistance to depression will result.'

Schaffer (1977) develops this theme; he describes how the child learns, through the prompt action of his caregivers, that specific activities have 'signal value'. He cries, and his mother enters the scene; he gurgles and coos and the people around him respond with various actions indicating delight. As Schaffer puts it:

> He thus finds out that crying and cooing each produce a particular effect, and that he can employ one or the other to manipulate his environment in particular ways. But possibly this is only part of the lesson he learns; much more importantly, he may develop a general expectation that he can indeed affect his environment. A baby therefore develops an 'effectance motive' as he acquires a general confidence that he can produce consequences—even in those instances where he has as yet had no chance to see whether a particular act will be effective or not. To develop such a motive a child's actions must be consistently and promptly reinforced, and it is one of the mother's functions to make this possible. Depending on the ability to do so, the child will in due course learn a generalized expectation either of control or of helplessness. (p. 62)

White (1959), among others, has marshalled data from various sources to demonstrate that even very young babies exhibit a need to be competent, to master or deal effectively with their own environment. He calls this need 'effectance motivation' and considers it to be related to such motives as mastery, curiosity and achievement.

Coopersmith (1967) provides evidence that the optimum conditions required for the achievement of high self-esteem in children are a combination of firm enforcement of limits on the child's behaviour together with a marked degree of freedom (autonomy) within these limits. As long as the parentally imposed constraints are backed up by social norms outside the home, this provides the youngster with a clear idea of an orderly and trustworthy social reality which, in turn, gives him a solid basis for his own actions. Coopersmith found that children with a high degree of self-esteem are active, expressive individuals who tend to be successful both academically and socially. Youngsters with low self-esteem present a picture of discouragement and depression and in general the opposite features of those defining high self-esteem children.

Technique: *A quick test of self-esteem.* Ask the child to write (or verbalize) on two themes. The first 'essay' is called 'Myself as I am'; the second is entitled 'Myself as I would like to be'. A dramatic discrepancy between the *actual* and *idealized* self-image may be indicative of low self-esteem.

Normative studies: emotional and conduct disorder

It is obviously very useful to know about the social norms and the norms of development when making a diagnosis. It would be a dramatic step forward if we could identify more reliably the periods when an individual child is most vulnerable to emotional problems. Knowledge of 'sensitive periods' in the child's development could alert the child's caretakers to the developmental tasks which put a heavy burden on his adjustive capacities. At least we have studies by Rutter *et al.* (1970) and Shepherd *et al.* (1971) which provide normative data for British children. The counselling of parents as to the normality of their children can produce a sense of relief and the detached handling which allows them to remain the transitory problems that they are when given sensible management. We know as a result of longitudinal studies that, for the most part, 'neurotic' children (children with so-called *emotional* problems such as fears, phobias and inhibitions) become reasonably well-adjusted adults; they are almost as likely to grow up 'normal' as children drawn at random from the general population.

However, there is another constellation of problems involving physical and verbal aggressiveness, disruptiveness, irresponsibility, non-compliance and poor personal relationships. This behaviour pattern has been referred to as *conduct* disorder. Youngsters with conduct and delinquent disorders demonstrate a fundamental inability or unwillingness to adhere to the rules and codes of conduct prescribed by society at its various levels. Such failures may be related to the temporary lapse of poorly established learned controls, to the failure to learn these controls in the first place, or to the fact that the behavioural standards a child has absorbed do not coincide with the norms of that section of society which enacts and enforces the rules. The long-term implications of persistent and intense non-compliant, and therefore antisocial, behaviour in children are serious (Robins, 1966; West and Farrington, 1973).

Ethical imperatives

Because behaviour modification is very directive and often quite powerful, it should only be employed as a specific treatment or management procedure after full and careful consideration of the desirability of the proposed changes. The objectives are decided primarily on personal, social and ethical grounds. The clinician has the special responsibility of acting, in a sense, as an 'advocate' for the child. This is particularly the case with the younger child who cannot speak for himself and defend himself against the sometimes unreasonable demands made of him.

Critics accuse behaviour modification of a variety of failings, but none so passionately as its alleged unethical manipulativeness. The simplistic fundamentalism of some purists of behaviourism is going to take a long time to live down. Doubtless, many in the helping profession have been put off from even a preliminary exploration of behaviour modification because they find the laboratory-based language of behaviourists alien and because the methods (especially described out of context) evoke images of a 'clockwork orange' scenario. The very words 'behaviour modification' sound sinister and dehumanizing. Gambrill (1977) comments upon the disadvantage of the popular term for the behavioural model of intervention—'behaviour modification'. After all 'people have been trying to alter the behaviour of their fellows since the beginning of time, but only in select instances could we say that a behaviour modification procedure was used.'

There is justifiable concern that the behavioural approach might encompass the ideology that people are mere pawns of the environment or that it imposes control where no control previously existed. This notion that people are mindlessly manipulated without their choice or say so, is, in fact, misleading, not to say insulting; it is almost impossible to change someone's behaviour *significantly* without his awareness. Of course, all therapists are in the business of trying to produce change, as are all helping professionals, no matter what their orientation. But they are out to change behaviour, not deep structures of personality. Fischer (1978) maintains that behaviour modification 'respects' the integrity of the client by focussing on observed behaviour and limiting itself to helping diminish maladaptive functioning and increase adaptive functioning. The client should be an active participant in the selection of objectives/goals within a behavioural model of intervention—a choice which is likely to be obscured if the therapy is based on the therapist's interpretation of hidden motives and desires of which the client himself is unaware.

The idea that controlling behaviour is in itself somehow immoral ignores the reality, as Bandura (1969) reminds us, that all behaviour is inevitably controlled and the operation of psychological laws cannot be suspended by romantic conceptions of human behaviour any more than an indignant rejection of the laws of gravity can stop people falling. From the therapist's point of view the issue to be resolved, with any kind of treatment, is not whether behaviour is to be controlled but where the controlling forces lie and to what extent he should intervene or encourage others to intervene in their operation. The moral issues of whether to intervene and if so what the aim of intervention should be, can only be answered with reference to the individual therapist's value base and that of his profession.

The source of influence in behaviour modification is well recognized and quite explicit. The approach should encourage the therapist to take care not to influence the client unduly in the selection of treatment goals and to make his thinking about the problem explicit. Non-recognition of influences allows their use in an unsystematic, covert way— the so-called hidden agenda. Behaviour modification is not an intervention entering a vacuum of free will. Its working philosophy can be deliberately underlined in order to enhance personal freedom of choice for the client; this is done by trying (in part) to analyse the processes of unwanted influence. Personal freedom of 'choice is further extended by the particular concern of behaviour therapists to provide the client with the ability for greater self-direction, by means of self-control and problem-solving training. (See Erwin (1979) and Stolz *et al.* (1975) for full discussions of these complex and crucial issues.)

Practical guidelines to ethical issues

(1) Obtain the full informed consent of the client or those responsible for him. Defining who the client is, raises some complicated issues in family-orientated work.

Ask yourself: (especially where a child is concerned) Who benefits from the programme if it is implemented? Who should decide what behaviours are desirable or undesirable?
Who (if anyone) has the right to define the situations as problematic, and thus request a change?
Is the child old enough or responsible enough to have a say in the decision to intervene? (At the Child Treatment Research Unit, Leicester, the child is privy to all the discussions about the actual programme, but not to intimate marital or personal parental matters.)

There are no simple answers to these questions; they depend on varying circumstances in individual situations.

(2) Ensure that the client's participation in the programme is voluntary.

(3) Give the client the clear option of withdrawing from the programme if he so wishes.

(4) Make sure that the client and/or other persons of significance to the client (e.g. parents, foster parents, care staff) are engaged in the selection of treatment objectives.

(5) Give decided preference to positive treatment procedures over methods with aversive connotations.

Step 14b	FORMULATE OBJECTIVES if and when you have made a decision that the problem requires an intervention

Having selected the goals of treatment it is necessary to specify them very precisely in terms of the responses to be produced and the conditions under which these should occur. An objective must contain four elements:

(1) Who will do
(2) What,
(3) To what extent,
(4) Under what conditions?

The goals of treatment are also specified as publicly observable responses. At the treatment level, a serious difficulty arises because of the tendency for therapeutic goals in some traditional therapies to be conceived in vague 'global' terms rather than specified as measurable targets. This makes it difficult to measure success or failure, and thus to validate or invalidate one's way of working. Or when improvement does not follow treatment it is easy to label the parents ('they're uncooperative, manipulative, ineffectual ... etc., etc.') and their children, by way of exculpation. Such diagnostic labelling places the origins of the intractable problem within the child (e.g. an inadequate personality, a character disorder, poor motivation) or his family, rather than the interaction between the child and his environment. Furthermore, failure to get better can be attributed to the shortcomings of clients rather than to the therapist's lack of skill.

Once treatment goals have been identified, they are ranked according to the negotiated consensus as to what the priorities are. Balanced against the proposition that treatment must begin with the most troublesome behaviours is the proposition that the parents's first intervention attempts should hopefully be successful. Maximizing the chances of success may be more important than beginning with the parent's first choice, because they may already have a sense of failure in dealing with the child. If they experience failure at the beginning of treatment such an experience is likely to reinforce the sense of despair and helplessness which caused the parents to seek professional help in the first place.

Remember: Your behavioural objective is a carefully specified goal which describes:
(1) The nature of the desired behaviour (e.g. the child, whose target behaviour is disobedience, should comply with a parental request without saying 'No!' accompanied by verbal abuse).

(2) The situation in which it should occur (e.g. when mother asks him not to get up from the table when eating, or not to grab his sister's food from her place).

(3) The criteria for deciding whether the behavioural goal has been achieved (e.g. acceding to mother's specific request—without comment—immediately, or after one repetition).

Step 14c DRAW UP A VERBAL AGREEMENT OR WRITTEN CONTRACT

Contracts (whether written down or agreed verbally) have the effect of structuring reciprocal exchanges. They specify who is to do what, for whom, under what circumstances (De Risi and Butz, 1975; Stuart, 1971). Reinforcement contingencies (to take one example) can be made explicit between individuals who wish behaviour to change (e.g. parents, teachers, nurses) and those whose behaviour is to be changed (students, children, patients). Reciprocal contractual agreements are not unnatural to most people; they exist in families and other groupings, whether explicit or implicit. Many of the problems that arise are due to the arrangements not being reciprocal or explicit enough.

The contract specifies the relationship between the behaviours desired by the individual who has called for a change in the child's behaviour and the consequences of such a change, i.e. the reinforcers desired by the child. Any of the reinforcers listed in Table V, p. 56, might be used in the contract.

Contracts contain five elements:

(1) Contracts should *detail the privileges* each party expects to gain from the contract. For example, parents may want a child to complete his or her work, attend school regularly, and so on. On the other hand, the child wants free time with friends, extra allowance, and other reinforcers.

(2) The target behaviours of the child must be *readily observable*. For example, if parents or teachers cannot determine whether a responsibility has been met, they cannot grant a privilege. Thus, some behaviours may not readily be incorporated into the contract system. Parents cannot always monitor whether (say) an adolescent visits certain friends, so it would not be advisable to include this in a contract.

(3) The contract imposes *penalties* for a failure to fulfil the agreement. The child must know precisely the conditions for failing to meet the terms of the contract and what consequences will follow. The sanctions are planned in advance (i.e. agreed to by all parties) and are applied systematically (i.e. consistently). There must be no arbitrary or *post facto* arrangements.

(4) A contract can provide a *bonus clause* so that extra privileges, activity, or extension of free time, are available as rewards for consistent performance over a prolonged period. Consistent performance often goes unreinforced in everyday life. Because adults expect such performance ('Why should I reward him for what he should be

doing anyway?') it often gets overlooked. For a child whose behaviour is recently acquired, it is crucial to provide reinforcement for consistent performance. Bonuses written into the contract serve this purpose.

(5) A contract should provide a *means of monitoring* the rate of positive reinforcement given and received. The records that are kept inform each party of the progress (or lack of it) of the programme.

Figure 11a, b shows two sample contracts.

This Agreement is drawn up between . . . . Therapist for the Child Treatment Research Unit, and Mr and Mrs B . . . ., parents of Johnny B . . . .
In keeping with the wishes of both parents (and Johnny), to work towards the goals set out below, Mr and Mrs B. . . . . .agree with . . . . to keep the following arrangements.

General goals: for Johnny (separate agreement between Johnny and parents)
1.   Regular attendance at school.
2.   Informing mother of his whereabouts after school.
3.   Returning home by 6 p.m. for his tea.
4.   Refrain from swearing at his mother.

                for Parents (separate agreement between parents and Johnny)
1.   Increase Johnny's pocket money to £1 per week.
2.   Allow him to go out on Saturday nights with his friends.
     (return by 11.30 p.m.)
3.   Allow him to stay up until 10.30 p.m.
4.   Refrain from criticizing Johnny's friends.
The specific plans and goals are attached.

On your part you agree to: On our part we agree to:

                    Appointments
Keep the appointments we arrange   Keep the appointments we arrange

                  Recordings
Keep records in the diaries   Explain the purpose and meaning of
and chart as arranged   assignments and graphs

Renegotiation Clause: The requirements and objectives are re-negotiable at any time on request by any party.

Signed. . . . . (Clients) Signed . . . . (Therapist).
Date . . . .

FIG. 11a   A contract for a non-compliant school refuser.

Morning arrangements for John Smith: agreed by John Smith and Mrs Smith

1. John woken by Mrs Smith.
2. John offered choice for breakfast by Mrs Smith (toast, cornflakes, etc.).
3. After a reasonable time (one minute) John makes final choice of breakfast and tells Mrs Smith. This choice cannot be changed by John or Mrs Smith.
4. John then has a bath for a reasonable time (15 minutes maximum).
5. Mrs Smith calls John out of the bath by using three minute warnings:
   a. Calls John three minutes before he is to get out.
   b. Calls John two minutes before he is to get out.
   c. Calls John one minute before he is to get out.
   d. Calls John out of the bath.
6. John has a reasonable time to dress (approximately four minutes) and then comes down to breakfast.
7. If John delays or refuses to get out of the bath and does not come down for breakfast, the breakfast to be thrown away.
8. If John comes down on time and all the stages above (1-6) are followed John is awarded one gold sticker to go on his chart (and his breakfast!).

Evening arrangements for John Smith

1. At 9.30 p.m. John is to begin to get ready for bed.
2. John is to have supper.
          get undressed
          go to the toilet before 9.45 p.m.
3. At 9.45 p.m. he is to go to his bedroom.
4. John may watch television, read, knit, if he wishes before sleeping — once he is in his bedroom.
5. John may not:
   a. Shout, demand, scream to his parents downstairs .
   b. Come downstairs again after 9.45 p.m.
   c. Disturb Sally in her bedroom.
   d. Disturb his parents in their bedroom.
6. Mrs Smith is to buy John a 'night light' for his bedroom.
7. These arrangements are for Monday, Tuesday, Wednesday, Thursday, Sunday. On Friday and Saturday, John may go later to bed — Mr and Mrs Smith to decide a reasonable time (always at least half an hour after Sally).

Signed. . . . .(John)
Signed. . . . . (Mrs Smith)
Signed. . . . . (Social Worker Witness)

Date . . . .

FIG. 11b   A contract for a hyperactive eight-year-old—a boy with problems of extreme non-compliance (Toone, 1981).

Note: *Contracts help the client:*
   *(a) to understand what the therapist is doing, and what is expected of him, and
        by means of the summary statement that they embody, to comment on the
        accuracy of the therapist's perception of his complaints;*
   *(b) to identify the problems jointly and break them down from the large and
        unmanageable problems they seem (vague and abstract too often) to a level
        at which they are specific, concrete and partialized; when they assume
        smaller dimensions they become less daunting;*
   *(c) to learn about negotiation and compromise; how to reach a consensus
        between people whose interests do not always converge;*
   (d) to take account of others' needs and wishes;
   *(e) to be more aware when a specific goal is reached and when a successful
        termination should occur.*

Step 15	FORMULATE CLINICAL HYPOTHESES
	Set up hypotheses to account for your observations and other data

In trying to explain problem behaviour you might draw on a wide range of factors—
depending on their relevance for the particular case (see Fig. 12). Deciding what is relevant
is a hard-earned clinical skill.

In some clinics it is customary to work up a report for a Case Conference.

The case study: the quasi-judicial method

It has been forcefully argued by Bromley (1977) that jurisprudence provides us with a
guide to procedures for an effective *scientific* study of individual cases. The quasi-judicial
method has much in common with a behavioural (functional) analysis, and is worth
looking at in the preparation of the clinical formulation for the case conference or case
study. A case study involves a reconstruction and interpretation of a segment of an
individual's life-story—based upon the most reliable evidence available. It is a theory
about how and why a person behaved as he did in a particular situation.

This theory should be tested:
   (a) by collecting evidence;
   (b) by marshalling rational arguments to support the claims made in the theory.

The quasi-judicial method requires (inter alia) *that:*
   (a) the main issues be stated clearly from the very beginning;
   (b) sufficient empirical data be available to support or refute any claims;
   (c) evidence be admissable and relevant to those claims;
   (d) arguments be relevant and rational;
   (e) conclusions which have important practical implications be backed up by a greater
        weight of evidence than conclusions of lesser significance.

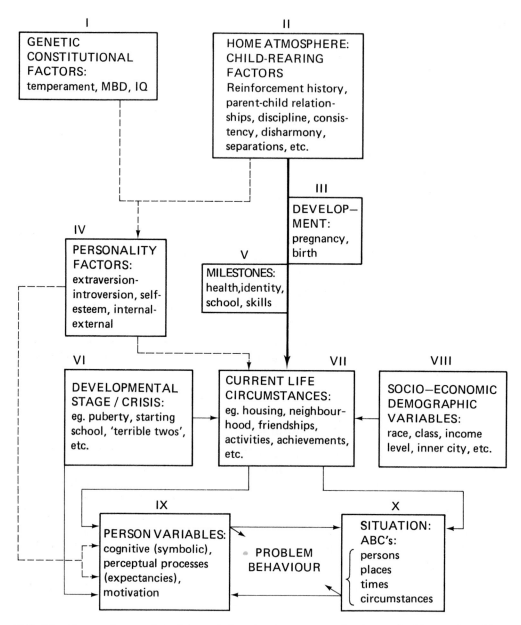

FIG. 12 The ten-factor clinical formulation, i.e. factors contributing to incidents of problem behaviour. (Adapted from Clarke, 1977.)

Rules

Bromley (1977) lists six rules for the preparation of a case study:

(1) Report truthfully and accurately: about the person, his life and circumstances—with attention to detail. (The author of this manual interpolates some 'don'ts'!)

    Avoid: Irrelevancies, trivialities, rhetoric and special pleading.

(2) State, at the outset, the aims and objectives of the case study—explicitly and unambiguously.

    Avoid: Global, vague or implicit (hidden) objectives.

(3) Include an assessment of the degree to which the stated aims and objectives have been achieved.

    Avoid: Confabulation—the attempt to fill in gaps in the history, or to make sense of the behaviour, where this cannot be done. Make clear the reasons for your inability to fulfil particular aims and objectives.

(4) Take the time appropriate to, and necessary for, the assessment. Some categories of information (vital for a good assessment) cannot be obtained in a hurry. This applies (*inter alia*) to intimate material of deep emotional significance to the individual. Trust may take time to develop. Data collection (of the less fraught kind) can also be time-consuming even for the skilful therapist. A representative sample of the client's behaviours/interactions takes time to record and observe.

    Avoid: Premature 'explanations' and prescriptions demanded by anxious clients or importunate 'seniors'.

(5) Focus on the person-in-situation (i.e. concentrate on an interactional approach). It is important to give a detailed account of the objects, persons and events in the client's physical, social and symbolic environment.

(6) Report findings in direct, objective language without resorting to meaningless jargon or an arid style. The report should retain its human interest by having (in a sense) a 'story line'. As Bromley (1977) puts it: 'The writer should present the individual's point of view, rather as a barrister presents his client's case in a court of law. This can be done with sympathy and imagination and with due regard for high standards of evidence and argument.'

    Avoid: Intruding your own personality into the report. Emotional bias is easy to detect and casts suspicion on the entire report.

Procedures

There are ten steps required for the explication of both individual cases and general laws (Bromley, 1977):

(1) State clearly the problems and issues.
(2) Collect background information as a context for understanding (1).

(3) Put forward *prima facie* explanations (conjectures/hypotheses) and solutions (pro-gramme formulation) with regard to the client's personality and predicament—on the basis of information available at the time, and on the basis of the *principle of parsimony*. Examine the simple and obvious answers first. They may, of course, have to be rejected if they don't stand up to critical examination. This guides the:

(4) Search for further/additional evidence. New hypotheses/explanations will have to be formulated and examined.

(5) Search *again* for, and admit for consideration, sufficient evidence to eliminate as many of the suggested explanations (hypotheses) as possible; the hope is that one of them will be so close to reality as to account for all the evidence and be contradicted by none of it. The evidence may be direct or indirect; but it is vital that it should be admissable, relevant and obtained from competent and credible sources.

(6) Enquire critically into the *sources* of evidence, as well as the evidence itself. Bromley (1977) makes the point that in the case of personal testimony, this is analogous to cross-examinations in a court of law; otherwise it amounts to checking the con-sistency and accuracy of all items of evidence.

(7) Examine carefully the internal logic, coherence and external validity of the entire network of associations and hypotheses formulated to explain the clients' predica-ment and proposals to solve the problems.

(8) Select the 'most likely' interpretation, provided it is compatible with the evidence (some lines of argument will be obviously inadequate whereas others will be possible or even convincing).

(9) Work out the implications of your explanations for intervention/treatment or some other action (or, indeed, inaction).* Work them out in clear, and specific terms with stated and explicit objectives.

(10) Prepare the case report as a 'scientific account' of the client. It should contribute to psychological or social work 'case-law' by virtue of the abstract and general *principles* employed in explaining the tactical adjustments or strategic adaptation of the person concerned. Psychological case-law evolves out of systematic comparison and contrasts between individual cases (Bromley, 1977, p. 173).

Interlude

Clinical formulation

A crucial stage in the assessment of Lorna (see p. 14) was the attempt to formulate reasonably precise hypotheses with a view to planning treatment. These were derived from all the information available.

---

*Always ask yourself about the implications (e.g. the risks involved) of making Type I as opposed to Type II errors in your assessment. Is it more damaging to your client if you risk Type I errors (i.e. asserting relationships falsely) than if you risk Type II errors, which deny relationships that do actually exist? The academic psychologist tends to minimize errors of incautious assertion at the expense of relatively common Type II errors. The clinician often acts on the basis of weakly supported propositions (see McWhirter, 1980) because of the dangers of ignoring potentially significant associations. But of course there may also be some risks in presuming relationships which do not have any basis in reality.

We were looking for possible antecedent and consequent stimuli which appeared to be instigating and maintaining the problem behaviour; we also examined other situations in which the child's behaviour differed from that in the problem situations (e.g. evidence of prosocial behaviour and the settings in which it took place).

The data upon which the formulation was based were also used in deciding that a behavioural treatment programme was appropriate. The case of Lorna was postulated to be one largely (but this was by no means the whole story) of defective stimulus control. As a result of discrimination learning, certain stimuli had come to signify the likelihood of particular reinforcement consequences, thus influencing the probability of Lorna's deviant response being performed. Mrs Green's words of command and denial, for example, were functioning as inappropriate discriminative stimuli (cues) for verbal disputations and other forms of attention (not to mention Lorna getting her own way). Such events were reinforcing her oppositional behaviour. There was also an almost complete absence of consistent sanctions contingent upon such behaviour. It might be said that Lorna was on an intermittent schedule of reinforcement for inappropriate behaviour. To put it another way: Lorna's mother was unwittingly reinforcing her maladaptive behaviour. Lorna's demands, with few exceptions, for being waited on, attention, etc., were acceded to following her display of tantrums and disruptive behaviours. The invariable outcome in the case of the oppositional behaviours was to increase the interaction between Lorna and her mother. The resulting attention was reinforcing these non-compliant actions. It was quite straightforward to identify favourable consequences: to take but one example, she was being allowed to veto activities she did not like. Conversely, in all examples of misbehaviour, there were no really aversive contingent consequences which might serve to extinguish them.

With regard to discriminative stimuli for the performance of problem behaviours, the most significant of these were the presence and actions of Mrs Green. The currency of her commands and threats had been debased; Lorna did not trust her words.* She had learnt that in her presence her wishes (for her undivided attention and for 'goodies') were likely to be met if she persisted long enough or escalated her coercive behaviours. Under normal conditions of socialization it would be expected that defiance of prohibitions given by her parents would be linked in the child's mind with unfavourable sanctions; but in Lorna's case ignoring or opposing mother's threats and commands had almost no aversive consequences.

As Mrs Green appeared to bear the brunt of most of Lorna's misbehaviour, it might be concluded that her father was able to exercise control over her. This was not so, in fact, Mr Green's small part in this analysis of the problem situation reflects his minimizing of the contact he had with Lorna—much to his wife's annoyance.

Organismic factors

Having attempted to identify the conditions controlling the problem behaviour, the next task was to try to explain their origins. The importance of this in a behavioural

*It is an interesting observation that many parents who wouldn't dream of letting their children (and themselves) down by breaking their word over a treat are quite willing to break promises (threats) over punishments.

approach is not so much to help the client achieve insight (although awareness may facilitate change) but rather to discover to what extent the original 'causal' factors continue to influence the current controlling conditions. Lorna's developmental history was analysed in order to seek any possible contribution to the problem by somatic or other factors. Physical conditions might produce problem behaviour directly or might contribute to it indirectly through the reaction of the child and/or his parents to any disability.

You may remember that Lorna, from early in life, had been a difficult and overactive child, and that from the day of her birth Lorna would cry day and night. The nights were particularly difficult. Mrs Green spent most of them nursing her. Being of such a commanding temperament, Lorna learned from early on the strategy of how to gain attention from her mother and the rest of the family. The parents always intervened when she was crying, shouting, screaming; when she was frustrated, disobedient and aggressive they often obeyed her commands for the sake of peace, to save time, or to avoid embarrassment. A variety of situations and settings became cues for verbal disputes and other forms of coercion (supermarkets, friends' homes, car drives). Here the parents were constrained even more than usual in responding to her oppositional behaviour.

Summary

Lorna appeared to be a child who had displayed a range of 'surplus' behaviours almost from birth; these have been shown to be closely linked with the development of maladaptive behaviours at a later age. In addition, her mother's ability to cope had been considerably reduced in a number of ways. First Mrs Green had been handicapped by her fatigue and depression and in particular by the fiercely protective (defensive) attitude she had toward this 'unwanted' child who had turned out to be so difficult. This (together with a philosophy of child-rearing which was a reaction to her parents' methods) had considerably limited her choice of disciplinary procedures at her disposal.

There was another vital factor: because of the parents' misreading of the child's difficult behaviour as reflecting a degree of mental subnormality, she was being subjected to inappropriate expectations in her play and other aspects of life. (We had ascertained that her IQ was 145, i.e. in the highest range.)

Levels of explanation

The trouble with the search for reasons or explanations is that there are several levels of explanation which may be applicable to a particular problem. This is illustrated by another child, Pam, who has a learning problem which is affecting her ability to read. On top of this, she has certain behavioural problems, and constant failure is causing her morale to sink lower and lower. Diagnostic tests carried out by the educational psychologist show that she has a visual-perceptual handicap. Remedial treatment is available to help her overcome her reading problem. The remedial teacher could teach her to recognize words and their meanings through the medium of her other sensory modalities. Here, the visual handicap is one explanation of the reading difficulty. Some clinicians would rest content with this level of causal explanation, justifying their decision on the grounds that they have sufficient knowledge to intervene therapeutically and help the child. This has been called the 'instrumental' level of explanation. The explanation is sufficiently precise to be instrumental in planning some therapeutic measures to mitigate the cause–effect sequence of events. Or it may simply be instrumental in providing the individual with a satisfactory account of some event. It is sufficient in that it *explains*, and raises no further questions in his mind.

While this explanation provides an account of an important antecedent condition in the problem—in this case the visual-perceptual handicap—other workers might claim that the diagnostician should search for the *original* cause. In this case they would feel it necessary to determine whether the visual problem was organic or psychogenic in origin.

To illustrate the many remaining strata of explanations, let us take only the organic possibilities. Pam may be diagnosed after further investigation as 'brain-damaged'. (It would be most unsatisfactory if the matter were left to rest here.) As we have seen, this term—like other 'hold-all' explanatory concepts such as 'poverty' and 'divorce'—is imprecise. It does not reveal the *specific mechanisms* whereby certain causal events are transformed into symptoms and disabilities; this makes it difficult to plan precise and detailed therapeutic strategies of a rational kind. Pam's reading problem—by now referred to as 'dyslexia'—is considered to be just part of a more general neurological condition called 'minimal cerebral dysfunction'. As it is explained to Pam's mother, her child is thought to have a 'different' kind of brain, which not only affects her behaviour adversely (in terms of a limited span of concentration and attention, and overactivity) because of its disharmonious functioning, but also makes it difficult for her to read. It processes incoming messages (stimuli) in such a way that Pam's visual perception of the outside world is altered—often in a way that makes the recognition of word patterns and sentence configurations difficult. We still have not exhausted the possible explanations to complete the chain of events. The neurological impairment itself must have some cause. The cause may be a biochemical irregularity which, in turn, could be traced back to genetic variations. Or it may be due to a lesion in the brain sustained during birth, or due to . . . and so we could go on and on, depending on the problem.

If injuries to the brain appear to be associated with epileptic symptoms, hyperactivity, uninhibited aggression and under-achievement in a particular child, there is likely to be a hierarchy of explanations (ranging from the neurological to the cognitive) for his problems. Therapy, too, is likely to range from the physical (e.g. epilepsy-inhibiting drugs) to the psychological (e.g. behaviour modification and remedial teaching).

Note: *In your attempt to arrive at an explanation of the problem before you, don't neglect the client's point of view.*

(1) Ask parents/teachers if they have a theory (or hunch) as to why the problem is occurring.
    You might say: 'I'm sure you've given the matter a lot of thought; have you any ideas or hunches about why Wayne is so rude and aggressive?'

Sometimes parents/teachers say they have no idea but their 'theories' are implicit in the way they've tried to deal with the problem.

(2) Ask parents/teachers about how they have tried to achieve their goals in the past.

You might ask: 'What have you done in order to stop Wayne being so rude and aggressive?' The answer: 'We've tried to stop him playing with the boys on the estate', might suggest some notions of modelling and 'bad influence'.

Ask: 'Have you ever asked Wayne outright to stop being rude and aggressive?'

Lesoff (1977) makes the point that parents who have unresolved conflicts do not make persistent demands on their children in these areas of conflict; they are often very successful in making demands in areas where they have no conflicts. So find out about any variations in the child's non-compliance! Remember that there *is* only one way to make a demand, with the imperative form of command: 'Stop doing X!' or 'Do Y!' The youngster is only defying directly if he has been given a clear and direct demand to which he has not complied.

Implicit in some parents' 'explanations' of the child's behaviour is the nihilistic view that he simply cannot control his behaviour. Parents commonly explain the problem in terms of the child's disability. Thus: 'Wayne cannot control his behaviour due to brain damage or, perhaps inheritance.'

Lesoff (1977, p. 11) links parents' ideas and behaviour together to show how they might prevent them from insisting that the child change his behaviour. 'I can understand that as long as you see Johnny as physically unable to control his behavior when he's angry, it wouldn't make sense to you to insist he stop having tantrums when he's angry. Just as it wouldn't make sense to insist a crippled person get up and open a door.'

Lesoff goes on to search for the sense/meaning that the child's behaviour (their perception of its causes) has for the parents. This might involve an interpretation that the parental 'theories' have a defensive role against their own angry impulses. 'As long as you see Johnny as unable to control his behavior, you can avoid being as angry with him as you might otherwise be. I can understand that as long as you feel you may be unable to control your behavior when angry, that you would want to avoid being angry.' Lesoff might make the following interpretation, for instance, in the example where the parent feels guilty or responsible for the child's behaviour. 'I can understand that as long as you feel Johnny's screaming is a device to get attention and you agree he should have more attention, it doesn't occur to you to insist he stop screaming whether or not he gets more attention. In fact you would see it as necessary that he get more attention before it would be reasonable for him to stop screaming.' The author would then go on to interpret that this idea helps the parent defend against his angry impulses. 'As long as you see Johnny's screaming as reasonable until you give him more attention, you can avoid holding Johnny responsible for his behavior and you can therefore avoid being as angry with him as you might otherwise be.'

Many therapists reject this interpretive approach as redundant to the therapeutic endeavour; others would say that the programme would run into difficulties without a reasonable understanding of the parent's conceptualization of the child's problem and child-rearing issues.

This debate takes us close to the issue of 'underlying causes'.

'Underlying' causes: symptom substitution

Many theorists and practitioners of a psychodynamic persuasion question the appropriateness of a behavioural approach because they believe that therapy for a particular problem must direct itself to the 'root cause' of the problem. According to this view, disorders of psychological origin should be treated by some form of psychotherapy. They regard as symptoms (the outward and visible signs of underlying disorder) what the behaviourally orientated therapists might take as the focus of treatment. It is often argued that a failure to deal with the underlying problems (e.g. intrapsychic conflicts) leads to 'symptom substitution'.

Just how one defines operationally indices of 'substitution'—clear-cut ways of specifying the links, symbolic or otherwise, between symptoms—is not clear. So the criticism is impossible to prove *or* disprove. In any event, as Goldfried and Davison (1976) compellingly argue, a determinant that is assumed to have its source in the unconscious, need not be viewed as more 'underlying' or 'basic' than a controlling variable that stems from the environment. Studies (e.g. Baker, 1969) designed *inter alia* to investigate whether *other* problems appear when behavioural programmes have successfully removed symptoms (such as enuresis—a problem which is amenable to treatment by bell-and-pad) do not indicate that such an eventuality occurs. And as Jehu *et al.* (1972) observe, it is one of the strengths of behaviour modification that treatment does not depend necessarily upon the discovery and understanding of the historical causes of the problem. He concedes that the identification of the current problem behaviour and its contemporary causes may be assisted by information about the client's history. However, this information is gathered primarily as a source of clues to these contemporary conditions rather than for such specific treatment objectives, as interpretations for insight-giving or 'working through' of problems. The behaviour therapist places most weight on providing his client with *new* learning experiences; if past experiences did contribute significantly to the manner in which (say) an adolescent is now behaving, in practice they are seldom still functional. That is to say, they no longer maintain current behaviour problems.

Ryall (1974) has described as the peculiar feature of delinquent (approved school) children the *quantity* of their law breaking. The sheer *intensity* of the offending of the persistent delinquent is at the centre of the treatment problem; for these boys delinquent behaviour has become a habit—a self-reinforcing learned behaviour pattern. Each delinquent act produces excitement, peer-group status, and possible material rewards. These consequences generate the incentives for further offences. Ryall accepts that young people present other serious social and psychological problems apart from delinquent actions. Many have tragic social histories, coming from broken or unhappy homes; some show marked signs of emotional disturbance. A majority appear to be personally or socially inadequate; a substantial number have serious educational problems. Of course, such problem areas are proper targets for treatment in cases where they might prove remediable. But the solution of the general problems is unlikely to deter the persistent delinquent from offending.

By comparison with the current events which are reinforcing the youth's delinquent acts, the history of early rejections, or the particular cause of his very first delinquent acts, recedes in practical importance. There is little, if anything, that can be done to remedy those situations. The therapist and his client have to come to terms with the present realities of what, in some way, is a rewarding life-style. The therapeutic problem is posed by the delinquent behaviour being not only habitual but also central to the child's self-image. As Ryall explains, 'being delinquent' not only gives the young person status in the eyes of his friends but it also gives him status in his own eyes. Indeed, delinquency may be the only area of activity in which the individual has any sense of personal adequacy or achievement. Another crucial aspect of the behaviour of the persistent delinquent is that his delinquency is buttressed by a self-consistent set of attitudes towards his social environment.

We return to the issue of symptom substitution in Step 20.

School environment

The school really matters as an influence for good or ill on the child; after all, he'll spend some 15,000 hours of his time at school (see Rutter *et al.*, 1979). In an important study of London secondary schools, Rutter and his co-researchers showed that they varied greatly with respect to rates of examination success, attendance, misbehaviour and delinquency. Research data indicated that the differences between schools in outcome were systematically related to their characteristics as social institutions. Factors as varied as the degree of academic emphasis, teacher actions in lessons, the availability of incentives and rewards, good conditions for pupils, and the extent to which children were able to take responsibility, were all significantly associated with outcome differences between schools. All of these factors were open to modification by the staff, rather than fixed by external constraints.

This is hardly surprising. As the authors point out, standards of behaviour in the school are set (*inter alia*) by the staff. Children have a strong tendency to imitate the behaviour of other people, especially those in positions of authority whom they respect and like. Not only do they copy particular actions, but they may identify in a more general way with those whom they follow, and adopt opinions, values and attitudes that they perceive as belonging to their models. It is not only a matter of how teachers deal with the children in their care but also the manner in which they interact with colleagues and the attitudes (by word and deed) they express about the school.

Home environment

The variations in home environment which can have an influence on the child's development of problematic behaviour are so multitudinous as to be beyond the range of this manual (see Herbert, 1975, 1980). We do know that when the family fails in providing appropriate and consistent socialization experiences, the child seems to be particularly vulnerable to the development of conduct and delinquent disorders. Typically the children with persistent disorders come from families where there is discord and quarrelling; where affection is lacking; where discipline is inconsistent, ineffective and either extremely severe or lax; where the family has broken up through divorce or separation; or where the children have had periods of being placed 'in care' at times of family crisis. Parents, especially fathers, have high rates of mental disorder, especially personality disorders of the aggressive type, and they show an unusual amount of rejecting, hostile and critical behaviour towards their offspring.

We know, also, that the children of parents with a chronic or recurrent mental disorder are at risk themselves of manifesting psychiatric disturbance; several forms of separation, loss and disturbed family relationships also contribute significantly to the genesis of different forms of childhood psychopathology. However, as was suggested above, it seems that it is family discord and disharmony (rather than the separation of death, divorce or some other break-up of the home) which are pathognomonic in the development of delinquent patterns. Different causal mechanisms and principles are probably at work, but understanding of them is limited. This is most true of the 'exceptional cases'—the children who are the exception to the empirical 'rule' that says 'by all accounts that child, in those circumstances, *should* be a problem!' Or the one that says 'Why on earth is that child a problem? He comes from such a good home!'

And it is here that a macro-analysis is of limited value and the micro-analysis (described in these pages) comes into its own. It is the detailed assessment of the individual child and his family and their social situations, and the exploration of current controlling events, that may provide answers to these puzzles.

Summary: background to the formulation of the nature of the problem

It is useful to distinguish the historical and the contemporary causes of problem behaviour. Let us see, in this summary, how they also link up.

The historical causes may have directly affected the client's bodily functioning, as in the cases of some genetic factors, injuries or infections, or they may have consisted of certain experiences through which he has learned some unacceptable way of behaving, in certain situations. What the child has done in the past is a fairly good indicator of what he may do on future occasions. Contemporary influences determine whether the child will perform the behaviour he has acquired.

Note: *Early formative (distal) influences have an historical but not a functional connection with present behaviour (see Fig. 1, p. 6). The distinction between distal and proximal factors in the explanation of the client's behaviour is crucial.* The reinforcement history (when primary and secondary reinforcers were being developed) may be helpful in explaining why 'universal' reinforcers don't motivate this particular child. The failure of rewards, normally associated with a response pattern, to cue this pattern in an individual is referred to as 'defective or inappropriate incentive systems'.*

The contemporary causes of problem behaviour may exist in the client's environment or in his own thoughts, feelings or bodily processes, and they may exert their influences in several ways:

(a) Certain antecedent conditions may be eliciting or reinforcing problem responses,

---

* It is of interest that the judicial method proper demands that explanations be formulated in terms of proximal events.

especially those of an emotional kind, while other such conditions may involve some lack of appropriate discriminative stimulus control over the client's instrumental responses.

(b) 'Inappropriate stimulus control of behaviour' (where a normally neutral stimulus acquires the capability of eliciting a dysfunctional response like anxiety) may arise— in part—from a history of classical conditioning. 'Defective stimulus control' over behaviour (notable for the inability of a stimulus, normally associated with a pattern of behaviour, to cue this pattern in a person) may stem from inconsistent discipline, *laissez faire* parenting, extreme permissiveness, or the lack of outcomes to actions— such as to make discriminating behaviour irrelevant or unimportant. There may be outcome conditions which either reinforce problem behaviour, or punish or extinguish desirable responses. 'Aversive behavioural repertoires' (such as violent actions, extreme dependency behaviours) may originate from learning conditions such as these, and others.

(c) Any of these inappropriate forms of antecedent or outcome control may be operating in the client's symbolic processes, rather than in his external environment or physiological changes. In the case of 'aversive self-reinforcing systems' the youngster sets high standards in evaluating himself, thus leading to self-depreciation and criticism rather than self-approval. Such punitive cognitions can originate from an early history in which the individual was taught to rely on stern standards of self-appraisal. (Example: depressed, suicidal individuals; youngsters low in self-confidence.)

(d) 'Defective or inappropriate incentive systems' (as we saw above) are characterized by the failure of rewards, normally capable of acting as an incentive, to influence a youngster. (Defective incentive systems are to be seen in the aloof and isolated child, the child who is indifferent to achievement and learning; inappropriate incentive systems are to be seen in the cross-dresser and some delinquents.) These developments may originate from early disturbances in the reinforcement history when primary and secondary reinforcers are evolving.

(e) 'Behavioural deficits' are observable in the absence of skills normally expected in a child of a particular age. There may also be an impairment in the child's problem-solving capacity. These problems may stem from physical disability, the absence of appropriate parental models, the suppression of such behaviour through punitive attitudes, or the lack of encouragement of social and problem-solving skills.

Note: *Behaviour modification is an educational exercise. Indeed, you may not always be able to fathom out the causes of the problem, and yet still be able to do remedial work by using the behavioural approach. The point is that behaviour modification provides new learning experiences. These experiences include a wide range of specific behavioural procedures that are in some degree related to the basic learning models of observational learning, classical and operant conditioning, and self-regulation. Examples of such specific procedures include modelling, imitation, desensitization, flooding and reinforcement techniques.*

SECTION 4

Methods of Treatment

Some criteria for selecting procedures

A treatment programme may include various combinations of antecedent and outcome procedures, environmental and self-control methods. There is no generalized formula or simple recipe approach to the choice of treatment procedures, such as X methods for Y problems. The planning of a therapeutic intervention is based upon highly individual and flexible considerations. Roger Morgan (1975) puts it in this way: 'Just as in a game of chess a limited number of possible moves are combined into a strategy which is adapted to fit a given situation, according to a behavioural analysis. A programme once initiated may continue or be adapted according to its progress or lack of progress, or unexpected practical exigencies.'

One criterion for the selection of treatment procedures is based upon whether the problem represents a deficit or excess of behaviour. Broadly speaking, the therapeutic task with deficit problems is (1) to increase the strength of a particular behaviour (response increment procedures) or to aid in the acquisition of new behaviour patterns (response acquisition procedures); whereas with excess behaviours, the therapeutic task is (2) to eliminate them or reduce their strength (response decrement procedures).

Note: *Behaviour excesses (like aggression) may be related to behaviour deficits in the sense that if appropriate skills are absent, the only way that reinforcement can be obtained is through deviant actions.*

Parents (and teachers) are concerned with deficit/excess issues like the following:

(1) How can I get him to do X?
(2) Now that he is doing X, how do I get him to continue doing X?
(3) How can I get him to stop doing Y?
(4) Now that he doesn't do Y, how can I get him to go on desisting from doing Y?

Remember: *Not to overlook direct and informal solutions. A child who is not getting enough sleep may be irritable and rude. An earlier bedtime may resolve the problem. Direct requests (or orders) to change may sometimes be sufficient, e.g. telling a child to stop picking his hair; explaining that blasphemy causes offence to some. Changes in the physical environment (separating two talkative children in the classroom) and changes in routine and responsibility (setting poacher to be gamekeeper) may work like magic in some instances.*

In less straightforward cases, the therapeutic method will be determined—in part—by the target problem in need of modification. You would not use a technique like desensitization on a truant who deliberately opts out of school because of boredom and under-achievement, rather than some fear of school-going. You might well use it on a school phobic. Thus methods are selected on the basis of knowledge of their therapeutic and directional effects, and acquaintance with the literature on the modification of particular problems (see Blackham and Silberman, 1975; Herbert, 1978). The behaviour therapist seeks out the strongest controlling variables in a problem situation, and in the light of this analysis, decides on the most appropriate procedures to bring to bear on these influences.

Remember: *Problems occur not only in the client's overt actions but also in his covert thoughts or feelings.*

There are (as was stated earlier) two basic learning tasks that are commonly encountered in child therapy. To be more specific they involved:

(1) the acquisition or learning of a desired behaviour in which the individual is deficient (e.g. compliance, self-control, bladder and bowel control, fluent speech, social or academic skills);

(2) the reduction or cessation—the unlearning—of an undesired response in the child's behavioural repertoire (e.g. aggression, temper tantrums, stealing, facial tics, phobic anxiety, compulsive eating) or the exchange of one response for another (e.g. self-assertion in place of timid withdrawal).

Each of these tasks may be served by one or a combination of four major types of learning: (a) classical conditioning, (b) operant conditioning, (c) observational learning, and (d) cognitive learning. Furthermore, they can be analysed (and a therapeutic intervention planned) in terms of antecedent events, consequent events, organismic and self variables.

The choice of therapeutic approach will depend not only on the nature of the target behaviour to be modified and the stimuli which maintain it, but also on the age and maturity of the child, the circumstances under which the child manifests the problem behaviour and the aspects of the environment which are subject to the therapist's influence.

Ask yourself: Who can best implement the programme—the client, a mediator, or yourself. A mediator is necessary if the client is unable to control the consequences of his behaviour, or is not in a position to implement the basic recording which is essential to the programme (e.g. very young children, mentally handicapped youngsters).

Remember: *Learning always involves knowing what to do (the appropriate response) as well as when to do it (under what stimulus conditions the response is appropriate).*

Let us look at the choices and what they mean.

Table VII   Methods for increasing behaviour

Procedure	Method
1. Positive reinforcement	Present a positive stimulus (a rewarding event or object) following the desired behaviour.
2. Negative reinforcement	Remove a stimulus (an aversive or noxious event) following the desired behaviour.
(1 + 2) Contingency management in the token economy.	
3. Differential reinforcement (including discrimination training and method of successive approximations).	Reinforce appropriate behaviours in the presence of the S^D; leave them unreinforced in the setting of inappropriate circumstances, S^Δ.[a]
4. Provide an appropriate model.	Get someone suitable to model the desired behaviour.
5. Remove interfering conditions (e.g. aversive stimuli).	Remove stimuli that are incompatible (interfere) with the desired behaviour.
6. Stimulus control and change (including cueing and prompting).	Determine (or develop) appropriate discriminative stimuli for the desired behaviour.

[a] See Appendix III for an exposition on these and other learning terms.

Methods for increasing behaviour

The methods shown in Table VII are designed for the child (and sometimes parent or teacher) whose responses and/or skills are absent from his behavioural repertoire, or too weakly, too inappropriately represented.

Remember: *Behaviour modification does not consist merely of specific treatment techniques which are applied in a routine manner to particular problems—it is not a 'cookbook' approach.*

It is probably not an exaggeration to claim that in a majority of behavioural programmes the parents have been taught how to decrease unwanted behaviour rather than how to increase desired behaviour with positive methods. It is a good idea, however, to emphasize the latter. Parents are encouraged to 'catch' the child doing something praiseworthy, rather than 'catch' him out in something bad. The same applies to their own actions—so many lack self-esteem or self-confidence and tend to make negative, disapproving self-statements. Positive methods are generally more effective. Produce a more rewarding child and you'll produce a more rewarding parent (and vice versa). You will also tend to get beneficial results going beyond your original targets of intervention— a kind of 'snow-ball' effect. So build into your programme the kinds of interactions/ situations in which the parents and child are likely to enjoy each other's company and in which it is probable that the youngster can be praised for desired alternatives to his present self-defeating behavioural style.

1. Positive reinforcement

Procedure 1	**POSITIVE REINFORCEMENT** *Arrange matters so that an immediate reward* *follows the performance of the desired behaviour.*

Applications

Choose positive reinforcement as a method of change when:

    (a) a new behaviour is to be incorporated in the child's repertoire;

    (b) when the strength of an already acquired behaviour pattern is to be increased; and

    (c) when by increasing the strength of a particular behaviour the effect will be to cause an undesirable incompatible response to diminish in strength.

Method

Positive reinforcement involves the presentation of a stimulus (a rewarding event or object) following the required act; thus it embodies the principle that the likelihood that behaviour will recur depends on its consequences. Circumstances are arranged so that the correct performance of an act (or an approximation of it) is followed closely in time by what are thought to be reinforcing (i.e. rewarding) consequences.

Reinforcers

There are, broadly speaking, four classes of reinforcer:

    Those provided by others

    (a) Tangible—material reinforcers (treats, privileges, sweets, money, crisps etc.).

    (b) Intangible (social) reinforcers (hugs, smiles, encouragement, etc.).

    Those provided by oneself from 'within':

    (c) Tangible reinforcers (leisure activities, treats to oneself).

    (d) Intangible reinforcers (self-praise, self-appreciation).

Adult attention is a powerful acquired secondary reinforcer for the child who has built up an association between adult attention and the provision of primary reinforcers, such as food, comfort, security. Children reinforce adults too. As was stated before, happy adult–child relationships result from mutually reinforcing interactions.

In the case of behaviours which are complex and difficult to perform, it is essential to reward the child for *trying* as well as for success. Reward often. Do not mix criticism with praise. You arrange for only the better approximations to the correct (desired) actions to be reinforced—as the child becomes more adept (see Procedure 3b). When the child becomes successful, reward for accomplishment rather than mere obedience. It is the approved behaviour that is being praised rather than the whole child; identify specifically (i.e. cognitively structure) what is being rewarded. To give a simple example: mother might say 'Thank you for letting your brother share your game' rather than 'You are a good boy'.

Contingencies

Let the child know what the contingencies are. Set up a 'contract' with the child (see Step 14) by word of mouth (or one written down) and make clear parental expectations of the child and the reciprocal obligations to him.

A contingency is a *rule* which stipulates that a particular consequence (reward *or* punishment) follows the performance of a particular kind of behaviour.

Ask yourself:

    (a) Are the rules clear?

    (b) Are the rules simple?

    (c) Does the child understand the rules?

    (d) Does the parent interpret and implement the rules fairly and consistently?

Children should be encouraged to think about the reasons for having rules so they have standards for judging their own behaviour, and learn to reason things out for themselves. Socialization is particularly effective when training is presented in terms of a few well-defined principles. The use of inductive methods—explanations and reasons—especially when they elucidate a few clearly defined principles, seems to enhance moral awareness and resistance to temptation. Conformity of behaviour to specific norms in particular situations is more likely to depend on sanctions attached to those particular situations than on the general parent–child relationships.

Remember: *Four important points:*

    (1) Do not assume that parents (or teachers) have a repertoire of effective phrases for giving praise or, indeed, give praise with the right degree of warmth, enthusiasm and eye contact. Check on this!

    (2) A child may become satiated to a reinforcer. It loses 'reward' value (see Procedure 1b).

    (3) Reinforce the reinforcer (build in treats and encouragement for the person/s mediating the child's behaviour, e.g. the caregiver).

    (4) Ultimately the child should learn to reinforce himself, i.e. become self-directed (this is a major objective in child-rearing).

Procedure 1b	**SUBSTITUTION** *When a reward is ineffectual, present it to the child just before (or as close in time to) the moment in which a more effective reward is presented.* **REINFORCING EVENT MENU** *Offer a variety of reinforcing stimuli so as to avoid reinforcer satiation; some therapists make use of the 'reinforcing event menu' which allows children to make a choice of reinforcers.*

Procedure 1b (continued)	**DEPRIVATION** *A little judicious responding to temporary states of deprivation may have the desired effect, increasing the potency of the reinforcement. (The thirsty child is more interested in doing a task for a glass of lemonade than the child who has just had a drink.)* **PRAISING IN FRONT OF OTHERS** *This adds to the value of reinforcers. The teacher tells the mother in front of the child how well he is doing.*

Timing of reinforcement

Timing of the reinforcers is crucial. Reinforcers should not be given before the child has begun to improve his behaviour. Immediate, rather than delayed reinforcement is generally more effective in establishing a conditioned response. Prompt reinforcement is essential to obtain *new* or improved behaviour patterns. In real life rewards are not always awarded immediately. Ways of tapering off the reinforcement to prepare the youngster for real life—learning patience and long-term commitment—are discussed in Step 20b.

Schedules of reinforcement

Responses that are reinforced on a partial or intermittent basis (the regime under which most of us learn in the natural environment) prove to be most enduring, in other words, resistant to extinction. Different rates of reinforcement produce varying results in conditioning procedures. In order to establish new behaviour as promptly as possible, it is crucial—initially—to reinforce immediately and often. When reinforcement follows each correct response, the schedule of reinforcement is referred to as *continuous*. In order to encourage a child to continue performing an established pattern with few or no rewards, ensure that the frequency with which the correct behaviour is reinforced, is gradually and intermittently decreased.

Reinforcement schedules may be categorized in terms of:

(1) the interval between reinforcements (determined either by time elapsed or the number of responses); and

(2) the regularity or irregularity of the intervals.

This classification gives four basic schedules:

(a) Variable-interval schedule: a programme used in which the individual is reinforced after an interval of time which varies around a specified average.

(b) Variable-ratio schedule: here the individual is reinforced after a number of responses which varies randomly around a specified average.

(c) Fixed-interval schedule: a schedule of partial reinforcement in which a response made after a certain interval of time is reinforced.

(d) Fixed-ratio schedule: a schedule of partial reinforcement in which every nth response is reinforced.

Variable schedules result in stable response rates which are difficult to extinguish (see Walker and Buckley, 1974).

Note: *Don't let people convince you that reinforcement is a simple matter of giving children smarties or stars. It requires a great deal of thought and planning.*

Informative function of reinforcement

The effectiveness of a reward depends partly on the child's expectation of success in a particular undertaking. During the course of learning, the child not only performs responses, but he also observes the variations in consequences that flow from his actions. On the basis of this informative feedback, he develops hypotheses about the types of action most likely to succeed. These hypotheses (expectancies) then serve as guides for future actions. We need to know about the child's reinforcement history and achievement in order to select effective reinforcers. Children vary in their interpretation as to whether rewards follow from, and are contingent upon, their own behaviour ('internals') or are controlled by forces—luck, fate—outside themselves ('externals').

Attribution problems

Some children are difficult to work with in terms of reinforcement programmes, be they externally or self-administered. They may have been habitually lavished with 'rewards' which have no link to their actions (non-contingent reinforcement); consequently they fail to recognize and attribute a causal connection—in the programme—between acceptable behaviour and rewards.

If the child has a low expectation of passing an arithmetic test, yet is successful, the value of the reinforcement occasioned by the triumph may be great. As McCandless (1969) observes, criticism or failure may serve as an excellent motivating device for the bright and able child yet discourage and handicap the child who is already doing poorly. Although reward does not do very much 'extra' for the bright and successful, it motivates the unsuccessful child highly. After all, the bright child expects to succeed, hence success and praise do not surprise him or raise him to new levels of performance. He does not expect to fail or be criticized; hence, when such things happen to him, the effect is great. The punishment, as it were, is so severe that he redoubles his efforts to avoid encountering it again. The failing child expects failure and criticism, hence it has little effect on him except to confirm his beliefs and reduce his effort. But an experience of praise or reward is so striking and sweet that he works doubly hard to encounter such a state of affairs again.

The effects of feelings of failure are somewhat more unpredictable than those of success. If a child does not achieve what he has expected to achieve but accepts failure in a realistic manner, he will lower his expectation for the next performance. Sometimes, however, a child will react to failure by raising his expectations. He may simply blame his failure on some external obstacle. The expectations of people important to the child also play a part in the way he reacts to failure. If there is pressure on him, he may continue to base his expectations at a level far above what is realistic. There are children who are unable to attain their own goals, or the goals set by their parents, because they are dominated by a fear of failure, and therefore avoid, at all costs, achievement situations.

Assessment implications

This matter of the child's own expectations of success or failure is important in determining his performance. You cannot make facile assumptions about reinforcement. You need to know about the youngster's subjective expectations of his future achievements and his likelihood of success in different situations; and you have to find out what they are by talking to him.

Summary of our guidelines

In planning to apply reinforcers, be precise; responses that occur just prior to the reinforced (to-be-learned) response will also be strengthened. Those nearest in time are strengthened more than those further away (this is the gradient of reinforcement). On the other hand, responses nearer to the point of occurrence of reinforcement tend to occur before their original time in the response sequence and crowd out earlier, useless behaviours. (This is the development of anticipatory responses.) Select your reinforcers carefully. They vary in potency according to the individual's tastes and his reinforcement history (see Step 12). Use a variety of reinforcers and arrange for there to be more than one *source* of reinforcement (e.g. mother, father, older siblings, relatives, teachers). Try to ensure that they are consistent, that they only reward after the correct response and then, promptly.

2. Negative reinforcement

Procedure 2	**NEGATIVE REINFORCEMENT**
	Arrange for the child to terminate immediately a mildly aversive situation, by changing his behaviour in the desired direction.

Applications

To get a child to behave in a certain (desirable) way, and conversely, to stop him from acting in another unwanted manner, the removal of an aversive stimulus is made contingent upon a required behaviour; this procedure is known as negative reinforcement. Like the application of positive reinforcement in operant conditioning, it tends to increase the required behaviour. Thus the mother says: 'If you don't say "please" when you ask for something, I'll slap your hand.' If the rate of saying please on appropriate occasions increases, the slap on the hand (that is to say the avoidance of it) has acted as a negative reinforcer.

Contingency management (rearranging consequences)

This is the generic title given to programmes involving the manipulation of reinforcement, positive (Procedure 1) and negative (Procedure 2). Flow chart 4 provides you with a step-by-step guide.

Note: *Although positive and negative reinforcement are distinctive procedures, they serve to maintain, strengthen or increase the likelihood that a behaviour will be*

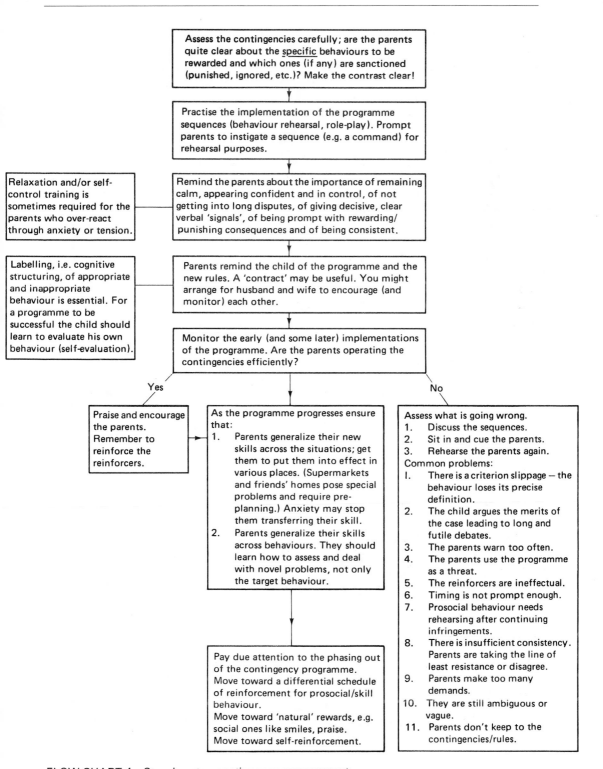

Assess the contingencies carefully; are the parents quite clear about the <u>specific</u> behaviours to be rewarded and which ones (if any) are sanctioned (punished, ignored, etc.)? Make the contrast clear!

Practise the implementation of the programme sequences (behaviour rehearsal, role-play). Prompt parents to instigate a sequence (e.g. a command) for rehearsal purposes.

Relaxation and/or self-control training is sometimes required for the parents who over-react through anxiety or tension.

Remind the parents about the importance of remaining calm, appearing confident and in control, of not getting into long disputes, of giving decisive, clear verbal 'signals', of being prompt with rewarding/punishing consequences and of being consistent.

Labelling, i.e. cognitive structuring, of appropriate and inappropriate behaviour is essential. For a programme to be successful the child should learn to evaluate his own behaviour (self-evaluation).

Parents remind the child of the programme and the new rules. A 'contract' may be useful. You might arrange for husband and wife to encourage (and monitor) each other.

Monitor the early (and some later) implementations of the programme. Are the parents operating the contingencies efficiently?

Yes   No

Praise and encourage the parents. Remember to reinforce the reinforcers.

As the programme progresses ensure that:
1. Parents generalize their new skills across the situations; get them to put them into effect in various places. (Supermarkets and friends' homes pose special problems and require pre-planning.) Anxiety may stop them transferring their skill.
2. Parents generalize their skills across behaviours. They should learn how to assess and deal with novel problems, not only the target behaviour.

Assess what is going wrong.
1. Discuss the sequences.
2. Sit in and cue the parents.
3. Rehearse the parents again.
Common problems:
I.   There is a criterion slippage — the behaviour loses its precise definition.
2.   The child argues the merits of the case leading to long and futile debates.
3.   The parents warn too often.
4.   The parents use the programme as a threat.
5.   The reinforcers are ineffectual.
6.   Timing is not prompt enough.
7.   Prosocial behaviour needs rehearsing after continuing infringements.
8.   There is insufficient consistency. Parents are taking the line of least resistance or disagree.
9.   Parents make too many demands.
10. They are still ambiguous or vague.
11. Parents don't keep to the contingencies/rules.

Pay due attention to the phasing out of the contingency programme.
Move toward a differential schedule of reinforcement for prosocial/skill behaviour.
Move toward 'natural' rewards, e.g. social ones like smiles, praise.
Move toward self-reinforcement.

FLOW CHART 4 Step-by-step contingency management.

JANE'S CHART	WEEK 1	BONUS	POINTS	WEEK 2	BONUS	POINTS
MONDAY		★	10/10		★	10/10
TUESDAY		★	10/10		★	10/10
WEDNESDAY		★	10/10		★	10/10
THURSDAY		★	10/10		★	10/10
FRIDAY		★	10/10			9/10
SATURDAY		★	10/10		★	10/10
SUNDAY		★	10/10			9/10

FIG. 13   A typical home-made reward chart.

emitted. Positive and negative reinforcement procedures generate four training methods: reward training, privation training, escape training and avoidance training. The procedures (all of which strengthen behaviour) involve the following characteristic statements:

(a) Reward training: *'If you make the response, I will present a reward';* (b) Privation training: *'If you don't make the response I will withdraw a reward';* (c) Escape training: *'If you make the response I will withdraw a punishment';* (d) Avoidance training: *'If you don't make the response I will present a punishment'.*

Self-reinforcement

Studies (e.g. Johnson, 1970; Lovitt and Curtiss, 1969) have repeatedly established that self-administered reinforcement is effective in maintaining various kinds of behaviour (see Procedure 20b).

Token economies

Figure 13 illustrates a typical home-made reward chart.

The token economy is, in a sense, a work-payment incentive system in which the participants receive tokens when they display appropriate behaviour. At some specified time, the tokens are exchanged at an agreed tariff for a variety of back-up reinforcers— items and activities. Kazdin and Bootzin (1972) list the following advantages:

(a) They allow the consequences of any response to be applied at any time.
(b) They bridge the delay between target responses and back-up reinforcers.
(c) They can maintain performance over extended periods of time when the back-up reinforcers cannot be administered.
(d) They allow sequences of responses to be reinforced without interruption.
(e) The reinforcing effects of tokens are relatively independent of the physiological state of the individual and less subject to satiation effects.
(f) They permit the use of the same reinforcers for individuals with preferences for different back-up reinforcers.

Applications

Token reinforcement procedures are not applied in isolation; they are usually supplemented simultaneously by rules, extinction, praise and response-cost. They have shown their usefulness in school classrooms and in specialized classrooms for disadvantaged, hyperactive, retarded, and emotionally disturbed children. There are many ways—witting and unwitting—to make a token system fail. Drabman and Tucker (1974) and Kuypers *et al.* (1968) suggest important procedures for pre-empting the things that go wrong. As the latter remark: 'A token system is not a "magical" method to be applied in a mechanical way.' Tables VIII a and b provide an example of a home token economy.

Table VIIIa   Home token economy chart
Name:_____ Dates:_____ Recorder:_____

	Points earned	Points lost	Comments
Monday			
Tuesday			
Wednesday			
Thursday			
Friday			
Saturday			
Sunday			
TOTAL:			

Table VIIIb

Behaviours that earn points	Points	Behaviours that lose points	Points
Good report note from teacher (as detailed in contract)	4	Hitting other children (as defined)	5
Leaves for school without complaint	2	Non-compliance (as defined)	3
Gets dressed himself without argument	2	Swearing/tantrums	2
Stays at dining table until meal ends	1		

Back-up reinforcers: 10 points: Mother reads extra long story (half-hour), *or* allowed to stay up an extra half-hour; 8–9 points: special treat at dessert; 5–7 points: Father has game of Ludo with him; 1–4 points: no TV; 0 points: goes to bed early 8 p.m.; Minus: Extra early 7 p.m.

Illustration 1

Group setting

McLaughlin and Malaby (1972) describe a token programme in a primary school class designed to enhance the academic performance of 25–29 pupils with regard to completing assignments in maths, spelling, language and handwriting.

Table IX indicates the 'earnings' and 'costs' of particular behaviours. Variations in points are related to variations in the performance, e.g. the number of items on a test. The pupils were encouraged to join in the selection of privileges, the choice determined by reinforcers naturally available in the classroom.

Table IX Behaviours and the number of points that they earned or lost

Behaviours that earned points	Points:
(1) Items correct	6 to 12
(2) Study behaviour 8:50–9:15	5 per day
(3) Bring food for animals	1 to 10
(4) Bring sawdust for animals	1 to 10
(5) Art	1 to 4
(6) Listening points	1 to 2 per lesson
(7) Extra credit	Assigned value
(8) Neatness	1 to 2
(9) Taking home assignments	5
(10) Taking notes	1 to 3
(11) Quiet in lunch time	2
(12) Quiet in cafeteria	2
(13) Appropriate noon hour behaviour	3

Behaviours that lost points	Points:
(1) Assignments incomplete	Amount squared
(2) Gum and candy	100
(3) Inappropriate verbal behaviour	15
(4) Inappropriate motor behaviour	15
(5) Fighting	100
(6) Cheating	100

Source: McLaughlin and Malaby (1972, p. 264).

Illustration 2

Individual home

Lorna's therapy included (*inter alia*) some contingency management: a home token economy.

We began the programme (Step 16) by recording carefully defined positive (desirable) behaviours, for which parents allocated stars on a chart. Lorna was to get a star for being 'good' (again carefully defined) for half an hour—to begin with. Each star was further reinforced by a sweet, an agreeable 'incentive' to Lorna. Every third star earned a special silver bonus star on her chart in the sitting room. An accumulation of three silver stars was further rewarded by a gold star—which meant going to an 'open sale' (a shop made out of a big box containing small books, chocolates, sweets, games, pencils, etc.) where she could choose what she wanted according to a tariff. Lorna, a bright child, understood all of this. Throughout, all the family were involved in providing immediate social reinforcement (praise, encouragement, smiles) for Lorna's acceptable behaviour. In other words, she received attention only when she behaved appropriately. To ensure this, all unacceptable actions (for example one target was called commanding behaviour) were followed by 'time-out'. After one warning, but without indulging in any verbal disputation or arguing, she was taken upstairs to the parents' bedroom for five minutes. Time-out often had to be extended, when a tantrum was occurring at the end of the five minute period. Time-out was used for temper tantrums and physical aggression.

The therapist spent six afternoons during the first and second week at the Greens' house to supervise the programme (prompting and cueing) and to give Mrs Green moral support. A telephone call was made every day to check whether Mrs Green was coping well, to encourage her and to give necessary advice. The main concern was to apply rewards and punishments in a consistent and continuing manner, in all kinds of situations and places (generalization). Lorna's playgroup leaders agreed to help her to integrate into all group activities in order to teach her some social skills and also to provide some more demanding learning exercises—according to her exceptionally high abilities (see Step 13). (Various strategies were adopted to take account of Lorna's special need for stimulation.)

Lorna's progress was reviewed regularly, and because of a marked improvement in her prosocial behaviour, it was felt necessary to make more rigorous the criteria for reward. After three weeks the time for getting a star was extended to one hour, and then to two hours, and later gradually faded out altogether. The treatment took three months, during which, defiance, verbal aggression, temper tantrums and other target behaviours decreased to an acceptable level.

We quote the mother herself:

> Since the treatment programme has been underway Lorna's screaming fits have dwindled to almost nil now. We understand her needs and frustrations and are able largely to cope with them. In responding to her vast intellectual needs and continually keeping her stimulated, she is rapidly developing as a normal four-year-old. Trips out are now taken without fear, although we are still slightly nervous. Supermarkets are visited with few qualms. She still has a rather low frustration-tolerance level, but this is at least 50% improved on the situation at the beginning of the treatment programme, and occasionally, she even laughs at her own mistakes and misunderstandings. Best of all though, is the way she now responds to affection, although she still has to make the first move. She will both give and receive cuddles and kisses. Mealtimes are no longer a battle and the dining table no longer a battlefield. Her aggressive fits are diminishing, although she can still be verbally aggressive, and is no respector of persons if something is done that is deemed silly or stupid. I can now leave her for increasingly long periods, visit the bathroom alone and do household chores without her hanging on to whatever part of me she can attach herself to.

3. Differential reinforcement

Procedure 3a	**DISCRIMINATION TRAINING** *Reinforce, in the presence of the S^D, appropriate behavioural responses. Never reinforce actions in inappropriate circumstances (S^Δ). In this way you help to bring about stimulus control over behaviour.*

Applications

When we wish to teach a young child to act in a particular way under one set of circumstances but not another (in other words, to develop new behaviour), we help him to identify the cues that differentiate the circumstances. This involves clear signals as to what is expected of the child and it presupposes unambiguous rules. The application of differential reinforcement can be used (especially with mentally handicapped children) to make—eventually—very fine discriminations.

Method
Make the appropriate situations (S^D) and the inappropriate ones (S^Δ) as different from each other as possible—at first.

Procedure 3b	SUCCESSIVE APPROXIMATIONS
	Reinforce approximations to the correct act. The successive steps to the final behaviour are reinforced according to an increasingly rigorous criterion. Only better and better approximations are reinforced, until eventually only the correct action is rewarded. Begin with a clear definition of what the child has to learn to do; then begin by reinforcing something he does that in some way resembles it.

Applications
Successive approximations (or, shaping, as they are called) make possible the building-up of a new response. (For examples see Appendix I, Case fragment 3.)

Method
Shaping involves the use of differential reinforcement and a shifting criterion of reinforcement. In order to encourage a child to act in a way in which he has seldom or never before behaved, the therapist works out the successive steps the child must and can make so as to approximate more and more closely to the desired final outcome. This last element, called 'shaping' or the principle of 'successive approximations', involves taking mini-steps towards the final goal. The therapist starts by reinforcing very small changes in behaviour which are in the right direction even if somewhat far removed from the final desired outcome. No reinforcement is given for behaviour in the 'wrong' direction. Gradually the criteria of the individual's approximation to the desired goal are made more rigorous.

Remember: *A slavish reliance on shaping procedures alone for teaching new ways of behaving, or novel skills, might well lead to frustrating delays. The apt provision of a model for the child to imitate could lead to a quicker solution, depending on the nature of the problem and the potential of the child.*

4. Exposure to appropriate models

Procedure 4	MODELLING
	Give the child the opportunity to observe a person who is interesting or significant to him performing the new and desired pattern of behaviour. 'Watch how he does it.' 'Do it like this.' Indicate that it is rewarding to behave like this.

Applications

Modelling can be used to change a wide variety of behaviours—in at least three situations:
(a) acquiring new patterns of behaviour;
(b) strengthening or weakening responses already present in the child's behavioural repertoire, by observing high status models demonstrating the appropriate behaviour;
(c) inhibiting learned fears, such as phobias of dogs, by observing a fearless model in the presence of the fear-object.

If the child never, or only very rarely, emits some desired behaviour and if this low rate is due to a deficit in the child's repertoire rather than inadequate incentives, then combinations of modelling, cueing, prompting, instruction and putting through (sometimes called passive shaping) should be used. You ensure that the behaviour can occur and then reinforce it. Danziger (1971) states that there is overwhelming evidence that children learn complex acts through cognitive processes based on observation rather than through being trained by external reinforcements administered by the parent. This does not mean that the reward and punishment of specific components of behaviour plays *no* role in social learning; it does mean that that role is defined in a context provided by the very special reactions that people have to people.

Children learn many of their actions and skills, either deliberately or inadvertently, through the influence of example. This provides you with a potent therapeutic tool.

Method
See Flow Chart 5.

Note: *Some exemplars (models) exert more influence over a child than others. It is usually possible to identify individuals in the child's peer group (or adults) of significance to him. Their behaviour is likely to be imitated because of the prestige they have, either for the youngster alone or for the entire group with whom he interacts (e.g. the popular child at school). Similarity is another important factor. There is evidence that student observers who perceive—or are told—that they have some characteristics or qualities similar to the model (e.g. sex, age and physical attributes) are more likely to imitate the responses of the model, than students who do not identify such similarities. Therapists can facilitate imitation by pointing out areas in common between the model and the client; a behaviour is more likely to be modelled if its complexity is not too great or too rapidly presented for assimilation, and if the child perceives that it has some components which he has already mastered.*

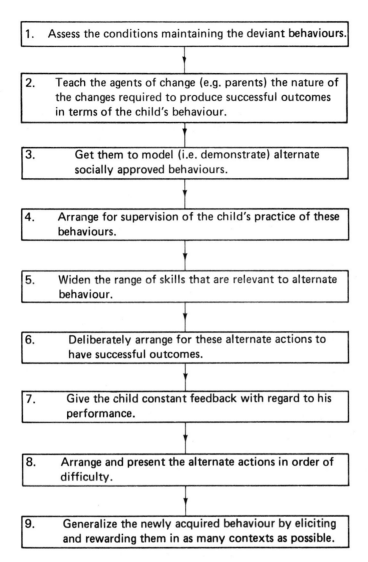

1. Assess the conditions maintaining the deviant behaviours.

2. Teach the agents of change (e.g. parents) the nature of the changes required to produce successful outcomes in terms of the child's behaviour.

3. Get them to model (i.e. demonstrate) alternate socially approved behaviours.

4. Arrange for supervision of the child's practice of these behaviours.

5. Widen the range of skills that are relevant to alternate behaviour.

6. Deliberately arrange for these alternate actions to have successful outcomes.

7. Give the child constant feedback with regard to his performance.

8. Arrange and present the alternate actions in order of difficulty.

9. Generalize the newly acquired behaviour by eliciting and rewarding them in as many contexts as possible.

FLOW CHART 5 Step-by-step modelling. Bandura (1973) provides these useful principles (put into step form by the author) as a guide to the acquisition, by modelling, of alternative behaviours.

One of the crucial influences on the extent to which a child will imitate a model is the consequence of that person's actions. Is the outcome successful, pleasant or rewarding?

5. Remove interfering conditions

Procedure 5	*Remove or reduce aversive stimuli associated with the problem behaviour; such a strategy may lead to an increase in desirable behaviour (and conversely a reduction in the undesired behaviour)— granted, a proposal easier to make on paper than to meet in practice.*

Applications
A large variety of aversive stimuli can set the stage for the development of problem behaviours—for example, bullying and teasing of a painful, threatening, or humiliating nature; deprivation of the child's proper nurturance, rights, and opportunities.

Method
A helpful technique therefore involves the defusing of aversive stimuli by diminishing their power to arouse anger in the child. This may be achieved (to take one example) by desensitization procedures. However, the harsh realities and constraints of the lives of many children and adolescents preclude the remedies which lie in reducing or removing misery, stress and temptation.

6. Stimulus control

Stimulus control refers to the extent to which an antecedent stimulus determines the probability of a response being manifested. Some 'triggering' stimuli are referred to as eliciting stimuli (see Appendix III). On the other hand, discriminative stimuli (see Appendix III) mark a time or place of reinforcement—positive or negative—being presented or removed. In other words, discriminative stimuli are markers as to when an operant will have reinforcing consequences.

Applications
A frequent complaint from parents is that their child 'won't listen' or 'knows what to do but just won't do it!' These are examples of faulty stimulus control. The child has a behaviour in his repertoire but will not perform it when the would-be directing stimulus is presented (i.e. at the appropriate time). The therapist and parents have to reinstate stimulus control. It is worth looking at the parents' requests or commands. They may be weak and ambiguous signals.

Method
A basic condition for correcting faulty stimulus control, as for establishing initial stimulus control, is to get the behaviour (or some approximation to it) performed while the child is attending to the stimulus which is to control it. There are ways to reinstate the discriminative stimulus, e.g. *cueing*.

Procedure 6a	CUEING
	Encourage the child to respond to cues for the correct performance just before the action is expected, rather than after he has performed incorrectly—in order to train him to act at a specific time.

Applications

Drives can act as responses (and become elicited by certain cues, and strengthened by reinforcement). This principle can be applied to remedy the poorly motivated, under-achieving child's performance.

Method

(a) Cues are among the most important behaviours used by the classroom teacher to control behaviour. A cue can be defined as anything used as a stimulus with the intent of evoking a response. The teacher cues (e.g. instructs, encourages) as a means of informing the pupils about the responses they should make (e.g. concentrating on the task to hand). To be effective, cues should serve to elicit a response which it is within the pupil's capacity to make. By presenting cues and withdrawing others (fading) the teacher can become an effective contingency manager, attaining stimulus control over certain crucial classroom behaviours. The association between a cue and a response is strengthened each time the response is followed by reinforcement. These preliminaries make up the stage of acquisition. Once a specific cue–response habit has been acquired, another cue which is similar in some way to the original cue, can also elicit the learned response (a phenomenon called 'stimulus generalization'). The teacher may give only the bricfest signal for work to begin.

(b) There are internal (intrinsic) cues as well as external cues. Drives can act as cues and elicit specific learned responses; thus a child with hostile impulses is helped to respond to signals from his incipient 'feelings' by training him to identify them and the situations in which they occur. You then take him through self-control procedures rather than letting him know he has gone wrong after he has lashed out at another child.

(c) In the case of those complex behaviours which are made up of a series of simple responses linked together in a behaviour chain (e.g. tying up shoelaces) you reinforce *combinations* of simple behaviours.

Procedure 6b	CHAINING
	Make reinforcement dependent (contingent) upon the emission of more than one behaviour in succession and then gradually require more behaviours in the chain to be emitted before providing reinforcement.

Applications

Chaining is often used when the client can perform the simple responses (or these can be taught by shaping) but does not combine them together.

Method

(1) Describe the steps to be followed clearly and minutely.

(2) Try to forge the chain from actions which already form part of the client's repertoire.

(3) Use differential reinforcement to increase the number of behavioural links in the chain.

(4) Backward chaining, beginning from the final link in the chain, is sometimes more effective than the reverse direction.

Procedure 6c	PROMPTING
	Coach the client—using verbal and/or non-verbal cues—to perform the required behaviour. Present a cue prior to the desired behaviour in a way which increases the probability that the behaviour will occur. It may sometimes be necessary to show him what to do or say.

It may sometimes be necessary to use prompts in training the child, in the sense of giving a child special cues that direct his attention towards the task the adult is trying to teach him.

In teaching a mentally handicapped child to speak it may be useful at the beginning of training to utter a word loudly while encouraging him to observe. This verbal prompt would eventually be faded (i.e. gradually removed) as the child becomes proficient in speaking. To take another example of prompting, the observant mother or teacher may notice that the child is fidgeting and draws his attention to the bladder signals, reminding him to go to the toilet. She may be required to help the child physically through the behaviour by prompts or verbal instruction.

Remember: *Attention is crucial to the establishment of stimulus control. A child will neither learn, nor have stimulus control, if he does not pay attention to the cues being used to direct his behaviour. Having established stimulus control, a special procedure is still required to maintain stimulus control under changing stimulus conditions. Fading is a procedure for slowly decreasing dependence on 'artificial' stimulus control—it involves the gradual removal of discriminative stimuli (S^Ds) such as cues and prompts in the child's environment.*

Fading Out Cues: If cues are withdrawn (e.g. prompting the child less and less) the procedure is called 'fading out'.

Fading In Cues: If new cues are gradually introduced this is called 'fading in'.

A basic objective in therapy and education is the goal of having learned behaviour emitted spontaneously rather than always as a response to a prompt or cue.

Illustration

Correcting faulty stimulus control

Guthrie (1935) gives the following illustration of faulty stimulus control and the method used to stop a child being untidy. The behaviour of the child was used to reinstate the S^D.

The mother of a ten-year-old girl complained to a psychologist that for two years her daughter had annoyed her by a habit of tossing coat and hat on the floor as she entered the house. On a hundred occasions the mother had insisted that the girl pick up the coat and hang it in its place. These irritating ways were changed only after the mother, on advice, began to insist not that the girl pick up the fallen garments from the floor but that she put them on, return to the street, and re-enter the house, this time removing the coat and hanging it up properly. The principle at work then is that the child must be made to perform the required act while she is attending to the stimulus which is to control it. In the example, the mother had been getting the response out in the presence of the wrong stimuli. The stimuli which were meant to control the response were those present *immediately* after the child entered the house. What was going wrong was that the 'tidy' response was being repeatedly and merely evoked in the presence of a stimulus—essentially an inappropriate one (an S^Δ)—the mother saying 'Please pick up your coat'.

Remember: *The role of the parent in ineffectual stimulus control! So often the problem is an interactional one—between the adult and the child. It may be necessary to train the parent to give more assertive, unambiguous verbal signals (e.g. commands). A parent (or teacher) may be ineffectual because he or she over-reacts to certain situations. A mother may feel depressed, hostile or anxious. You might ask her to record her own responses along with the child's (see Fig. 10, p. 53). Relaxation or self-control training could help her to remain calm and competent in these circumstances.*

Remember: *The teacher's role in ineffectual stimulus control! There exists within a classroom, as within any social setting, a substantial array of stimulus variables which can cue behaviour (discriminative stimuli), reinforce behaviour (reinforcing stimuli), or produce no effect on behaviour (neutral stimuli). It is the aim of a behavioural programme to manipulate these stimuli in order to modify behaviour. It may be possible to manipulate conditions already present in the situation, and/or introduce additional conditions into the existing arrangements.*

A closer examination of the teacher's sequencing of classroom antecedents and consequences may help you diagnose problems in classroom performance and management. The teacher's use of rules (for example) has been investigated for its effect on social and antisocial behaviour by the pupils.

Guidelines to stimulus control in the classroom

Altering stimulus conditions in classroom settings may take the form of posting rules or instructions as prompts for desired behaviours. Cues (rules) inform the pupils about what is required of them.

(1) Negotiate rules. Discuss the rules and the reasons for them with children who are old enough to participate in such a process. Rules are more likely to be obeyed if they are perceived as fair and seem to have a purpose. It may be possible to engage pupils in the formulation of *their* classroom rules. Negotiate a set of classroom objectives and clarify the function of rules in facilitating these objectives.

(2) To be effective rules should elicit responses which the pupils are capable of making.

(3) Emphasize rules that offer beneficial outcomes for appropriate actions.

(4) Select a few essential rules only—ones that can be enforced, and reinforced.

(5) Praise pupils who follow the rules, identifying the precise grounds for the praise. Rules alone are unlikely to be effective. Group reinforcers (privileges) might be built into a programme.

Some teachers arrange a competitive points system: one half of the class (say) competing with another for points and an eventual prize or bonus. Such 'team' endeavours can be highly successful but they carry the danger of group coercion against the individual.

There are other useful types of cueing behaviour such as modelling, prompting (physical or verbal), fading, chaining, successive approximations and using instructions.

Task Orientation Behaviours. The pupil needs to attend to the various cues which are presented to him in the classroom in order to perform the task successfully. The teacher has to present the class with cues which are orientated towards an educational task. Classmates and other distracting stimuli, on the other hand, might well present the pupil with cues orientated towards non-educational activites. The pupil's ability to attend to the *appropriate* cues will directly affect his ability to attend to the task itself.

Task Performance Behaviours. Each time a pupil performs the academic task which is set for him, he needs to attend to (say) the written cues which are a part of the task, as well as to the feedback from his own activity in carrying out the task; in this way he is able to detect and correct, as best he can, any error that arises in the course of that activity.

As the teacher cues behaviours, the pupils respond (hopefully) to these cues (attention to teacher) and initiate additional behaviours. They subsequently attend or fail to attend to the teacher's further cues (attention to task). However, as Friedman (1980) points out, it is often assumed that paying attention to the teacher is a necessary and sufficient condition for attending to the task. This is not always the case since it is quite possible for the pupil to attend to the teacher and then not attend to the task, or conversely not attend to the teacher but attend to the task; in the latter case the task to which attention is paid is likely not to be precisely the task the teacher had in mind for the pupil to perform. Friedman warns that it is important to distinguish between these two types of attending behaviour, as failure to do so may account for the inability of some teachers to understand the child's learning problems. A teacher may see the problem of attending only in terms of whether the pupils appear to be paying attention to him, whereas failure in performance may be due to inadequate attention to the task that is set.

Task Consequence Behaviour. The pupil needs to attend to the consequences of his academic performance in order to make progress. One of the most important of these consequences is the immediate feedback he receives from the teacher as to whether the response he makes is correct or incorrect.

Interlude

There is a more general, if you like 'background', aspect to this issue of feedback. It concerns the ethos of the classroom and the school. The feedback that a child receives about standards (expectations as to what is, and what is not, acceptable at school) constitutes a powerful influence on his behaviour. Here we enter the realm of norms and values in the school.

Thus the feedback may be direct and immediate, in terms of praise or reprimand in the classroom; it may be less direct and more delayed, in terms of annual prizes for work or sport; or it may be quite indirect, like putting children's work up on the walls. The findings of Rutter *et al.* (1979) showed that the most immediate and direct feedback in terms of praise or approval had the strongest association with pupil behaviour. Prizes for sport were associated with good attendance but not with any of the other outcomes, and prizes for work were quite unrelated to any of the outcome measures. The amount of punishment showed only weak, and generally non-significant, associations with outcome, and when the associations did reach significance, the trend was for higher levels of punishment to be associated with *worse* outcomes.

The researchers found outcomes to be better when both the curriculum and approaches to discipline were agreed and supported by the staff acting together. Thus, attendance was better and delinquency less frequent in schools where courses were planned jointly. Group planning provided opportunities for teachers to encourage and support one another. In addition continuity of teaching was facilitated.

Much the same was found with regard to standards of discipline. Exam successes were more frequent and delinquency less common in schools where discipline was based on general expectations set by the school (or house or department), rather than left to individual teachers to work out for themselves. School values and norms appear to be more effective if it is clear to all that they have widespread support. Discipline is easier to maintain if the pupils appreciate that it relates to generally accepted approaches and does not simply represent the whims of the individual teacher. The authors state that the particular rules which are set and the specific disciplinary techniques which are used, are probably much less important than the establishment of some principles and guidelines which are both clearly recognizable, and accepted by the school as a whole.

Table X   Methods for reducing behaviour

Procedure	Method
7. Extinction	Withhold reinforcement following inappropriate behaviour.
8. Stimulus change	Change discriminative stimuli (remove or change controlling antecedent stimuli).
9. Punishment	Present mildly aversive/noxious stimuli contingent upon (following) inappropriate behaviour.
10. Time out from positive reinforcement (TO)	Withdraw reinforcement for X minutes following inappropriate behaviour.
11. Response-cost (RC)	Withdraw X quantity of reinforcers following inappropriate behaviour.
12. Overcorrection	Client makes restitution plus . . .
13. Positive reinforcement: (a) Reinforcing incompatible behaviour (RIB) (b) Differential reinforcement of other behaviours (DRO)	 Reinforce behaviour that is incompatible with the unwanted one. Reinforce behaviour other than the undesired one on a regular schedule.
14. Skills training (e.g. behaviour rehearsal)	Various approaches. Simulate real-life situation in which to rehearse the child's skills and to improve them.
15. Gradual exposure to aversive stimuli (e.g. desensitization)	Expose child gradually to feared situation while secure and relaxed.
16. Avoidance (e.g. covert sensitization)	Present (*in vivo* or in imagination) to-be-avoided object with aversive stimulus.
17. Modelling	Demonstrate behaviour for child to copy.
18. Role-playing	Script a role so client can rehearse behaviour and/or a situation.
19. Cognitive control (cognitive restructuring including problem solving)	Teach alternative ways of perceiving, controlling, solving problems.
20. Self-control training	Various approaches.

Methods for reducing behaviour

When a particular behaviour occurs at a high rate (with excessive frequency) or with surplus intensity and magnitude, or where a response is emitted under inappropriate conditions, the therapeutic task is to bring the behaviour within a range that is more socially acceptable. Unlike the child with a behaviour deficit, who has to learn a response that is not in his repertoire, the child with excess behaviour has to learn to modify existing responses.

To facilitate this, the therapist has a choice among a variety of techniques which he can use singly or in combination—but, as always, in a clinically sensitive and imaginative fashion.

7. Extinction

Procedure 7a	**EXTINCTION**
	Arrange conditions so that the child receives no rewards following undesired acts; in other words, withhold reinforcements such as approval, attention, and the like, which have previously and inappropriately been contingent on the production of inappropriate responses.

Applications

Successful extinction brings about the relatively permanent *unlearning* of a behaviour (the elimination of a behaviour from a person's repertoire). It refers to a procedure by which reinforcement that has previously followed an operant behaviour is discontinued. For example, to stop a child from acting in an attention-seeking manner which is antisocial in its effects, conditions are arranged so that he receives no reinforcement (attention) following the maladaptive action.

Method

See Flow Chart 6.

Carefully analyse the contingencies operating currently to maintain problematic behaviour and plan the elimination of such contingent reinforcement. Often these contingencies involve social reinforcement. Ask the reinforcing agents (parents, teachers) to offer their attention, responsiveness, praise and smiles contingently upon behaviours *other* than the undesirable one and to 'grit their teeth' (turn their back, look away, leave the room, or divert their attention to something or someone else) when the maladaptive behaviour occurs.

Remember: The child may 'work hard' to regain the lost reinforcement and thus may get 'worse' before he gets 'better'. Warn parents of this distinct possibility or they may become disillusioned, and will not persevere with the programme long enough to obtain results.

The reinforcement history of the child is important in determing how much patience the therapist and parents are going to require. If the problem behaviour has been continuously reinforced in the past then extinction should be swift; after all it is much easier for the youngster to recognize that he has lost reinforcers than it is for the child on intermittent reinforcement. In the latter case, extinction tends to be slow.

Remember: The association between a cue and a response is weakened each time the response occurs and is not followed by reinforcement. Thus disuse alone does not lead to extinction. It is essential that the behaviour should occur in order for extinction to take place; for only then are the internal motivating factors truly weakened. So no restraint is put upon the child (see by contrast Procedure 9, Punishment). For this reason alone (there are others) give careful consideration to this procedure as in Flow Chart 6. Problem actions may provide intrinsic

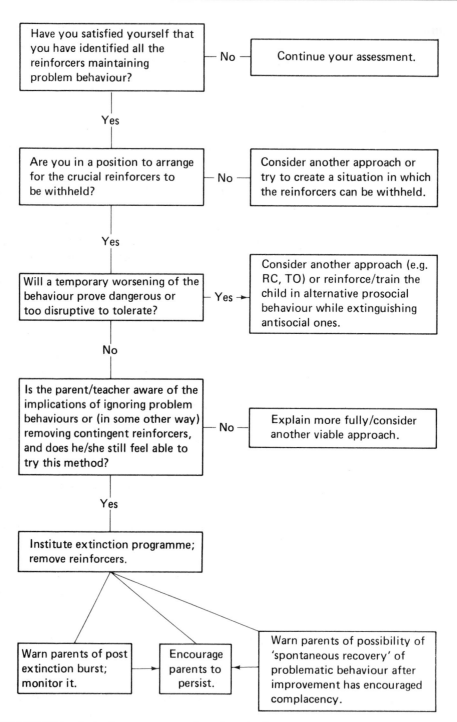

FLOW CHART 6   Extinction programme (e.g. ignoring).

satisfaction and pleasure (self-approbation) over and above the external re-inforcement inherent in the adult paying anxious attention to them. If a child plays up in the classroom the child may still obtain reinforcement from his peers although the teacher ignores his behaviour.

Involving others

Some behaviour is so disruptive of others, that it just cannot be ignored in isolation—in the hope that it will eventually extinguish. In some cases it has proved necessary to supplement extinction by procedures designed to short-circuit these difficulties; in other cases the help of sympathetic people has been enlisted. Carlson *et al.* (1968) reinforced classmates for ignoring certain aspects of the client's behaviour. Kubany *et al.* (1971) reinforced the client's peers contingent upon his improvement. It is often a good idea (given parental permission) to explain to friends and family (and sometimes neighbours) what is happening so that they do not unwittingly subvert the programme. Siblings can prove helpful in the furtherance of therapeutic objectives (Miller and Cantwell, 1976).

Avoid: Complacency. Sometimes the unwanted behaviour—which has apparently been successfully extinguished—returns after a period ... to everyone's dismay. This may occur when the child returns (say) to his classroom after a holiday. In learning terms this is referred to (paradoxically, for the parent and therapist) as 'spontaneous recovery'.

For reasons like these, extinction procedures are most suitable for the reduction of behaviours whose temporary continuance and (possibly) exacerbation before extinction can be tolerated. This would exclude high-intensity acts of assault and self-injury. Another consideration is the possibility of imitation by other children. If this is a major concern then extinction alone is probably not an appropriate choice of treatment procedure.

Try to facilitate the extinction process by combining the procedure with reinforcement for alternative actions (Step 12). The possibility of obtaining reinforcement by other means may hasten the renunciation of deviant behaviour.

Note: *Don't underestimate the difficulty of ignoring problematic behaviour, especially if it is disruptive and especially if one is teaching (and don't forget that extinction does not invariably work). Not surprisingly teachers are likely to attend to pupils when they are difficult and rowdy. Walker and Buckley (1973), for example, found that 18 % of a teacher's attention to 'non-problem' children was for inappropriate behaviour while 89 % of her attention to 'problem' children was for undesirable classroom behaviour. Furthermore, 77 % of the attention given to all the observed children was bestowed on the disruptive children.*

It is true, too, that parents provide attention, interest, approval, and positive physical contact as a consequence of behaviour such as shouting, hitting, and non-compliance in deviant children. The same pattern is seen in institutions for the mentally subnormal, where a child exhibits some form of undesirable (say self-injurious) behaviour and attendants terminate the behaviour by restraining the child. Such attention—a commodity which is very precious in an institution where stimulation, affection, and self-esteem are sometimes in short supply—may reinforce the self-mutilation.

In summary, to withhold reinforcers appears easy in principle. However, it may be difficult in practice, in the untidy and unpredictable world outside the clinic, to gain contingency control; the therapist has to assess whether he is in a position to arrange for the crucial reinforcers to be withheld.

Sadly, some children do appear to get worse rather than better when their parents ignore deviant behaviour and attend to more appropriate behaviour. Why should this be? Several explanations have been put forward. It may not be certain that attention by caretakers was definitely the reinforcer for the disruptive behaviour of the child observed. Thus it is feasible that removal of the parent's or teacher's attention following the deviant behaviour does not really constitute extinction. Even where it is considered unnecessary to introduce additional procedures in order to maximize therapeutic control over reinforcement, it is likely that residual minor sources of reinforcement for deviant behaviour may go unnoticed after withholding the more powerful reinforcers. These left-over low-potential reinforcers continue to subvert attempts to extinguish behaviours. There is still obviously a need for further research to make it possible to use combined extinction and reinforcement regimes with greater discrimination and effectiveness.

Procedure 7b	SATIATION
	Make the child (or allow him to) continue performing the undesired act until he tires of it.

Method
Get the child who is (say) destructive to tear up piles of newspaper until he sickens of the activity; the child who uses obscene language, to use the words over and over again in your presence (deadpan) until the 'shock' value of the words are lost. Welsh (1968) treated fire-setting by involving the child in lengthy and exhausting sessions of lighting matches and blowing them out.

8. Stimulus change

Procedure 8	STIMULUS CHANGE
	Remove or change the discriminative stimuli signalling reinforcement or cues signalling punishment.

Applications
Certain responses seem to occur only when specific conditions are present. Thus, by altering the antecedent controlling conditions, you may well eliminate the behaviour. Stimulus change is the process of changing the discriminative stimuli—the environmental cues—which have been present when problem behaviour has been reinforced in the past.

Method
Stimuli associated with rewarded undesirable behaviour are removed—a technique commonly practised by teachers. If a child continually talks to the student next to him,

the teacher generally moves his desk away. By moving the desk, the teacher is changing the stimulus-context (proximity) in which the talking took place. Stimulus change has the short-term effect of reducing undesirable behaviour. It gives the teacher a chance to get new behaviour going by using positive reinforcement. If the old stimulus conditions are simply reinstated (e.g. the child's desk is moved back), there is a chance the maladaptive behaviour will reappear.

9. Punishment

Procedure 9	**PUNISHMENT** *Follow an unwanted response with a mildly aversive stimulus.*

Applications

Punishment can be effective in controlling behaviour. It all depends on how we interpret the word and deed called 'punishment'. Both *withdrawal of positive reinforcement* (known as the extinction procedure) and *contingent application of an aversive stimulus* tend to decrease target problem behaviours. Occasionally a moderately aversive stimulus (e.g. a smack) administered immediately following an inappropriate behaviour, is justifiable in terms of quick and dramatic results, and because the consequences of not doing so can result in death or injury (e.g. a very young child putting a knitting needle down his infant brother's ear, or his fingers into a power point).

The trouble is that punishment always seems to be equated with hitting or hurting. Severe punishment tends to suppress behaviour rather than extinguish it! The behaviour is only likely to be performed a very few times, perhaps only once in the instance of intense punishment, before it ceases. The prediction is that punishment will be ineffective because suppressed behaviours tend to recur, whereas extinguished ones (see Procedure 7) do not—at least in the longer term. Such theorizing has led to the present emphasis upon the encouragement in the child of alternative behaviours that are mutually exclusive of the undesirable ones which are being punished. The training of these behaviours could take place during the period of suppression that follows punishment.

Punishment is not necessarily intense or indeed physical. Parents reprimand, shout at, isolate and withdraw approval or privileges from their children. There is no evidence that occasional spanking carried out in the context of a secure and loving home environment ever scarred a child's (or subsequent adult's) psyche. There *is* clear evidence that persistent, intense physical punishment carried out against a background of cold, hostile and rejecting parental attitudes, causes a great amount of harm.

The popularity of punishment as a means of modifying behaviour for parents and teachers, may be due—to some extent—to the fact that it is often reinforced by the immediate (if temporary) relief brought about by the prompt (and also brief) cessation of the misdemeanour. In other words it can be habit-forming! The more general and long-term consequences of punishment can degenerate in ways that are destructive. It is likely to be administered in ways which are ill-timed, extreme, inconsistent, retaliatory and without any accompanying choices and encouragement of more acceptable substitute behaviours. It has a nasty way of escalating. Because its effects are usually short-lived the child repeats the undesirable behaviour; parents repeat the punishment, somewhat more forcefully; soon the child is back to the same misdemeanour ... and there comes about another turn of the screw ... harsher measures, and so on and on.

Several researchers urge caution in the use of physical punishment with children. While it is true that intense punishment is more effective at suppressing behaviour than mild punishment, there are unwanted side-effects to take into account. Aggressive behaviour on the part of an adult (as part of the punishment) could provide an undesirable modelling experience for the child; there might be maladaptive emotional sequelae such as fear, tenseness, withdrawal and frustration. Punishment alone does not direct the child towards appropriate or desirable behaviour; indeed, as we saw, it does not even eliminate inappropriate activity but rather slows it down. A person who frequently uses punishment, might lose his own reinforcing value and stimulate avoidance activities (e.g. school phobia) or escape behaviour (e.g. truancy). Becker (1971) believes that punishment, used properly and humanely, can be effective in changing behaviour. In order to be effective, punishment (a) is given promptly, (b) relies on withdrawal of reinforcers (see below), (c) provides clear steps for retrieving these reinforcers, (d) makes use of a warning signal, (e) should be given in a calm, matter-of-fact manner, (f) is accompanied by plentiful reinforcement of actions incompatible with those being punished, (g) uses procedures to ensure that unwanted behaviours do not gain reinforcement.

Methods

The clinical application of punitive/aversive procedures is controversial from the ethical point of view. It is argued by proponents that distasteful as punishment may be to the therapist who is moved by compassion and the desire to relieve suffering, these very motives should force him to contemplate their use in certain cases. Self-injurious behaviour such as mutilation, head-banging, self-biting, induced vomiting, etc., have been successfully treated by the contingent application of aversive stimulation (see Sandler, 1980). 'The ends justify the means' is, however, a problematic and much abused slogan. The clinical application of shock or nausea-inducing drugs for addictive behaviour, sexual deviations and other problems, is felt (rightly or wrongly) to be outside the range of this manual, with its emphasis on community-orientated interventions and a naturalistic approach to life-difficulties. The more 'natural' sanctions, which are part of day-to-day child-rearing, are discussed in Procedures 10 and 11.

10. Time-out (TO) from positive reinforcement

Procedure 10	TIME-OUT
	Temporarily remove the child, following on the performance of the unwanted act, to a place devoid of people and objects of interest; in other words, a situation in which reinforcement is no longer available to him.

Applications

TO provides one means of sanctioning unwanted behaviour by the withdrawal of reinforcement. Removal of reinforcers is not only more effective than physical punishment

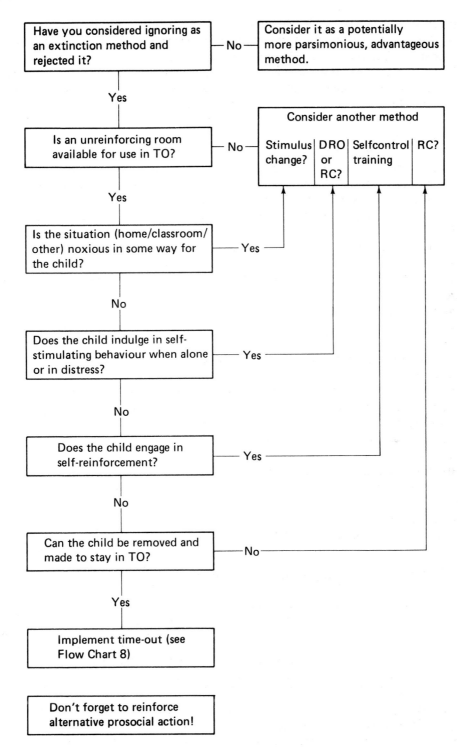

FLOW CHART 7   Some considerations in choosing time-out.

but it is free of the more undesirable side-effects. TO is a period of time during which the child is prevented from emitting the problematic behaviour (say a temper-tantrum) in the situation in which it has been positively reinforced in the past. (It has to be admitted that whatever technical definition learning theorists give to TO, children interpret it as punishment. Emphasizing potential self-control elements by referring to it as a 'cooling off' or 'think things out' period, may be useful.)

Choosing TO

TO sometimes leads to tantrums or rebellious behaviour such as crying, screaming, and physical assaults, particularly if the child has to be taken by force to a quiet room. With older, physically resistive children the method may simply not be feasible. So the procedure and its choice requires careful consideration (see Flow Chart 7). Very rarely are children destructive, but, if so, precautions have to be taken in the choice and preparation of the TO room. In some homes there just is no such room! Additional difficulties to be aware of are the possibility that the child may adapt to the TO situation by acquiring new means of obtaining reinforcement, such as self-stimulation or fantasy; and the likelihood that adults who have initial reservations about TO may use the procedure tentatively and inconsistently.

When the behaviour to be eliminated is an extraordinarily compelling one that all but *demands* attention (reinforcement) from those present, or when TO is difficult to administer because the child is a strong and protesting boy, an equivalent of TO may be instituted by removing the primary sources of reinforcement from him. So if the mother is a major source of reinforcement she could be advised to remove herself, together with a magazine, to the bathroom, locking herself in when her child's temper-tantrums erupt—coming out only when all is quiet. This ploy can be problematic if the child is also destructive.

Method

The child is warned in advance about those of his behaviours that are considered inappropriate and the consequences that will flow from them. See Flow Chart 8.

Timing

For younger children the time may be three to five minutes, for children of perhaps eight years and older, longer. Periods of 10 to 15 minutes are usually felt to be the maximum desirable duration. Ten-minute TOs are typically used in classroom situations. A stimulus associated with, and discriminative for TO, can acquire conditioned punishing properties, and thus lead to behaviour reduction. If so, the full TO sequence may not have to be administered in some instances. The presentation of the pre-TO stimulus which might consist of a verbal warning ('Stop that, or you'll have to go into time-out') a warning look, or a gesture may be enough to quell the target behaviour.

A child may or may not continue to display (say) a tantrum in the TO room; the point is that it is being ignored. *TO differs from extinction.* In the case of extinction, the reinforcers which are withdrawn are those specifically *identified* in terms of their maintaining function with regard to the deviant behaviour. TO, in contrast, involves the temporary withdrawal of *most* of the reinforcement currently available to the child. In a

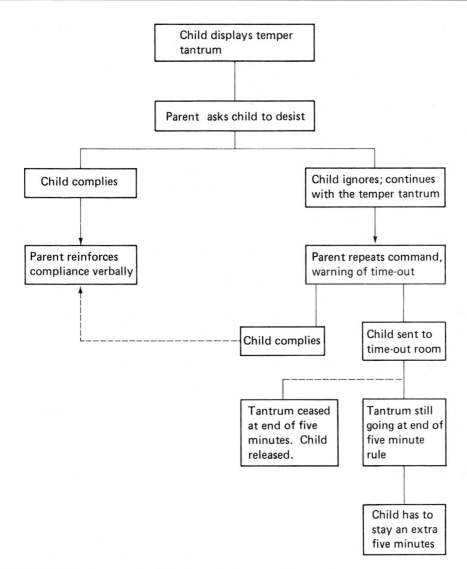

FLOW CHART 8   An example of the stages in the use of time-out.

sense, extinction by socially ignoring disruptive behaviours constitutes a focused TO. The TO room (sometimes referred to as a quiet room) is made non-reinforcing by being cleared of its entertainment value.

Note: *It is essential that the child sees that the mother is consistent and timely with her use of the procedure. This method is designed to help a child gain self-control; it should not become a game or be used frivolously for 'naughty' or 'annoying' activities, as opposed to serious maladaptive behaviour which has been subjected to thoughtful analysis and discussion.*

It is important to spend time in the home supervising the programme (especially in its early stages) and, when necessary, prompting the mother.

TO in the classroom

Time-out is a familiar procedure to the teacher: it has probably been used by most teachers at one time or another. Teachers have long used the procedure of placing a child at the side of the room, at the back of a room, or in days gone by on a dunce's chair. There is disagreement as to how far it is effective in changing unacceptable behaviour. It does have the advantage of providing both the teacher and the pupil with a breathing space in which tempers can cool, thus avoiding the use of harsher methods of control. TO has a number of counterproductive effects for the child. He is in the limelight, possibly acting the buffoon and therefore still the centre of attention. Or he is getting out of doing some unwelcome scholastic task. A lightweight screen for use in the junior classroom may overcome both these difficulties. Another disadvantage of TO is that it may prove to be more attractive to the pupil than the classroom, and thus act as a reinforcer of the behaviour it is intended to punish. If this is the case the teacher should have a hard look at his teaching and/or his interactions with this child.

Behaviour modification techniques such as time-out, which are designed to eliminate inappropriate or undesirable behaviour, are unlikely to succeed unless supplemented by the reinforcement of an alternative and more appropriate behaviour pattern. Time-out used in conjunction with extinction and positive reinforcement is effective in reducing a variety of deviant patterns of behaviour (see Appendix II).

Note: *Parents almost invariably state that they have tried (and often failed) with a version of TO. Sending a child to his room for unspecified periods of time is not TO, especially when the procedure is undermined by the presence of entertaining books and toys and (most important) the absence of clear-cut contingency rules. Nor is TO the unethical practice of confining him in a dark and frightening place.*

  TO should be used with caution. It is best not to use the child's own room as it could engender unpleasant connotations in his mind.

Self-control aspects

Although it was suggested that TO encourages self-control, there are procedures which allow the child to be more self-directed. By placing the subject in TO, the opportunity to make a decision is taken away from him and thus the self-control element is lessened. The mother, by placing the child in a quiet room, has made the decision for him and by the time he returns to the scene of combat, the provocative aspects of the situation are likely to have dissipated. The distinction between allowing the subject the opportunity to control his own behaviour and removing the opportunity to engage in additional unacceptable behaviour, is analogous to what is referred to as internal versus external control.

11. Response-cost (RC)

Another common punishment technique is response-cost, the contingent withdrawal of specified amounts of reinforcement. Parents ofen withhold love, approval, and privileges when their children are 'naughty'. This is an informal use of RC.

<table>
<tr><td>Procedure 11</td><td>RESPONSE-COST
Withdraw specified amounts of reinforcement from the child contingent upon his displaying unwanted behaviour; these must have been specified in advance. In effect the child pays a penalty for violating the rules; the withdrawal of reinforcers constitutes the 'cost' of the maladaptive action. Response-cost can of course only be used in a context where reinforcement in measurable quantities is being regularly used, as in the case of a token economy system (e.g. in a classroom).</td></tr>
</table>

Applications

RC is essentially a punishment procedure which seeks to reduce the future probability of a response. The method—in the form of loss of points, grades, money, tokens, privileges, etc.—is also applied in token economy programmes. The variety of applications is immense (see Appendix II).

Method

In order to put a RC contingency into effect:

(a) Some level of positive reinforcement must be administered to the child (so that there will be something to withdraw if necessary).

(b) The value of conditioned reinforcers such as tokens, points, or money has to be established for use in the programme.

It is essential to determine the reaction of each individual child and adapt the treatment programme accordingly. As with other procedures containing a punitive element, it is necessary to make clear to the child in advance precisely the 'cost' (in the form of fines, etc.) for each unwanted behaviour. Consistency, immediacy and knowledge of results (feedback) are crucial to a RC programme. The child has to learn that his maladaptive acts will be consistently punished; this involves applying the cost immediately after the unwanted act has occurred. Feedback means ensuring that the child has information about which of his actions produced the consequence of a penalty.

Avoid: Making costs too high and the reinforcement rate too low, or vice versa, otherwise the programme is likely to fail. It is common practice for prompts to be arranged. For example, in the classroom situation a card on the child's desk is used to list the deviant behaviours and the points he will lose if he emits them. In addition, the child should receive information about his performance, i.e. consistent and immediate feedback about the consequences of his behaviour.

In the use of RC, there is no time restriction before reinforcement is available as there is with TO. For example, a child may have to pay a fine for disruptive behaviour in the classroom. Having been fined, there is no fixed period of time during which positive reinforcers are beyond the reach of the child, as is the case if he is placed in a room for 10 minutes for the same maladaptive behaviour. Another difference between the RC and TO procedures is the amount of reinforcement lost. A *specified* amount of the reinforcers is withdrawn in the case of the former, whereas *all* reinforcers are withdrawn (for a specified time) in the latter.

Remember: That response-cost is an effective way of encouraging self-management, in that awareness of the rewards and losses of certain behaviour allows the individual to participate in the contingency system. (Incidentally, it is also a convenient self-discipline for the parent, e.g. contributing to a charity box after breaking a rule about shouting at the children over trivia and so on.) As with other punitive techniques, it needs to be used in moderation in order to avoid side-effects such as anger or avoidance behaviour, and to be supplemented by other techniques designed to reinforce appropriate behaviour.

RC may well be more practicable (and have less undesirable side-effects) than TO in classroom settings. Whether at home or in the classroom, there are at least two advantages of using RC. One is that RC does not remove the subject from the opportunity to engage in desirable behaviour. From that standpoint, any time spent in TO is, in a sense, wasted time. Because RC does not remove the subject from the ongoing events it avoids this particular problem. The second advantage is that by not removing the child from the situation which is unfolding, and which involves choices about whether to behave or misbehave, the child is provided with a more realistic learning situation. He is given the opportunity either to continue to perform the behaviour and be punished, or not persist in the undesirable behaviour and experience no punishment.

As with other behavioural methods there are individual differences in the reactions of children to RC procedures. The actual aversiveness of TOs and RCs appears to be a function of the child's interactions within a particular social context, the way in which the procedures are implemented, and his reinforcemented history.

A study by McIntire *et al.* (1968) illustrates the RC procedure in an after-school programme for elementary and junior high school boys. Each child had a counter on which a teacher could either add or subtract points. The child gained points for correct answers and lost points for disruptive behaviour. Whenever disruptive behaviour occurred, the instructor would turn on the counter associated with that student's name and allow the counter to continue to subtract points until the instructor felt that that student had corrected himself.

12. Overcorrection

A further form of response-cost or penalty is known as overcorrection. With overcorrection we have a method combining positive reinforcement and aversive control, which is used to discourage inappropriate or disruptive behaviour. This method requires a person to do something over and above that necessary to correct a situation resulting from inappropriate behaviour, or something that is incompatible with the unwanted action.

Procedure 12	(a) OVERCORRECTION (restitutional overcorrection)
	Require the youth to correct the consequences of his misbehaviour. Not only must he remedy the situation he has caused, but also 'over-correct' it to an improved or better-than-normal state. In other words, you enforce the perfor-mance of a new behaviour in the situation where you want it to become routine.
	(b) OVERCORRECTION (positive practice)
	Get the child to practise positive behaviours which are physically incompatible with the in-appropriate behaviour.

Applications

(a) A child who steals and breaks another youngster's penknife is required to save up enough money not only to replace the knife, but also to buy a small gift betokening regret. He is praised at the completion of the act of restitution. A boy who deliberately punctures another child's bicycle tyre not only has to repair the tyre but also must oil and polish the entire vehicle.

(b) A child who indulges in self-stimulatory behaviour is required to do something which is physically incompatible with the action (e.g. walking to counter rocking). Of course, alternative sources of stimulation would have to be sought.

13. Positive reinforcement: promotion of alternative behaviour

Procedure 13a	REINFORCEMENT OF INCOMPATIBLE BEHAVIOUR (RIB)
	Positively reinforce a particular class of be-haviour which is inconsistent with, or which cannot be performed at the same time as, the undesired act. In other words, to stop a child from acting in a particular way, deliberately reinforce a competing action.

Applications

To decrease a behaviour use positive reinforcement. Reinforcement, which is so crucial to the acquisition of behaviour, is also useful in eliminating unwanted responses. For example, the therapist can strengthen (by reinforcement) alternative acts that are incompatible with, or cannot be performed at the same time as, the maladaptive response (counterconditioning). There are very few occasions, as we have stressed, in which it is desirably only to reduce a given behaviour without at the same time training the child in some alternative prosocial act.

Method

Counterconditioning involves using principles of operant conditioning to supplant problem behaviours by reinforcing and thereby strengthening socially acceptable alternatives.

The advantage of this approach is the possibility of choosing a competing behaviour of a prosocial kind to strengthen while reducing the occurrence of the unwanted behaviour. The process may occur fairly slowly, and it may be helpful to attempt to accelerate the programme with a time-out or response-cost procedure.

If sufficient reinforcement is not made available in this way for adaptive behaviours, new strategies may be adopted—and possibly undesirable behaviours—as a means of gaining reinforcement. It is probably too much to hope that the youngster will necessarily, and of his own accord, turn to socially desirable actions once the target problems are extinguished. As with punishment procedures, extinction methods on their own do not indicate to the child the kind of actions that should replace the unwanted ones. The alternatives could indeed be as problematic, including aggression or absconding.

Procedure 13b	DIFFERENTIAL REINFORCEMENT OF OTHER BEHAVIOUR (DRO)
	Arrange for reinforcing stimuli to be contingent upon the occurrence of any responses other than the unwanted target behaviour.

Applications

As in Procedure 13a, except that DRO is simpler to use, involving the reinforcement of *any behaviour* other than the target behaviour. In the literature, target behaviours include disruptive, aggressive, hyperactive, self-injurious behaviours. DRO is indicated in circumstances in which it is desirable to discontinue reinforcement for an undesirable response, but it is unwise to decrease the quantity of reinforcement the child receives.

Method

Reward the child at the end of set intervals which are free of unwanted actions.

DRO and its disadvantages

The problem with DRO methods is their 'sledgehammer' properties. The fact that *any* behaviours other than the undesired one are equally reinforceable gives rise to the possibility that unwanted behaviours may be unwittingly encouraged. For instance, the hyperactive child may fail to perform some required academic task during the specified observation period, but because he is not out of his seat, shuffling his desk, or pinching his neighbour he remains eligible for reinforcement. This complication might be avoided by putting other patterns of undesirable behaviour on a DRO regime as well as hyperactive behaviour. Hopefully there will be enough intervals which merit reinforcement to allow the programme to work. Another problem in the use of a DRO regime is the so-called *behaviour contrast* effect. If hyperactivity is being dealt with by DRO procedures in one situation (say at school) but is rewarded in another situation (at home), then while it decreases under DRO conditions it may actually increase in the rewarded circumstances.

14. Skills training (e.g. behaviour rehearsal)

> **Procedure 14a** **BEHAVIOUR REHEARSAL**
> *Simulate real-life situations in which skills are to be developed.*
> *(1) Prepare the child.*
> *(2) Select the target situations (e.g. social skills to be learned).*
> *(3) Rehearse the behaviour in the security of the consulting room/child's home.*
> *(4) Get the child to try out the new behaviours in real-life situations—as 'homework' exercises.*

Applications

Many children, because of tragic and depriving life experiences, lack some of the crucial skills required to cope with life in a constructive and adaptive manner. If children can be helped to become more competent at social and other skills, then they may have less recourse to maladaptive behaviour (Foster and Ritchey, 1979; Goldstein *et al.*, 1978).

Method

During rehearsal:

(1) Demonstrate the skill.

(2) Ask the child to practise the skill. (Use role play. Provide a model if necessary.)

(3) Provide feedback as to the accuracy/inaccuracy of the child's performance. (If possible, it is advantageous for the youngster—and video equipment is most useful here—to evaluate the effectiveness of his own performance; see Thelen *et al.*, (1976).)

(4) Give homework assignments, e.g. real-life planned practice or the try-out at home of skills. Not only does behaviour rehearsal provide for acquiring new skills but it also allows their practice at a controlled pace and in a safe environment, and in this way minimizes distress. With increasing client skill in self-monitoring (sensitivity and accuracy of self-perception), the therapist hands over increasingly the evaluation and corrective actions to the youngster himself.

Trower *et al.* (1978, p. 80) provide a list of the basic skills; the technical details of social skills training are too multitudinous to include in a general manual such as this. However, there seem to be two basic attitudes which should be enhanced if friendships and other social relations are going to come with reasonable ease.

(a) Other people are perceived primarily as sources of satisfaction rather than deprivation.

(b) The child has opportunities for social interactions that reward and make enjoyable the giving, as well as the receiving, of affection.

Obviously, there are many strategies described in these pages which have a bearing on these attitudes. Careful assessment is required to determine whether skills are absent; to identify relevant situations; to determine whether there are discrimination problems in relation to when behaviours can most profitably be displayed; and to determine whether negative thoughts and irrational anticipations interfere with the display of effective behaviours. A variety of routes may be employed to gather assessment information, including self-report, role-playing and observation in the natural environment. And a variety of paths, including relationship enhancement (Goldstein, 1980) and attitude modification (Johnson, 1980) might be chosen for the mitigation of social deficits.

Procedure 14b	SOCIAL SKILLS TRAINING
	Coach the child so he calls on a new and more socially acceptable repertoire of skills, which will enable him to influence his environment sufficiently to attain basic personal goals (see Combs and Slaby, 1978).

Applications

The subjects (and by implication, problems) covered in the manuals and programmes on social skills training (e.g. Cotler and Guerra, 1976; Lange and Jakubowski, 1976; Zimbardo, 1977) typically include such topics as: improving powers of observation and accurate judgement; basic conversation skills such as listening, asking questions and talking; expressive skills such as the use of body language; social techniques for special situations, assertive training etc. These, and other skills, break down essentially into the three groups shown in Table XI.

Method

Role play (see Procedure 18a): Role-playing assessment may reveal that the child has many effective components of needed behaviours and it may be decided that these can be 'shaped' by offering further instructions and prompts during role rehearsal. Role rehearsal is a gradual process—building up skills by means of working out a hierarchy of component tasks. This 'pretend' sort of rehearsal provides an intermediate step in changing behaviour and developing new and more effective strategies. The end-point is when the child tries out the new skill or role *in vivo*. To take one application: the self-effacing, timid child may overcome these deficits by assertion training. Another application might be learning the social skills to conduct oneself to better effect with the

Table XI

Observational skills	Performance skills	Cognitive skills
Getting information	Listening skills	Planning
Reading social signals	Speaking skills	Problem solving
Asking questions		
	Non-verbal expression	
	Greetings and partings	
	Initiating conversations	
	Rewarding skills	
	Assertive skills	

opposite sex, a teacher or parents. (See Flowers and Booraem (1980) and Foster and Ritchey (1979) for discussions of role-play and social competence issues.)

15. Eliminating dysfunctional emotion

Emotional behaviour can be controlled by different stimulus sources. One is the emotional arousal evoked directly by conditioned aversive stimuli. To eliminate maladaptive emotional responses, repeated non-reinforced exposure to threatening events (either directly or vicariously) may be required.

Procedure 15a	GRADUAL EXPOSURE TO AVERSIVE STIMULI (variously referred to as desensitization, graded change, counter conditioning)

Expose the child gradually to the aversive (e.g. phobic) situation, using
(1) graduated imaginal stimuli (a fear hierarchy presented in imagery form); or
(2) graduated real-life stimuli (a fear hierarchy based on actual situations).
Expose the child, when
(1) he has been trained in anxiety-antagonistic responses such as relaxation or other anxiety-neutralizing conditions (e.g. while in the company of a trusted, reassuring person or while playing or eating); or
(2) he is feeling comfortable, but not after special antagonistic response-training, or measures. Reinforce the child for each successful attempt.

Applications
These methods are most useful for dealing with avoidance behaviour, e.g. fears.

The extinction of inappropriate avoidance behaviours (e.g. school phobia, animal phobia) is made difficult because the fear which is in need of extinction prevents the child coming into contact with the feared (phobic) object. This 'catch 22' stops the process of 'spontaneous remission' whereby most of our fears are extinguished or reduced. So we have to break down the phobic situation into manageable 'bits'.

Methods
Active participation procedures (so-called) emphasize the gradual approach to real anxiety-provoking cues. The emphasis here is on operant components rather than on relaxation-training. *Passive association procedures* include those desensitization techniques that emphasize the gradual pairing of anxiety-antagonistic responses with feared stimuli.

Hatzenbuchler and Schroeder (1979) speculate that these two types of desensitization are not distinct ways of overcoming fears but are best construed as two processes on one continuum of gradual exposure to aversive stimuli.

Procedure 15b	DESENSITIZATION—ACTIVE PARTICIPATION
	Help a child to overcome his fear of a particular situation by exposing him gradually and more closely to the feared situation while he is being rewarded or is feeling comfortable or secure— perhaps in the company of a supportive person.

The power of desensitization (in adults) is greatly enhanced by *in vivo* (real-life) exposures. Although one lacks the flexibility of fear hierarchies constructed for imaginal presentation, the real-life exposure training can of itself be most effective, especially when graduated and combined with modelling (see Procedure 17a).

Method
The child is helped to accomplish each stage successfully with minimal or no fear before moving onto the next step. The lowest item on the fear hierarchy is presented (say, a small dog) at a distance. Slowly, it is brought closer, pausing, if the youngster signals any apprehension. Gradually more fear items are presented in turn.

Procedure 15c	SYSTEMATIC DESENSITIZATION— PASSIVE ASSOCIATION
	A graduated approach (while physically and/or mentally relaxed) to feared objects/situations. In the procedure sometimes called 'systematic desensitization' the exposure to the feared situation (in imagined scenes) progresses in slow, gradual steps—graded by constructing 'fear hierarchies'.

Method
The most common procedure has been to arrange the anxiety-evoking stimuli in a hierarchy (see Table XII for an example) and to present them one at a time while the person is in a state of deep relaxation (see Jacobson, 1938) and at a pace at which he is able to cope with the stimulus without experiencing undue distress.

Rationale
Goldfried (1971) provides one of several alternative rationales for desensitization. For him it is a training in coping skills—a behaviour rehearsal of what the client is eventually to do in coping with anxiety in a real-life situation. This self-control procedure involves somewhat different emphases. The gradual exposure to the fear-provoking situation can

Table XII The fear hierarchy of an agoraphobic student (age 18). Items were rated on the subjective anxiety scale, 10–100, 100 representing extreme discomfort, 10 complete calmness.

100	Walking across the common at night (few people present)
90	Walking across the common at night (many people present)
80	Walking across the common at dusk (few people)
70	Walking across the common at dusk (many people)
50	Walking across the common in daylight (few people)
40	Walking across the common in daylight (many people)
10	Walking around the perimeter of the common
100	Walking from the Science Department to the Student Union (alone)
80	Walking from the Science Department to the Student Union (with strangers)
50	Walking from the Science Department to the Student Union (with friends)
20	Walking from the Science Department to the Student Union (with boy friend)
100	Taking a bus journey alone (a long distance seated toward the front of the bus)
100	Taking a bus journey alone (a short distance seated toward the front of the bus)
80	Taking a bus journey alone (a long distance seated by the door)
60	Taking a bus journey alone (a short distance seated by the door)
40	Taking a bus journey with boy friend (toward front of bus)
30	Taking a bus journey with boy friend (toward back of bus)
100	Shopping at the supermarket alone (crowded away from entrance/exit)
80	Shopping at the supermarket alone (crowded near exit)
70	Shopping at the supermarket alone (few people, away from exit)
60	Shopping at the supermarket along (few people, near exit)
40	Shopping at the supermarket (with boy friend)

occur either in the person's fantasy (imagining himself to be in various anxiety-related situations) or it can take place in real life (*in vivo*). In the former case, if anxiety is experienced, the imagined scene is extinguished, relaxation reinstated, and then the scene imagined again repeatedly until relaxation can be maintained in its presence. In this manner the child progresses along a hierarchy of imagined aversive stimuli until the relaxation can be maintained throughout, and the desensitization is generalized from the imagined to the actual phobic situation.

An alleged (but still unproven) problem with children is the difficulty of obtaining the required imagery, and indeed, the trained state of relaxation. Clear evidence for the effectiveness of any variant of desensitization with children is still lacking (see Hatzenbuchler and Schroeder, 1978). Some case studies suggest the successful reduction of avoidence behaviour; others failed.

It may be preferable with the child who shows intense avoidance behaviour so that his voluntary participation is inhibited, to emphasize (initially) responses (e.g. relaxation) which are antagonistic to anxiety. This relatively passive pairing of relaxation responses and the phobic object is thought by some to have a reciprocally inhibiting effect. Subsequently there could be more active participation of the child in approaching the feared object and less emphasis on the anxiety-neutralizing responses. With moderately avoident children—according to Hatzenbuchler and Schroeder (1978)—active participation is preferable because of the assured advantage of behavioural rehearsal.

Procedure 15d	RELAXATION *It may be possible to teach a child how to relax as a coping skill—when he becomes frustrated, agitated or angered. Relaxation has the advantage that it can be taught like any other skill. If the relaxation exercises have been well practised and successful, the person becomes relaxed when he says to himself, 'relax' or 'remain calm'.*

The precise role of relaxation as a therapeutic ingredient, either alone, or as part of a systematic desensitization programme, especially with regard to children, is currently in some doubt.

Procedure 15e	FLOODING (sometimes called implosion) *Bring the client into contact with the most feared item on the hierarchy, and keep him in contact with it until the fear has been extinguished. Essentially there is an immediate and sustained confrontation with the strongly aversive stimulus, either in vivo or in the imagination.*

Despite growing evidence for the effectiveness of this approach where children are concerned, the ethics of using it are questionable! Children may not understand the implications of the method even when it is explained to them; they are not always voluntary recipients of treatment.

16. Avoidance

Procedure 16	AVOIDANCE *Simultaneously present the child with the situation to be avoided (or some representation of it) and some aversive condition (or its representation).*

Applications

The purpose of this procedure is the opposite of the previous ones in the sense that you wish to reduce (not encourage) approach behaviour—because the object/situation is an undesirable one. To put it another way, avoidance tendencies are being built up.

Method

Approach behaviour is associated with aversive consequences—imagined or real.

Covert sensitization is the term given to the mental (imaginary) representation of noxious outcomes. The child may be trained to imagine vomiting and feeling nauseated by inhaling cigarette smoke (see Mahoney, 1974).

17. Modelling

Procedure 17a	MODELLING
	Systematically demonstrate in actuality (or symbolically—on film) a model displaying the required behaviour: a skill, an appropriate pro-social action, a coping strategy.

Applications

Modelling is the most frequently used and reliably effective strategy for reducing children's fears. However, it can be used in many situations including the teaching of new skills or alternative behaviours. It may have a promising preventive role in the area of stress-inoculation.

Modelling can be combined with other procedures; thus modelling combined with desensitization may be very effective in the treatment of phobias.

Method

In the case of modelling, the therapeutic intervention may be directed towards the relationship between the antecedent conditions and the deviant behaviour and/or between the problem behaviour and its consequences.

Procedure 17b	SYMBOLIC MODELLING
	An excellent example of this procedure is provided by Melamed and Siegel (1975). They use symbolic modelling to prepare children psychologically for surgery. Children view a 16-minute film of an initially fearful child who gradually copes with the situation and overcomes his own fears.

Procedure 17c	ACTUAL MODELLING
	An example is the reduction of aggression by exposing youths to models who demonstrate alternative ways of handling provocative situations; these models are more likely to be imitated if the consequences for the model are rewarding, than if they are followed either by an absence of reward or by adverse consequences for the model.

Applications

Brief symbolic modelling may be an effective aid in preparing children for dental and medical treatment (e.g. surgery) by reducing situational fears. Symbolic modelling refers (for example) to the viewing of a film.

Live modelling appears to be more effective than symbolic modelling, although there isn't much in it if one allows several therapeutic trials and several models and progressively varied fear stimuli.

Method

Modelling procedures become more powerful as additional controlled components are added to the basic technique. Thus you might use the package shown in Flow Chart 9.

As with reinforced practice and desensitization, children may or may not be trained in anxiety-neutralizing procedures and encouraged to use these self-control skills during exposure to feared situations. The severity of the anxiety may determine whether this is necessary. The more intense the anxiety, the more likely that training the child in skills for coping with anxiety will facilitate the reduction of anxiety and thus increase the probability of exposure to feared situations. Such training might also result in more generalized effects.

Lange and Jakubowski (1976, p. 180) provide some pointers for constructing modelling tapes for assertion training. (The tapes may of course be used for other purposes.)

(1) Select models (generally) of the same sex and similar in other crucial ways to the observing child (group members).
(2) Demonstrate not only assertive behaviour but that action resulting in reinforcing outcomes.
(3) Make the modelling scenes reasonably short (one to three minutes).
(4) Break down complex assertive behaviours into smaller more easily assimilable parts, capable of being remembered by the observer.
(5) Highlight key aspects of the modelled assertive behaviour, viz. simplify the modelling scenes so the key aspects are 'underlined' or include a narrative which directs the observer's attention to the salient characteristics of the model's behaviour.
(6) Include methods for helping the observer to develop codes or covert symbolic labels for the modelling sequence of behaviours (e.g. acknowledge the other person's point of view before making your own, possibly contradictory, view known).
(7) Follow the tape by individual (or group) discussion. Allow a period of practice— on personal adaptations of the modelled actions.

| Procedure 17d | **COVERT MODELLING** |
| | *Encourage the child to imagine a model coping with the feared situation.* |

In this way rehearsal of approach behaviour takes place.

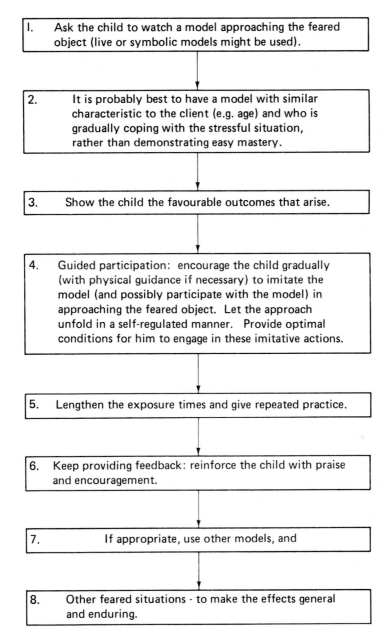

I. Ask the child to watch a model approaching the feared object (live or symbolic models might be used).

2. It is probably best to have a model with similar characteristic to the client (e.g. age) and who is gradually coping with the stressful situation, rather than demonstrating easy mastery.

3. Show the child the favourable outcomes that arise.

4. Guided participation: encourage the child gradually (with physical guidance if necessary) to imitate the model (and possibly participate with the model) in approaching the feared object. Let the approach unfold in a self-regulated manner. Provide optimal conditions for him to engage in these imitative actions.

5. Lengthen the exposure times and give repeated practice.

6. Keep providing feedback: reinforce the child with praise and encouragement.

7. If appropriate, use other models, and

8. Other feared situations - to make the effects general and enduring.

FLOW CHART 9   Modelling and reinforced practice (for fear reduction).

18. Role-playing

Procedure 18a	ROLE-PLAYING
	Role-play a problem situation (a feared event, a provocative confrontation, etc.) with the child. The adult (parent/therapist) can 'change' roles, child playing parent or vice versa. One or other can pretend to be the individual who is thought to be the source of the problem.

Applications

Role-playing is an effective technique for helping a person to learn new skills. Initiate rehearsal of the required behaviour under the direction of a therapist. A child will be explicitly asked to perform a normal role which is not normally his own, or asked to perform a normal role but not in a setting where it is normally enacted. The method is used to teach youths very basic skills, to help them become more effective in their interactions, and to help them to become more effective when extremely anxious (e.g. through enacting scenes such as using the telephone, going to an interview with an employer or dealing with provocation).

Procedure 18b	FIXED-ROLE THERAPY
	Encourage the youngster (or parent?) to 'try out' new behaviour patterns based upon a carefully 'scripted' role. A highly specific, fixed role is negotiated, and the client is encouraged to play this role in the expectation that by receiving new and helpful forms of feedback from the environment he will change the self-defeating constructs that control his behaviour.

Applications

This method of helping the client to test out the way he construes (and self-defeatingly misconstrues his world) is useful for youngsters who have low self-esteem, feel persecuted and socially isolated.

Method

(1) The client is encouraged to explored (by trying out) patterns of behaviour constrasted to his own. This is based on a fixed role sketch worked out with the client and derived from a compromise between what he is 'actually' like, and what he would like to be like.

(2) He is invited to practise these patterns in everyday life.

(3) From practice he gains an experience of how the environment can differ in appearance and 'feel', and how it reacts, when *he* behaves in a different manner.

(4) Practice generates new and more effective skills, supplemented by novel experience from the feedback he receives.

Devised by Kelly (1955), fixed-role therapy is a sophisticated behavioural-cognitive form of behaviour rehearsal. A case history fragment (Appendix I, Case fragment 2) provides an example of fixed-role therapy as described by a parent of a child in treatment at the Child Treatment Research Unit; it indicates something of the approach to designing and implementing the method.

19. Cognitive learning and control

Rationale
Behaviour is not always predictable from external sources of influence; cognitive factors, in part, determine what we observe, feel, and do at any particular point in time. Cognitive learning is a generic term for learning about the world by the use of reasoning, judgement, imagination, and various perceptual and conceptual abilities. Such learning makes use of images, symbols, concepts and rules. Cognitive processes involved in learning include attentional processes, the encoding of information, the storage and retrieval of information in memory, the postulating of hypotheses, their evaluation, and inductive and deductive reasoning. This category of learning has been neglected in behavioural formulations of childhood deviance, although there are signs of a growing interest in training children in problem-solving (Kifer *et al.*, 1974; Meichenbaum and Goodman, 1971; Spivack and Shure, 1973; Urbain and Kendall, 1980), and in cognitive control.

Kendall (1981) states that cognitive-behavioural interventions are not merely the simplification of the cognitive approaches employed with adults. Whereas the nature of the cognitive problems associated with adult anxiety and depression—to take two examples—can be conceptualized as *cognitive errors*, the cognitive problems and the focus of treatment in child cognitive-behavioural therapy are most often *cognitive absences*. Kendall explains that the child fails to engage in the cognitive, information-processing activities of an active problem-solver and refrains from initiating the reflective thought processes that can control behaviour. Indeed he may lack the cognitive skills needed to carry out crucial abstract, analytical mental activities.

Problem-solving therapies
The rationale for these methods is succinctly provided by D'Zurilla and Goldfried (1971):

> Much of what we view clinically as 'abnormal behaviour' or 'emotional disturbance' may be viewed as ineffective behaviour and its consequences, in which the individual is unable to resolve certain situational problems in his life and his inadequate attempts to do so are having undesirable effects, such as anxiety, depression, and the creation of additional problems. (p. 107)

Applications
Although some of the therapeutic procedures commonly used in adult cognitively-orientated work can be understood by adolescents, many of them would not be suitable for children. Nevertheless, youngsters can be taught rational thinking, stress-inoculation techniques and problem-solving strategies.

The learning theorist Estes (1971) is commenting on methods such as these, in a sense, when he writes that

> For the lower animals, for very young children, and to some extent for human beings of all ages who are mentally retarded or subject to severe neurological or behaviour disorders, behaviour from moment to moment is largely describable and predictable in terms of responses to particular stimuli and the rewarding or punishing outcomes of previous stimulus–response sequences. In more mature beings, much instrumental behaviour and more especially a great part of verbal behaviour is organized into higher-order routines and is, in many instances, better understood in terms of the operation of rules, principles, strategies and the like.... Thus in many situations, an individual's behaviour from moment to moment may be governed by a relatively broad strategy, which, once adopted, dictates response sequences rather than by anticipated consequences of specific actions. In these situations it is the selection of strategies rather than the selection of particular reactions to stimuli which is modified by past experience with rewarding or punishing consequences. (p. 23)

An example of this broader approach to therapy is the method designed to improve *social perspective-taking* in children. Piaget (1932) described the young child as egocentric, seeing the world from a self-centred, personal perspective—indifferent to and unaware of the point of view of others. The development of role-taking (decentring) skills is a maturational process that results from the youngster's active involvement with his environment. Treatment methods encourage role-taking skills by means of enacted roles, discussions, observations of films, writing, debating and helping (see Chandler, 1973; Furness, 1976; Van Lieshout *et al.*, 1976).

Interestingly, behavioural procedures may be among the most powerful methods of activating cognitive processes; they are recruited for the remediation of a wide range of intra- and interpersonal problems. There is a delightful irony about this finding. What we now find is a burgeoning literature on the cognitive aspects of behaviour modification (see Beck *et al.*, 1979; Mahoney and Arnkoff, 1978). Kazdin (1980) believes that the major difference between cognitive and less cognitive behaviour therapists lies not so much in their therapeutic procedures, as in their rationale and selection of a given procedure in an individual case. The more cognitively orientated therapist is inclined to employ a behavioural procedure appropriate to the 'cognitive restructuring' he presumes is required. Emotional reactions—for example—may be controlled by self-generated stimuli, i.e. by symbolic activities in the form of emotion-provoking thoughts about pleasurable or frightening events. This sort of emotional arousal is susceptible to extinction through cognitive restructuring of probable response consequences.

19a. Cognitive restructuring

You train the child to re-evaluate potentially distressing events so that when they are viewed from a more realistic perspective they lose their power to upset. This involves changing his characteristic ways of organizing his experiences, and then producing alternatives. What a person tells himself about his experience affects his behaviour. For example, one youth may tend to attribute the causes of what happens to him to forces beyond his control, while another may see himself as having a major influence and say on the unfolding events of his life.

Applications

Cognitive restructuring has been found to be effective in modifying depressive (helpless) states, decreasing avoidance behaviour and reducing subjective anxiety. Its usefulness might be restricted to older children and adolescents.*

Method

The cognitive-restructuring method (e.g. Ellis, 1962) encourages the individual to talk about past experiences involving (say) feared events. Irrational ideas underlying their fears are exposed and challenged, as in rational restructuring. In this way the client is engaged in prolonged verbal exposure to threatening situations. You encourage him to *relabel* threatening stimuli.

Essentially a rational explanation for the development of the fear is being offered. The youngster is encouraged to attribute fear to internal cognitions rather than to external events.

As with other behavioural methods for stress reduction, there is a redistribution of the fearful behaviour away from the feared event and onto the faulty conceptualization of the distressing sequence. There are various ways in which cognitive appraisals may subvert the possibilities of mobilizing effective coping strategies. The child or mother may perceive that only in certain situations is his/her behaviour effective. Or they may credit their achievements to external factors rather than to their own ability ('external locus of control'). At the Child Treatment Research Unit we have known a mother attribute the successful treatment to 'luck' rather than to her hard earned competence *and* hard work. (Such misperception represents a failure on our part as therapists!) Indeed, the effect of successful performance on a client's sense of self-efficacy could vary, depending on whether accomplishments were attributed to ability or to effort expended.

19b. Thought stopping

Applications

Some children cannot stop themselves indulging in recurrent unconstructive ruminations. Thought stopping may help the child to control the obsessive, intrusive ideas.

Method

The child is trained to identify negative thoughts, to tell himself (covertly) to stop them, and to focus on the task at hand or some rewarding memory or imagery. The potential of achieving control over one's thoughts can be dramatically demonstrated to clients by requesting them to verbalize their negative thoughts and by shouting at them, 'Stop!' Typically, their speech will be interrupted. This procedure is repeated with an inquiry each time as to whether the child's thought pattern was interrupted. If it worked then there was

---

*One of the features of Ellis's RET (Rational Emotive Therapy) is the notion that certain core irrational ideas are at the root of much emotional disturbance, and that these dysfunctional cognitions can be altered. Such ideas are:
  —that it is easier to avoid than to face life difficulties;
  —that one should be thoroughly competent, intelligent, and achieving in all possible respects;
  —that one has virtually no control over one's emotions and that one cannot help feeling certain things.

a blocking! The child gradually assumes blocking control himself, and learns to say, 'stop' (covertly after a few trials) when negative, self-defeating ideas and thoughts start to occur. Pleasant, positive ideas and imagery that are incompatible with anxiety are substituted for the morbid preoccupations.

19c. Problem-solving skills

Procedure 19c	**PROBLEM-SOLVING** *Select problematic situations. Give examples (or encourage the child to do so) of various reactions to these situations, and then identify the consequences generated by these reactions.*

Applications
The aim of training children in problem-solving skills is to provide them with a general coping strategy for a variety of difficult situations. The method has been used to help children and adolescents deal more effectively with a variety of conflict situations (e.g. arriving at mutually acceptable decisions with parents, developing cooperation with the peer group). Its prime advantage as a training method is the provision of principles so that the youngster can function as his own 'therapist'. It is a variant of self-control training, directed towards the objective of encouraging the youth to think and work things out for himself.

Method
Goldfried and Davison (1976) enumerate five stages in problem-solving:

(a) general orientation;
(b) problem definition and formulation;
(c) generation of alternatives;
(d) decision-making;
(e) verification.

(a) *Orientation.* Encourage the client to monitor his problematic circumstances (e.g. a diary of events/feelings) but also to accept the normality of problems as a function of life and growing up. Sensitize him to the problem areas by discussion—getting him to identify fraught situations when they first occur, and to think first and act afterwards. All this presupposes the initial recognition that there is a difficulty.

To the extent that the individual has a mental set that he can cope with his problem, the greater is the likelihood that he will find a solution. The feeling of being in control (and conversely, *not* helpless) is of great significance in working through difficult situations.

(b) *Problem definition and formulation.* Encourage the client

(1) to define all aspects of the problem in operational terms, i.e. in relevant concrete terms rather than in vague, global and abstract language;

(2) to formulate or categorize the elements of the situation in a manner that identifies the client's major goals and the obstacles that get in the way of fulfilling these goals (issues, conflicts, barriers). It is helpful to follow this analysis with a summary restatement of the problem.

(c) *Generation of alternatives.* Ask the client to propose as wide a range of possible solutions as he can think of, in terms of:

(1) general strategies (*what to do*), and later
(2) specific tactics to implement the general strategy (*how to do it*). Brainstorming—a free-wheeling (at first uncritical) generation of as many ideas as possible—can be a help. After this depict the criteria (values) by which solutions will be judged. Consider (with the client) possible solutions.

(d) *Decision-making.* Get the client to work out the likely consequences of the better courses of action he has put forward. What is the 'utility' of these consequences in resolving the problem as it has been formulated? (see d'Zurilla and Goldfried, 1971). Test out the proposals against other criteria formulated in (c). Plan the operation—who is to do it and how it is to be done.

(e) *Verification.* The client carries out his chosen course of action and monitors the consequences of his actions. He matches the actual (reality) outcomes against the hoped-for outcomes; if the match is satisfactory he 'exits' (to use the jargon); if not, he continues to 'operate'—which means that he returns to the sequence of problem-solving operations.

Schneider and Robin (1976, p. 160) give the following example of a child thinking through alternatives:

If I hit Johnny, the teacher will get angry. She will punish me, and it will ruin my day. On the other hand, if I choose to control myself and ask the teacher to help me get my toy back, the day will continue to be good, and I can show myself how big I am. If I rip my paper up because I made a mistake on it, I will only have to start again. Another choice is to cross out my mistake neatly and continue so I do not waste time. That way I will have more time to play.

Interlude

You will have noticed that some of the methods overlap with each other. Procedures are not usually exclusive to particular problems. Most treatment programmes combine elements of each of the types of learning enumerated in Appendix III. Thus, in treating a hostile, aggressive child a therapist might attempt to teach him alternative ways of interpreting 'provocative' incidents; train him to associate calm and relaxation with the anger-provoking stimulus, while also modelling non-aggressive behaviour under provocation and reinforcing any exhibition of pacific behaviour by the child. It should be noted that some courses of treatment involve sophisticated extensions of basic principles, such as treatments concentrating upon self-control of behaviour. Self-control (or regulation) is a potent source of control which covers all types of learning. It has proved to be a crucial development in behaviour modification.

20. Self-control training

Procedure 20a	**SELF-MANAGEMENT**
	Most self-management programmes combine techniques that involve standard-setting, self-monitoring, self-evaluation, and self-reinforcement (which also involves self-specification of contingencies and self-administration of reinforcement). Before a child can be taught to reinforce himself for a be-haviour pattern, he must learn to evaluate his behaviour correctly. In order to encourage a child to evaluate his own behaviour properly, he must be taught to use some sort of standard by which he can measure his own behaviour. He also needs to attend to his own behaviour, monitoring it accurately. For example, he will have to learn to 'read' the signs of his own feelings (anger or hostility) and to label them correctly. If he hits out at another child, he will require a standard for evaluating his act as antisocial and therefore as grounds for criticiz-ing (i.e. punishing) himself. Or, if he desists from lashing out, praising himself (reinforce-ment) for showing self-control.

Applications

Behaviour modifiers vary in the degree to which they plan external or self-control over the contingencies and the administration of reinforcing or punishing consequences, when it comes to the treatment of children. The field is still a very new one. Self-control refers to those actions an individual deliberately undertakes to achieve self-selected outcomes.

Rationale

Self-control techniques involve a crucial assumption—namely, that mediational processes operate in human learning and that these internal actions obey the same laws or principles as external actions do. Thus, a child can be encouraged to reward himself either covertly (by engaging in very positive self-thoughts and self-statements) or overtly (by indulging in a favourite activity). The sources of antecedent and outcome control may be in a person's own symbolic processes rather than his physiological states or external environment; the therapeutic endeavour thus becomes concerned with the manipulation of these symbolic sources of control. A person displays self-control when in the relative absence of immediate external constraints, he is able to resist a temptation—one to which he would previously have yielded.

The assumption of a correspondence between internal and external actions opens the door to a great variety of covert self-control procedures, such as (a) self-monitoring, (b) contingency management, (c) self-punishment, (d) self-reinforcement, (e) contract management, (f) self-confrontation, (g) self-administered behavioural analysis, (h) covert sensitization, and (i) altering the discriminative stimuli for the target response.

Self-monitoring provides the clinician and client with a baseline record of target behaviour for treatment purposes: in some instances the observed behaviour may actually change during monitoring in a favourable direction. Clinical practice has therefore attempted to utilize self-monitoring as a therapeutic technique.

Self-monitoring

(1) Request the youngster to keep a diary or log of events and situations (decided by both of you as pertinent) in the natural environment.
(2) Get him to note down the nature of the situation, what happened, what was said, what the child did.
(3) How comfortable—uncomfortable did he feel? (subjective rating)
(4) How satisfied was he with his actions on that occasion?
(5) What would he do differently if the event was still to come?
(6) Record any other comments: how he felt or thought.

Procedure 20b	SELF-CONTROL OF ANTECEDENT CONDITIONS
	Manipulate those eliciting, reinforcing or discriminative stimuli in the youngster's symbolic processes which influence his maladaptive behaviour.

Applications

There are several applications of self-control training (see Appendix II). One involves (as we saw) being able to resist temptation. From the therapist's point of view, the test of self-control is the ability (and inclination) of the client to minimize temptation by the early interruption of behavioural sequences which end up in the transgression of some self-imposed standard.

Rationale

Specific behaviours are performed in the presence of specific stimuli. Eventually, such an association leads to a situation in which the stimuli serve as cues for the behaviours and increase the probability that they will be emitted.

When behaviour is under maladaptive stimulus control it should be possible for a youngster to eliminate or weaken unwanted behaviour and increase desired behaviour by modifying his environment in certain ways. For example, the adolescent girl with a weight and eating problem might make a rule never to eat anywhere but at her place at the table and then at specified times; to remove herself from food stimuli wherever possible, by avoiding the kitchen, and by asking her siblings not to eat cakes and sweets in front of her.

Methods

There are several methods of stimulus control which involve building in appropriate stimulus–response connections. One such method is the technique of *cue-strengthening*. This requires that conditions be made favourable for the person to practise the response in a specific situation, where previously it was not associated strongly to any set of environmental cues.

The Schneider and Robin (1976) turtle technique for aiding self-control begins with a story to tell young children about a boy named Little Turtle. Little Turtle disliked school. In spite of his vows to stay out of trouble he always managed to find it. For example, he would get angry and rip up all his papers in class. One day when he was feeling especially bad, he met a talking tortoise. The old tortoise addressed him: 'Hey, there, I'll tell you a secret. Don't you realize you are carrying the answer to your problem around with you?' Little Turtle didn't know what he was talking about. 'Your shell—your shell' the tortoise shouted in his loud bellowing tones. 'That's why you have a shell. You can hide in your shell whenever you get that feeling inside you that tells you you are angry. When you are in your shell, you can have a moment to rest and figure out what to do about it. So next time you get angry, just go into your shell.' The story continues with an account of how the next day when he started to get upset Little Turtle remembered what the tortoise had told him so he pulled in his arms close to his body, put his head down so his chin rested against the chest, and rested for awhile, until he knew what to do. The story ends with the teacher coming over and praising him for this reaction and Little Turtle receiving a very good report card that term.

Following this story, the teacher demonstrates the turtle reaction. The children now practise it to various imagined frustrating experiences. In this way the child learns a new reaction to the cue of anger or frustration. This is combined with teaching the child relaxation skills, again employing the story of Little Turtle. The story is taken up where Little Turtle returns to the tortoise, telling him that he still has some angry feelings, even though he has used the turtle response. Starting with the stomach muscles, the children are given practice in tensing and relaxing major muscle groups of their body. Tensing and relaxation are then incorporated into the turtle response by tensing the body when assuming the turtle position, as a count is made from 1 to 10, followed by relaxation of the muscles, which is maintained for a few moments. The children are encouraged to use frustrating experiences as a cue to employ the turtle reaction.

Learning the turtle reaction is combined with teaching the child problem-solving methods (see Procedure 19c). Problem-solving instruction sessions are held daily in class, during which recent problem situations are discussed. Cues are provided for the children, such as the teacher asking, 'What are your choices?'. The children are instructed to incorporate problem-solving efforts during use of the turtle technique; that is, to use this time to imagine behavioural alternatives to their frustrating situation and the consequences of each. In this way, the child learns to expand his range of alternative coping strategies. Children in the peer group are rewarded for supporting other children's efforts to employ the turtle method. They are encouraged to praise and applaud the child who is using the technique, and to cue fellow pupils to use the turtle method in situations that might lead to a fight. Peers, in turn, are reinforced by the teacher for their support. Training sessions are held for about 15 minutes each day for about three weeks and are then reduced to twice a week. Within a few weeks after introduction of the turtle technique, children start 'doing turtle in my head' without prompting and without going through the physical withdrawal reactions. It is important that children learn to discriminate when they should employ the turtle technique and when they should assert themselves.

Further procedures

At the Child Treatment Research Unit we are studying the effectiveness of various training exercises which have the purpose (1) of helping the child to develop better self-control, thus reducing the frequency of outbursts of overexcitement, aggression, and impulsive acts, (2) of teaching the child to exercise better control over his body movements, and (3) of developing body awareness with a view to increasing his consciousness of his body movements and activity level, e.g. fidgeting, running, shuffling, arm flapping, and so on. Further aims are (4) to give the parents some means of controlling their child during 'crisis' periods of excessive activity and excitement, (5) to help the child with coordination problems such as those associated with the description 'cross-lateral' which applies to many hyperactive children, and (6) to improve attention through breathing control.

The exercises are divided into three types, each concentrating on a different problem area. Within each group are several exercises, any number of which may be used depending on the individual child's needs and capabilities. The three types are as follows:

(1) body control and awareness;
(2) self-control;
(3) coordination.

All the exercises are based on learning principles and make use of behaviour modification techniques. Both response increment and response decrement procedures are used in order to ensure the child's cooperation and effort, such as positive and negative reinforcement (including self-monitoring and reinforcement), star charts, shaping, and response-cost.

In group (1) the child is required to do the following exercises for progressively longer periods, and which are themselves progressively more difficult.

(a) Keep parts of the body and then the *whole* body still.
(b) Move parts of the body in turn; keeping all others still.
(c) Move very slowly on the spot, copying the therapist's arm and leg movements, etc. and at the same time 'talking through' the exercise. For this, the three stages in verbal control of the inhibition of voluntary motor behaviour described by Luria (1961) are utilized.
(d) The 'talking through' procedure is also used in the final stage of this group of exercises, where the child is required to carry out various instructions including gross movement actions, such as making a cup of coffee, fetching objects, etc.

The procedure being tested here is similar to that described earlier and used by Schneider (1974) and Schneider and Robin (1975/6): 'turtle imagery' to foster self-control in hyperactive children (see below). The main imagery used in these exercises is perhaps more topical for the children seen at the Unit, i.e. that of the TV characters—the Bionic man and woman. The procedure is very similar to that used by Meichenbaum and Goodman (1971) who evolved a treatment paradigm for training verbally mediated self-control in children.

In group (2) (self-control exercises), a procedure similar to thought-stopping is used. Whenever the child feels the first signs of a reaction within him, such as an aggressive outburst or mounting overexcitement possibly leading to a loss of self-control, he is instructed to stop on the spot and to count slowly to ten, at first aloud and later to himself. The child monitors and reinforces his own behaviour. The other type of exercise in this group, which is at present being developed and investigated, is role-playing, where the subject may be instructed, for example, to take the role of a quiet, submissive child.

Group (3) consists of various coordination exercises, e.g. simple finger exercises for a child with fine motor control problems.

Self-instruction

This is another method of self-control of antecedent conditions.

Applications

Children are taught to instruct themselves as a means of regulating their own behaviour. Eventually, the child's covert or inner speech comes to assume a self-governing role (see Meichenbaum, 1977).

Method

Instruct (say) the hyperactive, impulsive child in the concept of talking to himself. Gain the child's attention by using his natural medium of play. For example, while playing with the child, say: 'I have to land my airplane, now slowly, carefully, into the hanger'. Encourage the child to have the control tower tell the pilot to go slowly, etc. In this way help the child to build up a repertoire of self-statements to be used on a variety of tasks. Tranining begins on a set of tasks (games) in which the child is somewhat proficient and for which he does *not* have a history of failures and frustrations. Employ tasks that lend themselves to a self-instructional approach and which encourage the use of cognitive strategies.

The method of self-instructional training is flexible and usually follows the principle of successive approximations. Initially, the therapist models and has the child rehearse simple self-statements such as 'Stop! Think before I answer', 'Count to ten while I cool off'. Gradually the therapist models (and the child rehearses) more complex sets of self-statements.

Illustration

Here is an example of a self-instructional package which Bornstein and Quevillon (1976) used on three overactive, four-year-old, pre-school boys. Scott was described as a 'disciplinary problem because he is unable to follow directions for any extended length of time'. He could not complete ordinary tasks within the pre-school classroom setting and often manifested violent outbursts of temper for no apparent reason. Rod was described by teachers as 'being out of control in the classroom'. He displayed several problems and behavioural deficits, including short attention span, aggressiveness in response to other children and a general overactivity. Tim was reported to be highly distractible both at home and in pre-school. Most of his classroom time was spent walking around the room, staring off into space, and/or not attending to a task or instruction.

After an eight-day baseline period of observations, the children were seen individually for a massed self-instruction session lasting two hours. Each child worked with the therapist for about 50 minutes, was given a 20 minute break, then resumed work for another 50 minutes. The self-instructional training was as follows:

(1)   the therapist modelled the task while talking aloud to himself;
(2)   the child performed the task while the therapist instructed aloud;
(3)   the child then performed the task talking aloud to himself while the therapist whispered softly;
(4)   the child performed the task whispering softly while the therapist made lip movements but no sound;
(5)   the child performed the task making lip movements without sound while the therapist self-instructed covertly;
(6)   the child performed the task with covert self-instruction.

The verbalizations modelled were of four types:

(1)   questions about the task (e.g. 'What does the teacher want me to do?');
(2)   answers to questions in the form of cognitive rehearsals (e.g. 'Oh, that's right, I'm supposed to copy that picture.');
(3)   self-instructions that guide through the task (e.g. 'OK, first I draw a line here . . .');
(4)   self-reinforcement (e.g. 'How about that? I really did that one well!').

The entire training session was presented in a story format.

The results of this study were measured in terms of on-task behaviour, defined as those behaviours directed towards the assigned tasks. It was expected that the child would be attentive and silent during teacher's instructions. When asked to participate during a work period (e.g. figure-drawing exercises, story-reading etc.), on-task behaviours included performing the prescribed and accepted classroom activity. Off-task behaviours included engaging in movements about the room, playing with toys, shouting, fighting, kicking, and leaving the classroom without permission.

On-task behaviours increased dramatically with the introduction of the self-instructional package. The therapeutic gains were maintained $22\frac{1}{2}$ weeks after the baseline was initiated.

Procedure 20c	SELF-CONTROL OF OUTCOME CONDITIONS
	Teach the youngster to rearrange contingencies that influence behaviour in such a way that he experiences long-range benefits, even though he may have to give up some satisfactions or tolerate some discomforts at first.

Methods

(1) *Self-control* involves a precise analysis of the behaviour to be controlled and (as with any other behavioural analyses) its antecedent and consequent conditions.
(2) It is necessary to identify behaviours which *enhance* appropriate responses as well as those actions which *interfere* with the desired outcome.
(3) It is necessary to identify positive and negative reinforcers which control these patterns of behaviour.
(4) Reinforcement is applied to alter the probability of the target behaviour.

There is evidence that children may be able to modify or maintain their own behaviour by administering rewards and punishments to themselves in a contingent manner. These consequences may occur in the child's environment or in his symbolic processes. The self-administered rewards and punishments may be overt or covert. Sometimes a point system is very effective in instituting a programme of self-reward. A youngster can provide himself with a point immediately after a response, and that point in turn can be exchanged for a variety of reinforcers.

Empathy is one facet of prosocial behaviour which should be of concern to social and clinical psychologists. It involves the child's capacity to control his behaviour by considering its effect on the experiences of others, particularly the potential victims of proscribed behaviour. Little is known about the development of this attribute, although presumably it has some of its antecedents in parental statements involving explanations of the effects of one's behaviour on others. The capacity for empathy requires object permanence, considerable abstract ability and represents a rather advanced state in the development of self-control and moral behaviour.

SECTION 5

The Intervention

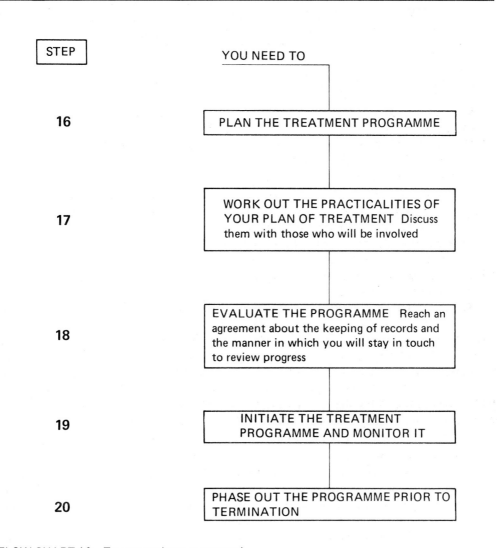

STEP	YOU NEED TO
16	PLAN THE TREATMENT PROGRAMME
17	WORK OUT THE PRACTICALITIES OF YOUR PLAN OF TREATMENT Discuss them with those who will be involved
18	EVALUATE THE PROGRAMME Reach an agreement about the keeping of records and the manner in which you will stay in touch to review progress
19	INITIATE THE TREATMENT PROGRAMME AND MONITOR IT
20	PHASE OUT THE PROGRAMME PRIOR TO TERMINATION

FLOW CHART 10   Treatment: how to proceed.

Step 16a	PLAN YOUR TREATMENT PROGRAMME Choosing specific methods for modifying behaviour

Essentially behaviour modification is an educational process; it provides new learning experiences through the manipulation of those contemporary factors which initiate and maintain the problem behaviour and its more acceptable alternatives.

Planning treatment

Jehu (1972) provides an excellent account of the considerations determining the precise details of the treatment plan. Several decisions are required before treatment commences with regard to the *choice of therapeutic agent* and *setting of treatment*, the behavioural *procedures to be employed* (and in what combinations and sequences), and the *measures* necessary to maintain improved behaviour after the intervention ends.

In previous steps you will have decided which principles of behaviour modification, and which procedures, you should employ to achieve the behavioural objectives of the programme. In working out your treatment, delineate clearly, as a matter of fundamental principle, how you will demonstrate that treatment has been effective.

Step 16b	TREATMENT PLAN Take into account relationship and other 'non-specific' therapeutic factors
	In addition to those procedures that are relatively specific to behaviour modification, there are other factors that operate not only in this but also in most other forms of treatment. Among these non-specific factors are the therapeutic relationship, the client's hopes and expectations of being helped, the attributes of the therapist, and the treatment setting.

Albino (1980) maintains that psychotherapy is not a natural science, even though the value of its methods may often have been empirically evaluated. He states that there seem to be three psychological principles commonly in use in all forms of psychotherapy:

(1) persuasion, which rests on practical knowledge or practice wisdom. It offers reasons why the client should change his beliefs and/or behaviour. This manual does not eschew the arts of persuasion. Subject to the ethical constraints discussed in these pages, and the process of negotiating goals with clients, it is an important component of therapy to voice clear opinions based upon valid information and knowledge of the developmental literature and of hard-gained practice wisdom and experience.

(2) *teaching*, which entails the offering of information and training in skills of acting. The client may not be able to act without instruction, training and monitoring. Because some actions (e.g. child-training techniques) are so ingrained in parents' repertoires (being anchored by ideology or habit, or constrained by lack of skill), it is not usually good enough to simply *advise* parents to change. Demonstrations, rehearsals, instructions and practice may be required in order to provide clients with the equipment for change.

(3) *providing explanatory 'stories'*,* which help the clients to re-order their beliefs about the nature of their problems. Attempting to change a person's beliefs, desires and actions, as Albino points out, is a commonplace activity in ordinary life. The therapist is particularly interested in providing helpful explanations ('stories') or changing existing belief systems which he considers to generate distressing, self-defeating actions on the part of the client.

Non-specific factors

The therapeutic relationship

Any form of therapy (be it psychotherapy or behaviour therapy) involves psychological influence—implicit or explicit—deployed in the setting of a relationship between client and therapist. A false (or forced) dichotomy is often drawn between (a) interpersonal and relationship factors (sometimes referred to as placebo or non-specific factors) and (b) techniques; false because it is doubtful whether these two major components in the therapeutic enterprise can ever be isolated in pure and separate cultures.

Do not disregard non-specific factors in your programme of behaviour modification. Awareness of them allows you deliberately to enhance the effectiveness of their contribution to treatment. What is crucial is to conceptualize them more adequately, and to identify the processes by which they contribute to therapeutic outcomes. Relationship (for example) is a means to an end—neither an end in itself, nor a means to which one attaches as much significance as to the specific methods of behaviour modification. It is regarded as facilitative rather than a necessary or sufficient condition for therapeutic change.

For someone who favours a social learning approach to the understanding of human problems and their remediation, there is no question of denying the importance of social influence in therapy. After all, social learning is concerned with explaining the development of behaviour in interpersonal, social settings. Influence is implicit in all social interaction because of the interdependence of human beings living in society. Helping, cooperative and therapeutic relationships are no exception, all being based upon mutual influence. Therapists influence clients and vice versa.

The therapist's influence upon the client may have its source in the provision of information or interpretations; changing behaviours, attitudes, values, and perceptions; teaching problem-solving and social skills; altering the client's attributions concerning past and present behaviours. Among the therapist qualities associated with 'healing'

* Albino refers to these (agnostically) as 'myths'.

properties are understanding, respect, acceptance, genuineness, empathy and non-possessive warmth. These attributes are stressed in the client-centred literature and their effect is related to fairly global aspects of the client's well-being, such as self-esteem.

Whether a trained professional has special access to these qualities (or some unique deployment of them) is thrown into doubt—surely even for those who give most weight to the relationship factor in therapy—by the absence of substantive differences in the results of professional as opposed to non- or para-professional therapists. Durlak (1979) reviewed 42 studies comparing the effectiveness of professional and para-professional therapists/helpers. Para-professionals, overall, achieve clinical outcomes equal to or significantly better than those obtained by professionals. To quote the author:

> In terms of measurable outcome, professionals may not possess demonstrably superior clinical skills when compared with para-professionals. Moreover, professional mental health education, training and experience do not appear to be necessary pre-requisites for an effective helping person.... Unfortunately, there is little information on the factors that account for para-professionals' effectiveness.

Strupp (1977) makes the point that the psychological techniques employed by the professional psychotherapist are similar to psychological principles by which any person influences the feelings and behaviour of another. As he puts it, the therapist's operations may be much more sophisticated, subtle and direct, but he has no 'special' forces at his command. The professional behaviour therapist would minimize the role of social influence and other so-called 'non-specific' factors in his work. The 'special forces' at his beck and call would be (in his view) a rational and empirically based methodology. Nevertheless, an awareness and use of placebo effects can enhance his therapeutic potential. Such factors may be an intrusion in evaluative research; they are a welcome ally in day-to-day clinical practice.

Contributing to (and countering) the placebo effects inherent in the therapist–client relationship are:

Therapist variables
  (a) Attitude to the client (e.g. interest, empathy, warmth, sympathy, liking, friend-liness; or their opposites).
  (b) Attitude to therapy (e.g. enthusiasm, conviction, commitment, interest, belief, faith, optimism; or their opposites).
  (c) Attitude toward results. Experimenters (and therapists) may 'obtain' the results they want or expect.

Client variables
Free-floating anxiety is characteristic of persons who are responsive to placebo effects. But contrary to popular opinion researchers have failed to find a correlation between suggestibility and placebo effects; furthermore the attempt to relate placebo effects to the client's personality has also failed.

Expectations of help

The importance of expectancy as a critical factor in behaviour change, especially the expectation of help, is well recognized as one of the more powerful placebo effects. In both psychoanalytic and client-centred therapy there is a marked decrease in symptomatology as soon as the client enters psychotherapy. Evidence for a psychological placebo effect is shown also in various groups designed as controls for systematic desensitization, implosive, operant, and aversion therapies.

Client's expectations of help seem to operate in all forms of psychotherapy. This finding has some practical implications. Expectations of help in therapy might be viewed as artifacts to be eliminated in research studies but in the clinic (as we said before) they should be encompassed with gratitude, as grist to the mill of achieving the changes desired in all forms of intervention.

Non-confirming experiences

Many clients have non-adaptive beliefs about the world. These beliefs often play a critical role in creating the problems that bring the individual for help. Since all forms of psychotherapy seem to involve changes in belief systems, a powerful tool in therapy is the provision of non-confirming experiences, as a result of which non-adaptive beliefs can be replaced by more effective ones. Behaviour modification—especially in its deployment of real-life role play (see Procedure 14a)—makes use of this therapeutic principle.

Personality of the therapist

The factors which play a part in the social influence of the therapist are his:

Credibility: This depends upon perceived
(a) expertness;
(b) reliability (dependability, predictability, consistency);
(c) motives and intentions;
(d) expressions of warmth and friendliness;
(e) dynamism of the communicator (confident, forceful, active);
(f) opinion of the majority of other people concerning the expertness and trustworthiness of the person.

Attractiveness: This depends upon perceived
(a) cooperativeness and goal facilitation;
(b) physical appearance;
(c) liking;
(d) similarity;
(e) competence;
(f) warmth;
(g) familiarity and propinquity ('to know them is to like them').

> ## Step 16c TREATMENT PLAN Assess the resources for treatment
>
> *Are the persons involved in the programme likely to give it the priority, support and concern it requires in order to 'get off the ground'? Motivation for treatment is a significant factor in the successful outcome of a therapeutic intervention, so the assessment of resources explores the child's (and his parents') personal attitudes, competencies, and limitations with regard to treatment.*

The child

Your assessment might include his degree of motivation, capacity for self-regulation, and any skills which might be capitalized on for treatment purposes. In the case of the younger child, there is the question of how much he should be directly involved in the intervention. There is also the issue of how intensive treatment should be. This will depend on the parents.

The parents

Ask yourself about the severity of the problem and current parent resourcefulness. Practical help like a playgroup or child-minding services may give an exhausted mother (especially in a single-parent family) the 'break' she needs to take on an onerous programme. Other significant persons in the family, such as grandparents or siblings can be an aid (and sometimes a hindrance) to the implementation of a programme. These matters must be calculated.

In some clients there is minimal responsiveness to social cues and reinforcements, a problem given the significant contribution of social persuasion and reinforcement in behavioural work.

There are various family attitudes to assess. How do they see the behavioural methods which have been explained to them? What is their attitude to the child and the work (and possible stress) a therapeutic intervention may involve? How realistic are parental (or teacher) expectations of the child and of the therapy? Persons suffering from serious personal problems or an unhappy marriage may find it difficult to act as agents of change for others. There are variations in the sophistication and comprehension of clients to take into account.

Staff

As assessment of staff and other resources (available for *this* case) in the treatment agency is another requirement. Part of the calculation must take into account the fact that behavioural treatments are not like fixed items on a medical prescription to be implemented in an inflexible manner. There is a creative element to the planning of an overall treatment programme and a human (and therefore fallible) component in its application.

Working environments

The naturally occurring incentives for mediators of change in some working environments (e.g. some wards, residential establishments, classrooms) are few and far between. This may be due to poor pay, lack of encouragement, low status, or indeed, plain overwork.

> ## Step 17 WORK OUT THE PRACTICALITIES OF THE TREATMENT PROGRAMME
> Work them out in detail and discuss them with your clients (let the child know what is happening)

Many a programme has foundered on some apparently trivial *practical* detail. But, first, a theoretical one: many children get 'worse' before they get 'better' when on an extinction programme: the theoretically predicted post-extinction burst. Warn parents of this or you will lose them.

Practical problems

Can the mother use time-out as a really viable strategy or is there no suitable room to use? If she lives in a thin-walled terrace house, a yelling child trying to coerce her into submission, could make time-out a tough proposition (one imagines phone calls to the N.S.P.C.C.!). How do you get a heavy, resistant child to go into time-out? Anticipate the difficulties, but better still (being human and unable to foretell the future and every bothersome hurdle) stay in touch, especially in the early part of the programme. Try to 'nip in the bud' the unexpected problems, before they assume serious proportions.

Remember: *The importance of feedback. The significance of giving learners feedback accords with the cybernetic model of human behaviour which suggests that the behaviour of an organism depends upon the feedback information available to him about the accuracy of his performance. This stops him perpetuating errors which might interfere with additional learning. Knowledge of results may be very reinforcing especially if correct responses outnumber errors (another reason for the therapist's presence!).*

> ## Step 18 EVALUATE THE PROGRAMME Put your hypotheses to the test by monitoring what happens after the treatment intervention begins

There are different ways of doing this. The use of graphical records is helpful (see Fig. 14). Without an objective assessment and record-keeping system, it is not possible to evaluate accurately and reliably the progress made by the child in the therapeutic situation. It is

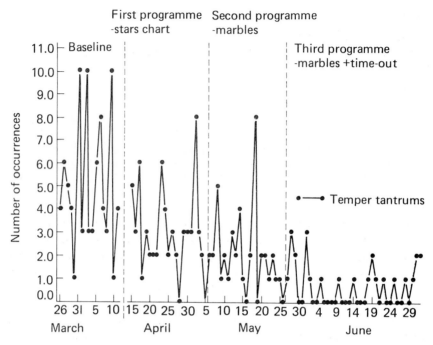

FIG. 14 A typical ABC design graph.

clear that many children's problems are transient, and often change can occur as a function of time and non-specific placebo effects. For these reasons, a controlled evaluation of the therapeutic process is essential. Objective data make possible two important objectives: determining whether a child in treatment is changing, and the direction and extent of change. They also make possible an assessment of the relationship between different kinds of intervention within the overall therapeutic programme.

An important function of the review of a programme, based upon data relating to the target behaviours, is the indication that a change in the treatment plan is required. A programme should be flexible. If target behaviours are showing *no* signs of change within two or three weeks (depending on the problem—there is, in fact, no set time guide) you would be wise to review all aspects of the programme.

There are widely divergent views as to the purposes of psychotherapy (see Gurman and Razin, 1977). Differing conceptualizations of objectives lead inevitably to different therapeutic *operations*. Different goals lead to divergent *outcomes*. Global questions such as 'Is X therapy effective?', 'Does casework of the Y variety work?' are meaningless. They beg several further questions: effective for whom; to what purpose, in what context, for how long ... etc., etc. Failure to specify clear-cut objectives in therapy (and social casework) means one cannot validate or (more important) invalidate the way one is working. There is no need to define change in restrictive terms, as many behaviourists have done, but it is necessary to stipulate that (1) change must be demonstrable; (2) it must be relatively permanent; and (3) it must be attributable to the interpersonal transactions between patient and therapist.

What is needed is:

(1) an assessment of changes in the client over time, and
(2) a demonstrated link between these changes (dependent variables) and particular therapeutic operations (independent variables).

Baseline

The pre-treatment record, as we have seen, is known as a 'baseline' and is useful in defining the problem and (by comparison with treatment records) indicating progress. How long must a baseline be to be sufficient for adequate data collection? This is difficult to answer and exposes the tension between a service *vs.* research orientation. The client's interests and your own purposes must be taken into account. Baseline (and other pre-treatment) assessment procedures serve to anchor behaviour in time so as to provide a *standard* against which to measure change. There are no hard and fast rules regarding the length of time baseline conditions should be followed. A theoretical guideline is to look for stability, to persevere until the behavioural measure varies only within a certain well-defined range. Sidman (1960) suggests preserving baseline conditions until the baseline behaviour is stable within a 5 % range of fluctuations. However, in practice stability remains an ideal rather than a realistic consideration in most psychological endeavours, and frequently we do not have the requisite technology to reduce variability to the 5 % level suggested by Sidman. For hyperactive children, 'up-and-down' behaviour is a way of life. One strategy is to extend the baseline to understand better the variability of the child's behaviour. However, some behaviours are intolerable and a quick response is required from the therapist. He may have to be content with only a few days of baseline recordings, taking the slope of the best-fitting line as an indication of direction (see p. 164). Treatment can be started when a baseline is ascending if the intention is to *decrease* the strength of the behaviour (say hitting), or when a baseline is descending if the intention is to increase the strength of the behaviour (say attention in class).

Ongoing measurements

Treatment records are meant to indicate progress towards a specified goal. The literature is replete with studies in which change has been demonstrated along only one dimension. It is generally agreed that it is preferable to evaluate the effects of intervention by multiple criteria. Child and family variables need to be assessed before, during, and after the parent-training programme, and the assessment designed to cover several dimensions of child and parent functioning. The change should have social *and* clinical significance. Measures should be based on instruments which are acceptable in terms of reliability and validity.

Side-effects of behavioural interventions

It would be naïve to assess the principal target behaviours alone as if changes in those areas can be encapsulated and isolated from any effects on behaviours of other kinds, in the child, and on the adjustments of other persons. A positive change in a target behaviour (say, a reduction in school refusal) if accompanied by negative features (say, an increase in disruptive classroom behaviour and consequent confrontations between teachers and parents) cannot be claimed as a 'success story'.

Given such possibilities you should build into your programme a systematic monitoring of behaviours and interactions which indicate acceptable and unacceptable side-effects of your intervention. Look out particularly for undesirable reverberations on the target child's siblings. They may feel that the client is monopolizing his parents' attention, or that he is rewarded for doing things that are taken for granted when *they* perform them (e.g. compliance to rules). Such complications require ingenuity on the part of the therapist and the parents to mitigate their effects.

Evaluation of interventions

How far you take this important principle of trying to validate your work (or invalidate it, in cases where you are getting it wrong) depends upon your role and function, and the opportunities you have to 'stand back' and examine the therapeutic process critically. You should *always* monitor your work at some level. If you are training students, or wish to publish your results on a particular client group or problem, or with regard to a new elaboration of therapy, then you should demonstrate your work by means of the appropriate experimental designs. In addition, parents and children might be interviewed before and after treatment, by an independent assessor not involved in the intervention; the purpose of such an enquiry would be to ascertain (in a detached manner) the significance of any changes that have occurred, as well as to assess their importance as viewed by the family.

None of the research designs will be of much use unless you ensure the highest degree of reliability for your data, as is possible (see Jackson *et al.*, 1973; Kent and Foster, 1977).

The most rigorous test of the usefulness of any treatment is long-term assessment. Follow-up visits (and/or phone calls) over gradually lengthening intervals should be conducted for at least 12 months in all cases, possibly as many as 24.

Systematic variation of treatment

A particular advantage of the single-subject ($N = 1$) experimental design (as it is known) is that it maximizes opportunity for innovation and flexibility in treatment, while laying the basis for the formulation and testing of hypotheses. There are problems connected with the approach (see p. 164) but it does allow comparisons to be made between a child's behaviour under one condition and the same youngster's actions under different conditions. The manner in which the therapeutic interventions are systematically varied directly affects the conclusion that can be drawn from the manipulation.

AB and ABC designs (examples are provided in Appendix I)

Symbol A represents a baseline during which the problem behaviour is monitored under uncontrolled conditions and the symbols B, C, D, etc., represent different treatment programmes (one may, of course, find one sufficient). The experimental design involves a comparison of (say) the frequency of the problem behaviour under a pre-treatment baseline condition and its frequency after the application of a treatment programme or a series of treatment strategies. Designs of this type determine whether a change in the level of the behaviour has occurred, and the approximate magnitude of that change. The child's behaviour is recorded, with the resultant scores (counts, or ratings) plotted graphically. When the therapist decides that the baseline measures represent the child's typical behaviour (and it has to be remembered that some children change during baseline recording) an intervention is initiated, designed to modify the deviant behaviour observed during the baseline period. Observations of the target behaviour are continued during treatment (see Fig. 14).

If you had a reducing baseline you would wait to see whether the improvement was consolidated over a period of time (and, indeed, discuss it with the family to try to work out the reasons for it) rather than starting a treatment programme.

Golden Rule: Don't interfere with something that is getting better; try to understand the process, capitalize on it, and if possible, consolidate it.

The principal limitation of both the AB and ABC designs is the inability to be certain that any reduction in problem behaviour is due to the therapeutic intervention rather than to other change-inducing influences. As service-orientated clinics are concerned primarily with treatment rather than with the constraints of research into its efficacy, this is not a vital limitation; nevertheless, it remains a useful routine check on the progress of your work.

Reversal designs

The reversal (or ABAB) design has a characteristic form; the baseline performance is measured first and identified as the A phase. Next the independent variable (behavioural intervention) is introduced. This is the B phase. Then the independent variable is removed. The return to baseline conditions when the independent variable is temporarily removed is frequently referred to as the reversal or the probe. Because these conditions are allegedly 'identical' with the baseline conditions, the phase is also labelled A. The independent variable is once more introduced. This reintroduction of the treatment condition is again labelled B. You will see how the reversal design comes to be referred to as an ABAB design. If, during the third stage when the intervention is discontinued, the target behaviour does indeed approximate to the original baseline level, then you have support for the notion that the problematic behaviour would have persisted without the treatment. The fourth stage should be followed by another reduction in the deviant behaviour. If such a result is obtained, it *suggests* that it is the intervention which is producing the change in behaviour. What this kind of design yields is essentially correlational evidence of an association between a treatment and a reduction in problem behaviour.

However, it is still not *certain* that fluctuations in target behaviour which accompany the application and withdrawal of the treatment are in fact a function of this treatment. The changes might still be due to the operation of other factors which happen to covary with the treatment and baseline conditions. In any event, because behaviour does not

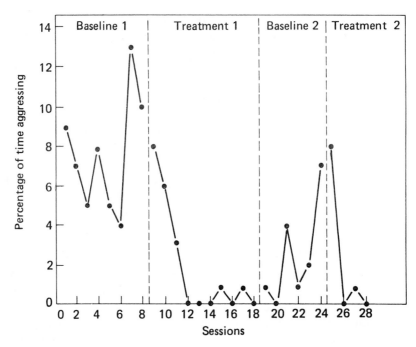

FIG. 15   Rate of aggressive responding during treatment periods when positive responses were rewarded and injurious actions were punished by brief social exclusion. The figure shows the reductions in physical aggression achieved by a mother in her five-year old son (Zeilberger *et al.*, 1968).

always reverse when the treatment contingency is altered or withdrawn, the reversal design may not always demonstrate a causal relationship between behaviour and therapeutic events, even when a contingency *was responsible* for the initial change. There are situations in which the logic of the reversal design breaks down because the target behaviour would not necessarily be expected to reverse in a reversal phase. The aim of treatment is usually to produce an irreversible reduction in some target behaviour—one which persists after treatment ends. If this is done successfully, then it will not be possible to return to the original baseline level of behaviour by withdrawing treatment in the third stage. Certain behaviours, once developed or altered, are maintained by beneficial and rewarding consequences which result directly from their performance. Figure 15 gives you an idea of what a reversal design record looks like.

Perhaps a more important problem related to the use of reversal designs in treatment is the ethical dilemma of deliberately attempting to reverse any beneficial therapeutic changes by successive replications of the baseline conditions. Even if willing, parents and teachers as contingency managers, may be unable to behave in the same way they behaved before an intervention. They may become more authoritative, confident, rewarding, in a way and to a degree, that there is no 'going back' to being tentative, fumbling or punitive.

Successive replications may also train the child to return to his deviant behaviour more quickly, and may make it more resistant to extinction because the replications constitute

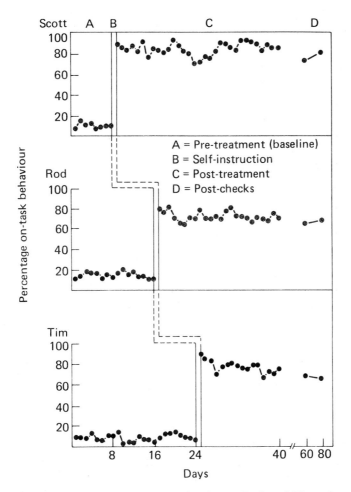

FIG. 16 Daily percentage on-task behaviours for Scott, Rod and Tim across experimental conditions (from Bornstein and Quevillon, 1976).

an intermittent reinforcement schedule. They may also breed distrust and suspicion in the child because of the apparent capriciousness of the adults operating the programme.

Multiple-baseline designs

Multiple-baseline designs involve comparing and contrasting change in those behaviours which have been treated, with other behaviours which have not been treated. For example, a child who manifests three relatively discrete behaviour problems such as aggressiveness, oppositional behaviour, and extreme attention-seeking might be treated specifically for the oppositional behaviour and extreme attention-seeking; changes in respect to these behaviours can then be compared with fluctuations in the problem which has been left untreated.

If, however, only one category of deviant behaviour (say aggression) was involved, the same treatment is applied in sequence to several baselines for different forms of aggressive behaviour. Alternatively, an intervention can be made across a number of behaviours but in only one of several settings, while the behaviour is monitored in all the settings. For an example of the design across children, see Fig. 16.

A thorough review of the problems associated with these designs is provided by Greenwald (1976), Hartmann and Atkinson (1973), O'Leary and Drabman (1971) and Kazdin and Bootzin (1972) in excellent review articles. Curve fitting is the simplest and best known approach to the analysis of your data, and is one way of analysing the structure of a baseline (Gottman *et al.*, 1969). It involves fitting the data to the *least squares* straight lines. In this procedure the slope and intercept of the best-fit straight lines obtained during baseline and intervention are calculated. A test of significance is performed on the difference between these two lines.

There are two more designs you might consider in monitoring specific behaviour problems:

   (i) the changing-criterion design (Hall and Fox, 1977); and
  (ii) the multi-element baseline design (Ullman, 1975).

There is insufficient space to elaborate these statistical or design methods here. They require a study all of their own! (See Gottman and Leiblum (1974) for the 'know-how' to assess the statistical significance of post-baseline changes.)

The analysis of magnitude of change

Some studies—by way of illustrating the impact of a planned intervention—simply give a graphical presentation of data with no statistical analysis performed. For this reason correct graphical methods are vitally important. A common mistake is to use units of measurement which do not reflect equal amounts of observation time. For example, it is misleading to quantify the home-based number of aggressive episodes on a daily basis, when the child is at school Monday to Friday and is only observed for five hours per day as compared with 13 hours on Saturday and Sunday. Some form of ratio unit (e.g. aggressive episodes per hour expressed as an average) is required.

In many cases, behaviour change is dramatic. Careful visual inspection of a graph sometimes reveals that behaviour during baseline does not overlap with behaviour during the treatment phase. In other words, during the programme the rate of behaviour does not approach the baseline. In instances such as these there would be a consensus that change has occurred. There may be changes which are less clear-cut, thus necessitating more subjective evaluation. One essential criterion for deciding whether a significant behaviour change has occurred or not, is its *practical* importance. If the behaviour has been altered enough to satisfy parents, school teachers, and the therapist, then *that* criterion has been met. Such a criterion of clinical and social significance should be decided, as far as possible, before the treatment programme; this is to avoid any subsequent bias in assessing the results.

Control group design

The most efficient procedure to control for systematic differences between groups (before a treatment programme is evaluated) is to randomly assign children to one of the two groups. One receives the experimental therapeutic programme (the experimental group) and the other does not (the control group). If subjects are not randomly assigned to groups, the likelihood is greater that the groups may differ in terms of the target behaviour prior to the therapy being implemented. And, if so, any differences (changes) in the target behaviour that you achieve may occur for reasons other than the effect of the therapeutic intervention.

Step 19   INITIATE THE PROGRAMME—with a good deal of help to the clients

There are many things that can go wrong in the beginning stages of a programme. It is one thing to plan the campaign quietly around a table; it is another to put it into effect in the hurly burly of family life.

Criteria of behaviour for rewarding or sanctioning no longer seem so clear. Parents may require prompting, reassuring. It is helpful to be around when the programme begins or within reach for consultation.

One of the frustrations of doing home-based behaviour modification is the 'I've tried it' syndrome! This is the price of using concepts and methods that are on a continuum with their day-to-day child-training practices. 'Time-out', 'Oooh, I've tried that'; 'Response-cost', 'I've tried that'; 'Over-correction', 'That didn't work', and so on. Of course, parents may not be aware of the small print of learning principles; matters of definition, of timing and the need for careful specification and contingency analysis. It is just these issues that require careful monitoring if the programme is to be successful.

Several of the procedures described in Section 4 are usually combined into a comprehensive treatment programme for implementation in an atmosphere of concern and care for the child. The actuality of behavioural work (as opposed to the neat and 'tramlines' way it is often written about) is a highly individualized, proactive but also reactive, undertaking. A programme once initiated may continue, or be adapted according to its progress or lack of progress, or unexpected practical obstacles.

Each programme is designed to produce an enduring decline in self-defeating actions together with the acquisition, performance and maintenance of acceptable alternatives. This behavioural approach can be contrasted with more traditional attempts either to suppress unacceptable behaviour by means of physical punishment, or to encourage its expression (in cases like aggression) in approved situations (the sports field) in the hope that it will decline elsewhere.

Step 20a   PHASE OUT AND TERMINATE TREATMENT   Do this with care: the durability of any improvements depend upon it

The decision to terminate treatment should be made jointly with your client. The time for the programme to end depends upon the goals established at the beginning of treatment.

Try to ensure natural, intermittent reinforcement in the child's different settings. A guideline is to teach only those behaviours which will continue to be rewarded after training, provided they are adaptive in the sense of contributing to the child's well-being and efficiency, and that of the community.

If a behaviour is defined as part of the treatment goals but is not functional (i.e. useful and rewarding) for a child, then a treatment programme may produce only a transitory effect. When the therapeutic procedures are withdrawn there may be nothing to maintain the behaviour and it will disappear.

Note: *Parents should not (and usually do not) expect the child to acquire and maintain certain lessons without setbacks and frequent reminders. Although some therapists pay lip-service to returning the child to an environment which will 'naturally' maintain the target behaviours, precise attention is not always paid to whether this actually happens. And when it does not, the therapy of the child has somehow failed. What has failed is the modification and maintenance of an environment that will promote the new behavioural repertoire of the once-deviant child.*

Parents tend to take a long-term view of rearing their offspring, continually encouraging their desirable actions, while chiding them for 'deviant' behaviour— month in and month out, and sometimes year in and year out. This goes on until the child has certain crucial social behaviours (or the control of antisocial behaviours) as habitual (internalized) parts of his repertoire. Other behaviours will always remain, to varying degrees, under the control of external contingencies. Time-scales vary, depending on the age and maturity of the child and the nature of the behaviour or task.

The termination of a programme is set—in theory—in advance of the treatment programme, by the negotiation of objectives. In practice it is a bit like jazz, a matter of 'playing it by ear'. It is so difficult to be precise, despite one's best efforts, in setting *goals* for future behaviour; *skills* are somewhat easier to specify. Deciding whether problematic behaviour (especially ones like aggression, manifested to some degree by all children) has changed enough is difficult. A clinician needs to know how different the terminal behaviour is from what is 'normal' (see Tables IV and VI) for a child of the client's age and sex, and in his particular situation. How far should the changes go? The *total* elimination of anxiety or (in a three-year-old) of tantrums—as a treatment objective— would be extreme, unrealistic and unattainable. So you might decide to terminate when there has been an improvement. But what constitutes an improvement? How much of an improvement will suffice? Should certain problem behaviours be eradicated altogether in all situations and forever? Or should the therapist be satisfied with a more modest reduction in the frequency of deviant behaviour, say, a 25 % or 50 % decrement. There is no simple answer. It depends on the problem behaviour, its implications, the context within which it occurs and so on. As with the criteria of what constitutes a problem it is more a value/social question than a scientific one; as at the diagnostic phase of your contact with your clients you have the special responsibility of acting as an 'advocate' for the child.

Symptom substitution

Some theorists would be concerned at the behaviour therapist's willingness to terminate the programme at the point at which the 'surface problems' (or symptoms as they see them) have been alleviated. The belief in symptom substitution ignores the fact that physicians from time immemorial have applied themselves diligently to symptom relief and removal in both functional and organic ailments. In the absence of empirical evidence to support the idea of symptom substitution but with plentiful evidence for the successful treatment of 'symptoms' or (as the behaviourists would prefer) alleviation of problems, we suggest that *sympton relief* is a legitimate goal in any therapeutic intervention. After all, in most cases, this is exactly what the client is asking for. Indeed, practitioners have found, as we have at the Child Treatment Research Unit (Herbert *et al.*, 1981), that children treated behaviourally often show improvements in areas that had not been specific targets of the behaviour therapy. It may be that serious problem behaviour blocks the child from engaging in activities that might be a source for him of positive reinforcement from his parents and peers. The absence of the mutually rewarding social interactions might well hinder his socialization and development of a repertoire of prosocial behaviours.

The answer to fears about symptom substitution is to avoid metaphors such as 'underlying' and 'deep-seated' causes, and rather to carry out rigorous and comprehensive assessment into *all* the contributory causal factors which have a bearing on the planning of successful therapeutic interventions. The 'safety net' is to engage in thorough and systematic follow-ups after the intervention is terminated.

Labelling

Be cautious about labelling or you may find it difficult to begin, let alone finish, therapy. Behavioural theorists find labelling almost entirely unnecessary, as becomes obvious from a study of the functional analysis of problems carried out by practitioners. Being tautologies (re-namings) in most instances, they tell us very little about the child and only too often are therapeutically pessimistic. Parents and teachers are sometimes told that a particular child's difficulties at home and at school are 'a result of brain damage', suffered perhaps as early as at birth. This is no more helpful than for a general practitioner to tell a mother her child is 'physically ill' when she takes him along for a diagnosis of a bodily malaise. Certainly no programme of rehabilitation—remedial teaching or behaviour modification—could be planned on the basis of such a vague diagnosis as 'brain damage'. What is needed, in describing a child, is not a meaningless label but precise information about his specific physical and intellectual problems, and also about any emotional difficulties which have a bearing on his ability to learn. The resistance in behaviour therapy to labels such as 'mentally ill', 'psychopathic' or 'abnormal', reduces the possibility that such labels will become self-fulfilling prophecies setting up a chain of responses that reinforce expected patterns of dysfunctional behaviour.

A classic example of this last situation can be seen in the case of Robert, an 'autistic' ten-year-old boy referred to the Child Treatment Research Unit. His parents were told that to expect anything other than bizarre and aggressive behaviour from an 'autistic' child was being unrealistic; as a result, for years, they made no attempt to check or prevent his more antisocial behaviour.

This child was successfully treated using a behavioural programme which assessed his 'autistic' behaviour in the same way as any other behaviour would be assessed. By changing certain antecedent and consequent events the therapist was able to reduce his 'irrational aggression' (which in behavioural terms could be quite rationally explained by looking at the reinforcement it was receiving) and similar antisocial behaviours. Eventually, he was able to start mixing socially with peers, and begin to develop the potential he did have, without the label 'autistic' getting in the way.

Summary

Change is the operative word for assessing your work and deciding on an appropriate point to terminate the programme. You might plan to make use of several indices of change (Gordon, 1975). The chosen intervention may bring about considerable changes in the home which are pervasive as well as specific. Multiple criteria are therefore suggested to assess the outcome of intervention:

(1) *Inspection of graphed records.* A significant change from baseline to termination, greater than fluctuations in the baseline, is required. There are statistical tests of significance which researchers apply to their data. An 'eyeball' test will probably have to suffice for the busy clinician (nevertheless see Jones *et al.*, 1975).

(2) *Therapists clinical judgement.* This is the therapist's assessment of the child and his family as functioning better or more happily than before intervention or the same, or worse, as the case may be. The judgement requires specific criteria which are of real clinical and social significance, i.e. they should represent meaningful gains in adaptive functioning.

(3) *Parents' assessment.* Parental perceptions of change are by far the most simple measures of outcome to obtain, and they should not be neglected.

   (a) The parents evaluation of improvement (or its absence) in their child's behaviour and relationships with them, can be assessed using either a questionnaire or a structured interview.

   (b) Semi-structured interviews might provide information about changes in the family's social activities (e.g. visits outside the home; changes in the child's play and other social interactions with his peer group; enjoyable outings by the family; being able to leave the child with a babysitter, or take him to a supermarket or indeed, visiting).

Improvement may be defined as a change in the child's target behaviours toward the goals set for those behaviours; it may be specified in terms of parental activities, or parent–child interactions. The goals may not be all met, but a definite change must be reported by the clinician, parents and be apparent in the graphical records.

The degree of improvement in (say) the child's behaviour might be refined into categories:

(1) All goals are reached and the parents and therapists are fully satisfied with their child's improvement ($+2$).
(2) Only some goals are reached or partially reached, or the parents/therapist are less satisfied ($+1$).
(3) No change occurs (0).
(4) There is a moderate deterioration (-1).
(5) There is a significant deterioration (-2).

There is a great deal of unpredictability in the effects of behavioural interventions. The therapist soon learns that techniques which yield the most impressive results are not always effective with all types of problem or with all children. Furthermore, to his (and everyone else's) frustration, a given technique may, on one day, produce complete control in the case of a particular child, but on the next have no apparent effect at all.

McAuley and McAuley (1980) make an important observation:

> The behaviour therapist, like most persons, is motivated by success and because of this he is liable to prefer working with younger children. The social behaviour of the young child, because of its immaturity, is generally quite flexible. There is also the added advantage that since he spends a large percentage of his day in the home, treatment usually need only involve the parents and family. In contrast the older child's behaviour is more complex and comes under a much wider range of influences. Practically the therapist is often faced with attempting to change problems which have been present (or developing) over many years. Only in few instances will he have any control over diverse influences such as the peer group and other reinforcers outside the home. In fact, because of this the older child's co-operation in therapy assumes great importance. (p. 43)

So does a knowledge of the literature on self-management and self-control.

Facing failure

Sadly for you, but more distressingly your client, you are going to fail on occasions to achieve significant change. Understandably, clinicians publish their success stories when writing up single case-histories. But failure rates can be depressingly high (see McAuley and McAuley, 1980). If you believe that behaviour is lawful, and presumably you do if you are reading this manual with serious intent, then there are several possibilities:

(1) You may have got the 'story' wrong; failed to understand the key determinants of the problem; omitted key items/persons in the assessment; prescribed the wrong remedies; initiated the right remedies but with insufficient support, reinforcement for the mediator, or attention to transfer and maintenance of effects.
(2) The client is resistant to change (see Gottman and Leiblum, 1973) and you have not been sensitive enough to the signs (homework assignments not performed, lateness for appointments, criterion slippage) and therefore not tried to deal with it as a problem in its own right.
(3) The client lacks crucial skills, resources (help, health, energy, incentives) to see the programme through to the end.
(4) The behavioural approach is not a panacea; it may simply not accommodate the ramifications of your client's problems.

Before giving up, you might take the example of Gottman and Leiblum (1973) who, when all else fails, try the 'force field analysis'—a problem-solving approach which assumes that things are 'stuck' because there is an equilibrium between the forces facilitating change and those that are opposing and restraining (p. 128).

What you do is:

(1) List facilitative forces for change;
(2) List restraining forces for change;
(3) List alternative intervention strategies for:
   (a) strengthening facilitative forces;
   (b) adding new facilitative forces;
   (c) weakening or removing restraining forces;
(4) List the advantages and disadvantages (including costs) of each intervention.

Step 20b   FADE OUT THE PROGRAMME GRADUALLY

An abrupt transition from a rich reinforcement schedule, in a behaviour modification programme, to a lean one following treatment (or indeed, one in which *no* provision is made for the administration of reinforcers), is often the equivalent of placing the desired target behaviour on an extinction schedule. A gradual modulation is possible using *fading procedures* or other scheduling techniques.

Technique: Gradually increase the delay between reinforcement and the target behaviour—in order to maintain improvements.

Fading procedures change the environmental stimuli so that they approximate more closely those natural conditions that are likely to prevail following the end of formal treatment. Reinforcement schedule transitions have to be introduced *gradually over a period of time.*

Preventing the child's behaviour from reverting to pre-treatment patterns soon after the cessation of treatment is one of the most intractable problems associated with behaviour modification programmes. Gelfand and Hartmann (1975) point out that if such a reversion occurs, the child will have benefitted only briefly from the programme; he and his family might become unduly fatalistic and disillusioned about the possibility of his ever improving. In other words, in some instances an untimely relapse might worsen an already distressing situation.

It is possible to reinforce behaviour in ways which are likely to facilitate its persistence. An intermittent schedule of reinforcement might be used, as behaviour which has been reinforced in this way (see Step 12, p. 54) requires fewer reinforcements to maintain it, and it takes longer to extinguish after the cessation of reinforcement. Similarly, we have seen how artificial reinforcers in treatment such as tokens or material rewards are gradually replaced by others like social attention and approval which are more likely to apply after treatment ends.

Gelfand and Hartmann (1975, p. 251) offer advice on how to proceed in order to maintain the level of behaviour achieved during the therapeutic intervention at that critical termination juncture:

> The wise therapist incorporates increasing intermittency of reinforcement into the treatment whenever circumstances permit.... If you have been applying a fixed-interval or fixed-ratio prior to termination introduce a less predictable variable schedule prior to termination. The variable schedule more nearly matches most naturally occurring schedules and so blends well into the child's everyday routine. If you have applied a variable schedule since the inception of treatment, increase its intermittency until the natural environment's schedule is closely approximated.... It is advisable to thin the schedule gradually. Sometimes the process of thinning the reinforcement schedule produces a performance loss. This problem is relatively easily remedied, however. Should the target behaviour decrease appreciably in rate following an increase in performance requirements to earn each reinforcer, you must revert to the immediately preceding schedule, restabilize this behaviour, and then introduce a less dramatic schedule change. (Note that this procedure is similar to that employed whenever introduction of a new performance requirement disrupts the process of shaping.) Insofar as possible, avoid large magnitude and sudden reductions in the frequency of reinforcement of the desired behaviour.

In another approach the therapist fades out special and perhaps artificial discriminative stimuli used in the behavioural programme so that the targeted behaviour is evoked in situations where the control is exerted through appropriate and natural cues. These should be present in the child's day-to-day environment.

Where treatment has been conducted in the clinic, it may be possible to promote stimulus and response generalization by making the treatment setting as similar as possible to the child's natural environment. This involves stimulus generalization; similar situations tend to elicit the same behaviour, and the more parallel the situations can be made, the greater is this tendency. With regard to the response side, it has been shown that a situation which elicits one response is likely to evoke similar responses. There is a gradient of response generalization according to the degree of similarity between responses. One way to programme response maintenance and transfer of training is to develop the target behaviour in a variety of situations and in the presence of several individuals. If the response is associated with a range of places, individuals, situations and other cues, it is less likely to extinguish when the settings vary. (See Jones and Kazdin, 1975; Wildman and Wildman, 1975.)

It is not always necessary to arrange special measures for the purpose of prolonging treatment effects; the intervention may strengthen skills or remove inhibitions so that the client gains access to existing sources of reinforcement, or it might reduce the aversiveness of his behaviour for himself or others and thus entail reinforcing consequences. This sounds easy but is extremely difficult to do in practice—especially with the volatile, highly coercive children, who are so quick to seize the 'main chance' and who make up such a large proportion of a clinical population. The fading out programme can so easily degenerate into a haphazard pattern which approximates the original unhappy situation. At the Child Treatment Research Unit we have made use of *overlearning* as a protection against relapse; it involves erring on the side of plentiful (and redundant) practice well beyond the point at which the child has acquired new behaviours and skills.

Motivation and participation

One of the most critical problems to overcome in implementing a successful therapeutic programme is stimulation and maintenance of the parents' interest and motivation to participate in the joint work. We soon found that it was crucial to involve the father from the beginning. Contracts (not used in every case) proved useful and gradually became almost standard practice. Cooperation of the parents was further increased by involving them as much as possible in decision-making about their child's programme. Although this is not necessarily part of a triadic behavioural approach to therapy, it appears important, not only because the parents feel more involved, but because it requires a certain level of understanding, on the parents' part, of the principles involved. Such an understanding may well help the parents (or it may be teachers) not only to use the techniques during the programme, but also to provide them with a framework within which to plan ways of handling future problems as they arise. This level of comprehension may be a desideratum for people dealing with multiple and fairly persistent or chronic childhood problems (e.g. conduct disorder, mental handicap or hyperactivity). Whatever else you achieve in your therapy you want to make the parent and child more mutually rewarding. In this notion we have the concept of a 'behaviour trap'. You aim to produce a behaviour pattern which, once begun, produces environmental consequences that maintain the behaviour. Guiding children into behaviour traps appears to be highly desirable if behaviour change is to persist in the environment. Having claimed that it is unlikely that techniques designed to delay extinction or relapse can have permanent success unless the changes are supported by the environment, we must also underline the necessity for developing procedures for training parents to deal with their problem children themselves.

Parent training

Ayllon and Azrin (1968) propose a guideline: 'Teach only those behaviours which will continue to be reinforced after training' The therapist's aim in using behaviour modification procedures is to introduce the child to behaviours which are either intrinsically reinforcing or which make reinforcements available to him which he was not previously experiencing. In a sense there are two therapeutic objectives in working with children:

(1) To enhance a child's responses to the controlling factors in his environment without deliberately altering the latter. Assuming a family environment to be essentially satisfactory, one might attempt to adjust a child to it.
(2) To change the controlling factors in an unsatisfactory learning environment as a means of modifying problem behaviour.

Where the latter strategy is predominant the therapeutic objective is to programme the environment so that it sustains the child's (and parents') 'improvement' after the formal programme is terminated. The long-term purpose of this phase of therapy is to help parents to become more systematic in their own behaviour, so as to be more effective in managing their children.

There are several levels at which parent training might be pitched; four of which are listed by Gardner (1976) as follows:

(1) *The applicator* is able to apply specific behavioural techniques under circumscribed conditions to solve particular problems.

(2) *The technician* is able to apply a broader variety of techniques but still under limited conditions to solve specific problems.

(3) *The generalist* has the 'know-how' to apply theory and techniques to a wide spectrum of problems with a minimum if supervision.

(4) *The consultant* is the person who trains others in behavioural theory and methods.

Of course the rationale of the desire to train parents to the generalist level is the belief that the parents' ongoing contact with the child and possession of new skills might facilitate generalization of treatment effects across time. Haynes (1976) points out that clients learn not only a new model of behaviour—a construct system which emphasizes the significance of behavioural consequences and environmental causality—but they assimilate new *methods* of understanding behaviour. They learn a new language for communicating about behaviour and a more precise way of specifying, defining, observing and thinking about behaviour—environment relationships. Various people are researching into the cost-effectiveness and cost-benefits of training parents in different ways. Sadly, the evidence in the area of temporal generalization is mixed: positive with regard to long-term persistence of favourable effects in some studies (see Giffin and Hudson, 1978), negative or minimal in others. A further hope is that thorough parent-training will enhance the transfer of skills applied to one problem in the child's behavioural repertoire area to novel problems manifested by the same child. This expectation is difficult to translate into reality. The evidence is a little more positive when it comes to generalization across children.

The cost-effectiveness of group versus individual training procedures has yet to be evaluated. At the Child Treatment Research Unit the didactic element was covered by individual consultation and also (although somewhat haphazardly) in groups. Sadler and Seyden (1976) have published a helpful guide for teaching child management to parents. They enumerate several basic course concepts:

(1) More learning occurs when people feel comfortable, relaxed, and in friendly supportive surroundings.

(2) It is best to remove as much social anxiety as possible.

(3) A fun-filled atmosphere heightens the interest and excitement of the workshop.

(4) People learn better by actually doing rather than talking about something.

(5) Parents' reluctance to take tests can be overcome with innovative quizzes.

(6) It is helpful to work on parental attitudes as well as behaviours.

(7) Some simple exposure to and practice in communication skills is useful to many parents.

(8) It is somewhat destructive to self-esteem when parents see this kind of training only as remedial therapy for 'Problem Parents and Children'.

(9) Parents make major contributions to the course itself.

Parents' groups

The setting up of a parents' group might be initiated to help with training, the maintenance of parental behaviour, and also to help cope with those cases in which treatment has failed. The group (ideally) becomes a self-supporting group: its aim is to bring parents together, not only to discuss the management of problems and child-rearing practices, but also to meet socially and to share experiences—notably to do with the often heavy burden of bringing up a difficult child.

Our parents' group kept close contact with the Child Treatment Research Unit aiding us with both current and follow-up cases. Developmental counselling and the teaching of contingency management techniques in group sessions became possible, as a complement to individual consultative training. An advantage of the group is that mothers who had used a management programme were introduced to mothers about to begin one—reassuring those who were apprehensive or sceptical. Words of encouragement and support, or the assurance that things could get better—from someone who had experienced (say) the depressing 'post extinction burst'—were useful aids to therapy.

No formal evaluation of the effectiveness of the group was made; however, personal reports from parents who became involved were positive, with several of them finding new interests and friends (many were socially isolated) as well as sought-after support. It proved particularly supportive of those with whom we failed.

Follow-up of cases for at least a year is crucial for maintaining results; *brief* booster programmes (or simply contact) are usually sufficient to put right any relapse—according to Child Treatment Research Unit findings.

Step 20c	**YOU MAY DECIDE TO CHOOSE OTHER METHODS FOR PERPETU-ATING FAVOURABLE CHANGES** (e.g. Self-management training)

Self-direction

A promising approach to the generalization problem is represented by attempts to provide the child with self-regulating strategies which can be applied across a number of situations. The goal of treatment increasingly incorporates the development of a child's cognitive as well as his instrumental repertoire in an effort to establish the foundations for self-sufficiency and further growth. At the highest level of functioning, mature individuals regulate their own behaviour by self-evaluative and other self-administered consequences. A further dimension concerns the *attribution* of any favourable changes that have been brought about. If a client perceives himself as mainly responsible for his improvement during treatment, he is more likely to maintain these advances.

Early manifestations of self-control are encouraged during childhood training by many parents, especially in middle-class families. The common disciplinary and other child-rearing methods for developing resistance to temptation have been reviewed by the author (Herbert, 1974, 1980). The profusion of research and theory into the mechanisms of socialization reflects the centrality of this issue for understanding the transition of the infant from an impulsive, uncontrolled organism into a social being who is able to exert a reasonable degree of self-restraint. Just as the development of self-regulation has been viewed consistently as one of the most important objectives of the socialization process, therapeutic procedures which can be brought under the control of the individual himself are most beneficial.

Technique: Tangible, self-reinforcement and symbolic rewards can be used to maintain new patterns of behaviour until they become a source of personal satisfaction. While this may be a desideratum of treatment, especially with more mature individuals, the behaviour of children is very much under the control of external contingencies and the relative generality of responses (implicit in self-regulation) is the exception rather than the rule.

APPENDIX I
Case Studies

Case fragment 1: Wayne, age two

To see the twins, Jimmy and Wayne Grant, * together—on one of our home visits—is to understand something of what the paediatric term 'failure to thrive' means. Jimmy is a chubby, rosy-cheeked, boisterous two-year-old. He appears to be a happy, mischievous boy, running, playing, talking and laughing. He comes to his mother for help and comfort and cuddles up to her spontaneously. He responds readily to her attention and affection. She smiles at him, picks him up, sits him on her lap, plays with him, answers his questions, watches his movements, warns him when he is in danger.

On the edge of the room, like a stranger, stands Wayne—posture rigid, staring fixedly at us. He is a sad, lethargic looking child, very small and extremely thin. His pale face throws into relief the dark shadows under his eyes. He remains in one spot, as if at attention. Later he gazes unswervingly at his mother. She takes no notice of him. When asked to call Wayne over to her she looks in his direction; as she does so her face hardens and her eyes are angry. She addresses him with a dry command; when he hesitates she shouts at him.

Our observations of his interactions with his mother (several visits over four weeks) which gave us baseline data, indicated that she *never* smiled at him, *never* picked him up, *never* sat him on her knee, *never* played or read to him. The only physical contact came about when she fed, bathed or dressed him, and at such times, her handling was rough and silent. When she approached him he appeared to be frightened and occasionally burst into tears.

He would never come to her for comfort or help and she never approached him except to carry out the bare essentials of care and control. The children were both meticulously clean and well-dressed.

Home-based observations allowed us to see that when the father returned from work, Wayne brightened a little, he became somewhat more alert and lively, especially when mother was out of sight. When she entered the room he stiffened up. Jimmy and Wayne don't play together. Jimmy frequently pushed his brother and smacked him, Wayne's cries were largely ignored by his mother.

Looking at Wayne and Jimmy it is hard to believe that they are twins who were of the

---

*These names are purely fictitious. The case is described by Herbert and Iwaniec (1980) in the *Australian Journal of Child & Family Walfare*, and is reprinted with permission.

same weight at birth. Wayne's small stature was now reflected in a height and weight that were below the third percentile curves of normal growth. Wayne had been hospitalized several times because of his failure to gain weight. During the latest hospitalization Wayne's mother refused to visit him and requested his reception into care; she appeared to be very depressed and said that she could no longer cope with trying to feed him (he would refuse food, or spit it out screaming loudly). She added that she could no longer tolerate his behaviour ('defiance', whinning and crying) and her hostile feelings towards him. At the stage of our entry into the case Wayne had to be fed by a combination of the health visitor, father or a neighbour.

Failure to thrive

'Failure to thrive' has become a popular term to describe infants and children whose growth and development are significantly below expected standards. It is thought of as a 'syndrome' of severe growth retardation, delayed skeletal maturation, and retarded psychomotor development which is frequently associated with a specific disturbance of maternal behaviour and family disorganization. Certainly, in Wayne's case, it was clear (after the essential exhaustive medical tests) that his retarded growth at this stage of his life was not due to organic disease.

Studies of such children and their families have shown that the most commonly identified forerunners to these problems are emotional disturbance and environmental deprivation—with the wide range of psychosocial disorganization that these concepts imply. The deprivation often involves rejection, isolation from social contacts and neglect. Occasionally, physical abuse enters the picture. Wayne showed, on several occasions, severe bruising. The health visitor had placed him on the 'at risk' register.

Wayne was hospitalized five times during his two years and three months of life. Altogether he had spent 68 days in hospital. The first admission was at the age of four weeks. He had been a difficult baby to feed from the start. He vomited frequently and seemed to cry or scream incessantly for the first few weeks of life. He was suffering from pyloric stenosis. After the operation he improved a little. His sucking became more vigorous although he took a long time to feed. The situation deteriorated when solids were introduced at the age of five months. He persistently refused to take them and gradually stopped taking liquids as well. From that time onwards, feeding time became a battle.

Wayne was 14 months old (weight 6 kg, height 69 cm) when his mother finally found it impossible to cope with his reluctance to eat. She screamed at him, smacked him, shook him, getting angrier and angrier. When she forced him to eat, he screamed, vomited immediately and then had diarrhoea. Soon Wayne began to scream at the sight of his mother. She could not touch him or come near him. In anger and helpless despair she would take him upstairs and leave him there for hours. Wayne took some food from his father and nextdoor neighbours and was fed only when they were available. Because he was losing weight rapidly, he was admitted to hospital for investigation. In hospital, Wayne cried a lot, was at first unresponsive to nurses and movements around him. When not crying he looked blank and lethargic. Gradually he began to take food and became more alert and lively, doing well enough in the end to be discharged. This pattern of 'failure to thrive', improving in hospital and deteriorating soon after going home, was to be repeated several times. All of this increased his mother's feelings of hostility and rejection towards the child, not to mention her feelings of inadequacy as a mother. He seemed better all round when he was in different places with different people. In the end she refused to have Wayne back home from the hospital.

The Grant family—now in acute crisis—were referred to the author (and a colleague) for a form of assessment and a broadly based form of behaviour therapy which we call 'behavioural casework'. This family-oriented approach, which combines behavioural methods of assessment and modification with family-casework methods which include discussion, clarification of problems, developmental counselling and task-setting is prac- tised at the Child Treatment Research Unit (CTRU).

In order to be able to institute a full programme of assessment and treatment, we had to teach Mrs Grant to relax and to structure small, manageable daily tasks to counter her tension and her inertia and apathy. We diagnosed her depression as learned helplessness (see Seligman, 1975). So as not to exacerbate her feelings of helplessness and demoraliza- tion, we underlined the point that we were not there as 'experts' to take over the burden of the child's problem from the parents, but that we would be partners in a cooperative venture with a major part of the responsibility rightfully in their hands. A period of counselling and support-giving and relaxation-training was embarked upon and covered seven weeks. We arranged for full-time attendance by the twins at a day nursery.

Looking at the history we took at this time, it seems likely that the child learned (on a classical cum operant basis) to avoid food by associating feeding with painful experiences, e.g. forcing, hurrying, shaking, smacking, scolding and throwing. Finally, mother's person became a stimulus to evoke fear which (in proximity) brought physical symp- toms like vomiting and diarrhoea, if she was angry. He screamed sometimes even at the sight of his mother approaching him. Given a history of social isolation and a paucity of stimulation, it is not surprising that Wayne manifested serious developmental delay in speech. His brother was more generally advanced but also showed speech retardation.

Treatment programme

Before we could initiate a programme dealing with the aversive interactions between Mrs Grant and her child, we had to cope with the crisis issue of the mother feeding her child. After all, Wayne was wasting away.

Phase I

This was tackled in a highly structured (and thus, directive) manner. Mealtimes had to be made more relaxed. She agreed (albeit reluctantly and sceptically) to desist from screaming, shouting and threatening the child over his meals. The period of eating was made quiet and calm. Mrs Grant was asked to talk soothingly and pleasantly to him. This was extremely difficult for her to achieve. (The social worker joined the family for a few meals, helping to reassure Wayne, prompting the mother to help him eat in a gentle manner when he was in difficulties.) Mrs Grant was encouraged to look at him, smile, and occasionally touch him. If Wayne refused his food she was to leave him if she couldn't encourage or coax him by play or soft words. The food was arranged decoratively to look attractive.

This aspect of the programme (lasting several weeks) was purely 'instrumental' or 'symptomatic' in the sense of encouraging the child to eat by creating less fraught circumstances. As long as the mother kept to this schedule, Wayne would eat (not much, but a life-supporting amount). If she broke the rules because she was moody or unstable, Wayne would not sit in his high chair. We added another rule (on the basis of this observation), that she never fed the twins when feeling acutely angry or tense. There should be a period of quiet relaxation (using the relaxation tape and the training we had given her) if this was difficult to achieve.

Phase II

This phase (as with earlier stages of treatment) was discussed in detail—rationale and method—with both parents. A contract was drawn up specifying the mutual obligations and rules for the family and ourselves.

Objectives.
(1) To deliberately, and in planned fashion, increase positive interactions and decrease negative interactions between mother and child;
(2) To desensitize Wayne's anxieties with regard to mother's caregiving (and other) activities;
(3) To desensitize mother's tension, anger and resentment when in Wayne's company;
(4) To increase and make more general the intra-familial interactions (e.g. as a group, between Wayne and his brother etc.).

Methods. Mrs Grant agreed to play exclusively with Wayne every evening after her husband returned from work, for 10 minutes during the first week, 15 minutes during the second week, 20 minutes during the third week and 25 minutes during the fourth and subsequent weeks. The father took Jimmy for a walk, or to another room, while Wayne had this period of play. Afterwards they would join in for a family play session. The mother was asked to play with Wayne on the floor—this was demonstrated and rehearsed—and she was encouraged to talk to him in a soft reassuring manner, encouraging him to participate in the play.

She was also instructed to smile at Wayne, look at him, touch him, briefly, or praise him for each positive response she detected from him. (His tentative approaches toward her were 'shaped' by just such a series of successive approximations.) After a period of weeks she was guided to seek proximity to him by hugging him briefly and then holding him on her lap for increasing intervals of time, eventually holding him close, but gently, while reading him a story.

There is no doubt that Mrs Grant found all this difficult, and, at times, distasteful, but they became gradually less so as time passed and especially as Wayne began to seek her out shyly and to smile and chat to her. We had to provide a good deal of support and encouragement to both parents during frequent visits or by phone calls. (Reinforcing the reinforcer is criticial in this work!!). Three months were occupied by this stage of the intervention.

Phase III

The final phase took two weeks and deliberately involved an intensification of Mrs Grant's interactions (now much improved) with Wayne.

(1) She was to take him almost everywhere she went, whatever she was doing from morning until night. She was instructed to chat as much as possible to him in a soft measured way, smiling and cuddling him at approximate times. (These had to be discussed as Mrs Grant frequently put Wayne in a double-bind by giving contradictory verbal and non-verbal cues.)

(2) She was asked to read to him and Jimmy, encourage them to play together, and read to them both at bedtime. *Their* positive interactions were to be reinforced socially.

The formal programme was faded out gradually (over a period of several weeks) after discussing with parents the importance of a stimulating environment and a rich reinforcement schedule for the maintenance of the improvements they both detected in the family interactions, and mother's feelings and attitudes (these were monitored for us by herself). Our perceptions of Wayne's improved health, weight and height (and indeed his general psychological well-being) were confirmed by the assessments of the paediatrician, the nutrition consultant, and a health visitor. Mrs Grant's sense of attachment to Wayne had returned. What is of interest is that although we discussed her feelings and attitudes with her they were not the primary focus of treatment. She found it difficult and, in the end, refused to discuss them. We hoped that old feelings of affection and nurturance would return if we countered the avoidance situations (and sense of helplessness) which stood in the way of her learning to love him again. Feelings (and insights) *followed* actions!

Case fragment 2: Tommy, age four

Tommy was difficult from early in life, something not helped by the fact that his mother was ill both with urinary infection and post-natal depression. Her capacity for coping with a new baby was understandably diminished.* This was not made easier when Tommy proved to have a volatile temperament. He suffered from colic and his frequent and prolonged screaming drove his mother to distraction. Picking Tommy up and nursing him were means by which the mother could hope to at least have some calming effect on her child and herself. This she had to do a great deal. By the time we saw Tommy (aged four) at the CTRU his problems consisted of: severe negativism, temper tantrums, and attention-seeking behaviours; what made them serious enough to merit treatment was their frequency, intensity, persistence, and pervasiveness.

In the words of his mother (Mrs M):

by the time his sister Claire was born, Tommy had got used to being the king-pin in the family. He liked all the attention that illness brought him, enjoyed the privileges of being an only child, and he was beginning to learn the art of getting his own way. These things, coupled with the fact that Tommy was obviously a sensitive and vulnerable child by nature, had already caused a few problems of behaviour even before Claire was born, but things rapidly got out of control after

*This case is reprinted (although in an expanded form) by permission of John Wiley and Son (see Herbert, 1978).

her birth. He was intensely jealous of the new baby. Feeding times with Claire were a nightmre with Tommy taking advantage of my immobility to throw tantrums, be disobedient, and to be aggressive towards myself and Claire. He couldn't bear her to be held close, and was so spiteful I daren't leave him alone with her even for a few seconds. He threw things into her cot, pulled, poked and scratched. Occasionally he tried to tip the cot over and on one never-to-be-forgotten occasion, threw, with tremendous force, a metal dinky car at Claire and me while I was feeding her. She was only six weeks old. The car hit her on the forehead just above the eyes, causing severe bruising. What little control I had left finally snapped. Perhaps I had been too patient, too tolerant of his jealousy, I don't know. I screamed at him but was so violently angry myself that I didn't dare go near him. I thought I would kill him.

As time went by Tommy developed into a despot. He developed a general aggression, a degree of wilfulness, and various other unacceptable behaviours. He whined, clung like a limpet, was insecure and anxious, and worst of all for me, was incessantly disobedient.... The situation deteriorated rapidly, compounded by an increasing tiredness on my part. This gradually deepened into general depression for which my doctor prescribed drugs. They didn't help; in fact feeling slightly drunk and rudderless made coping even more difficult. I was tearful, tense, often unreasonably angry, erratic and emotional, and then silent and withdrawn in turns. The tension in the house was painful. Tommy wouldn't go out without tears, unless to a well-known place and he became inordinately frightened and nervous of strangers; and all the time his behaviour got worse. We were trapped in a vicious circle. Finally, after yet another winter of ill-health, Tommy added another cruel refinement with which to torture himself and me. He had learned to 'play' sick brilliantly and, of course, I couldn't see it at all. Life was so miserable for me at this time that when I think back I can still feel the emptiness inside, the feeling of isolation, the constant fear that I would totally lose control and hurt Tommy. I was really desperate. It was an effort to go out, even to the shops. I looked awful, felt awful. Sometimes the loathing I felt for Tommy spilled over and I would find myself wanting to tell him 'Go away out of my life, I hate you. You've ruined my life'. Sometimes I would start and have to bite back the words, remembering that I did love him. Afterwards I would feel consumed with guilt that I could even think these things. And overall was this dreadful sense of failure. Failure as a mother and failure as a wife, even failure as a woman. I have never been so close to a total breakdown.

For the two therapists at the CTRU who worked with the family, watching Tommy at home was an object lesson in the coercive use of intense and more subtly disruptive behaviours to monopolize the limelight or to hold his mother's undivided attention. She, for her part, was tentative and highly sensitized to every nuance of his behaviour repertoire. The father appeared equally unsure of himself.

Tommy gave the appearance of being an unhappy child. He rarely smiled. This situation seemed unlikely to improve if he exhibited the target problems at school (which he was soon to attend) or in peer-group situations.

Tommy had learned that certain antisocial behaviours were guaranteed to gain attention from his parents. This lesson, applied in the school situation, could have aversive consequences for him and reduce his ability to learn. It was our opinion that they had affected his social development adversely—his manner was babyish and off-putting. From the point of view of other members of the family, Tommy's monopolistic and immature behaviour was undoubtedly undermining their well-being. His sister was beginning to imitate some of his behaviours. As his parents saw things, they had endeavoured to provide 'the best' for Tommy and yet they were faced with a situation in which they no longer enjoyed their child. They increasingly quarrelled over how to deal with the situation. These considerations, among others, contributed to the decision that an intervention was required. Much of Tommy's behaviour represented an insatiable search for attention. He was certainly receiving a large amount, but much of it took a negative form. It was precisely because of the endless round of disputations between parent and child that Tommy was precluded from many of the usual range of symbolic rewards or social reinforcers which belong to happy and meaningful family communications. Tommy, as a somewhat delicate child, had made constant demands on Mrs M's self-doubts. Her fears (buttressed by father's) kept her always close at hand so as to nurse him. Both parents feared that they might 'lose' Tommy. He received inordinate amounts of attention (positive reinforcement) during his illnesses which generalized to other areas of his life. His demands for his mother's attention seemed to her incessant. There was a symbiotic quality to the mother–child relationship: temperamentally, they acted like barometers for each other's moods. Thus Tommy's worst days often coincided with the days when his mother felt particularly low. The parents' child-rearing philosophy was such that they wanted to treat Tommy as an individual in his own right. They were determined not to be intrusive or dominating. Therefore they tended to give commands to Tommy as if he had a choice, although in reality there was often no choice—in the sense that he only knew how to act in one way—in an immature manner. The hesitant way in which their 'commands' were often issued made for ambiguous signals. For example, mother would say 'Tommy, would you mind clearing your toys up as I want to hoover now?', or 'Darling, won't you stop doing that?'. A command in the form of a question is likely to invite the answer 'No!'

Tommy's mother now takes up the 'story' of the intervention:

From the beginning of the psychologist's visits my feelings were ambivalent. First of all there was a feeling of relief. Something was at last being done. Something concrete. I was going to be helped. For a short while I felt euphoric ... but I was defensive as well because I knew that I must accept a certain responsibility for the way Tommy was. I did not want to do that. I had had enough of failure. But I recognized I would have to face up to the truth if I went ahead with a management programme. It was quite a struggle at times and my pride took quite a battering. I was very pleased that all the work in the programme was going to take place in the home. It seemed natural and logical that it should.

There were problems in initiating the programme as Tommy's mother says:

At the beginning of Dr H's intervention, however, I was unable to cooperate effectively. I was desparately unhappy and depressing with no clear understanding of how I came to be so. Each day I moved through a suffocating fog of failure, inadequacy, frustration and guilt. I hated Tommy whose parasitical behaviour had triggered these feelings, and myself whom I saw increasingly as an unattractive and undersirable individual. I felt that my intellect had atrophied. My daily round of housework and child-rearing held no rewards, but left me bored, frustrated, and exhausted. Against this background a natural shyness had developed into a real fear of going out and talking to people. The fear of rejection was greater than the fact of loneliness. My home had become a prison. Because of these feelings Dr H. decided to work on two levels: with the family on Tommy's management programme and with myself. After the initial discussions which did much to relieve the pressure and tensions within me, three broad problem areas emerged: my bored frustration at having no intellectual activity or stimulus; a total lack of social and personal confidence with its resulting social isolation for the children as well as myself; the accumulating and destructively suppressed anger, guilt, and tension from failing to cope with Tommy.

The latter feelings faded gradually and naturally as Tommy's programme progressed and I learned to express the resentment I felt when Tommy misbehaved, but in a more controlled manner, by giving appropriate commands. The first was also relieved, at least on a temporary basis, by my involvement with the programme. Dr H. encouraged me to widen my growing interest in psychology by reading and by discussing psychology with me in general and problem behaviour and learning principles in particular.... We discussed child-rearing and why I had become so tentative in dealing with Tommy. We also discussed my parents' way of bringing me up and how it had influenced my attitudes. The hardest problem to deal with was the self-doubt and isolation. Being depressed for several years and feeling an inadequate failure had eroded my self-confidence and produced a profound dislike for myself. It was necessary to change that before I could look up and outwards.

Dr H. asked me to role-play as a means of learning new ways of coping with my fears and suspicions of people. I started by writing a self-portrait. (Rereading it recently I was struck by its negative qualities.) Dr H. took each point and changed it to some extent. Where I was serious, introverted, careful, I was to be rather more spontaneous and impulsive, even a little frivolous— without 'overdoing' it. I was to think and act like an attractive woman; in fact we created a different 'persona' and role to my usual ones, but not too far removed (he said) from reality to make the task impossible. We went over it in great detail like a script.

The next step was not easy. What I had to do was go out and live my role daily. Privately I thought Dr H. was probably insane! It was certainly very difficult at first. You feel like a second-rate actor with severe stage-fright. But the remarkable thing was how it gradually became easier; and when the results were good I felt elated. I discovered casual conversations with local mothers, in the park or at the shops, soon unearthed common interests and I gradually developed new friendships with women in similar circumstances to myself, all with children for Tommy and Claire to play with. For the first time since Tommy's birth we were making regular visits outside the immediate family. Social skills are like any other. The more practice you get the better you become. As my confidence grew with each success so Tommy also relaxed and he began to look forward to these visits eagerly.

Throughout this period, during which there were regularly held discussions about my own situation and problems, we also worked with Mrs R. [another therapist] on Tommy's problems. Six main target behaviours were decided upon and there followed a week or so of careful charting to establish a baseline.

(We shall return to Mrs M's narrative shortly. The author and his colleague were also busy with a behavioural assessment).

Selection of goals for treatment

Treatment objectives were negotiated between the therapists and the parents. The first goal was to reduce the frequency of six target behaviours specified during assessment: (1) non-compliance, (2) aggression, (3) whining, (4) interfering, (5) tantrums, (6) 'lunatic' moods (so-called by Mrs M., and being episodes of hyperactive behaviour). All were operationally defined. The second goal was to increase adaptive behaviours in certain specified situations, as identified by the parents, with the main aim of creating opportunities for Tommy to win positive reinforcement for socially appropriate behaviour. There were four specified situations, one of which was tidying up his toys.

Treatment programme

With regard to the reduction of the six target behaviours, a programme was designed to change both the stimulus and consequential events associated with Tommy's problems, using mainly modelling and operant techniques.

(a) *Stimulus events*

Mrs M. was instructed in the modification of her methods of issuing commands to Tommy. Rather than using repetitive, pleading, and question-like 'commands' put in a hesitant manner, she was asked to give a simple, firm command to Tommy in those situations that required compliance. These situations were discussed with Mrs M. Modelling and behaviour rehearsal were also used.

Another alteration involved the timing of setting events during the day. Mrs M.'s day had all the periodicity of a school teacher's timetable. The baseline recording indicated that Tommy's target behaviours reached peaks at certain times of the day. His mother was advised to try to alter the pattern of the day in order to pre-empt the onset of target behaviours, particularly the lunatic moods.

(b) *Consequent events*

It was predicted after discussion with the parents that, for a variety of reasons, ignoring would not be feasible for use as an extinction procedure. So time-out was chosen. It was applied as a sanction after one warning given at the earliest onset of a target behaviour (e.g. at the first display of a defined category of disobedience). If Tommy failed to heed the warning, his mother made him go to an upstairs room for a five-minute period. One of the therapists spent the first day of the programme with Mrs M. helping her to initiate it (and when necessary cueing and modelling commands). This initiation process was somewhat painful for the mother.

As Mrs M. comments:

> I was very nervous while Mrs R. was with me. I wanted to tell her how difficult it was to act naturally with her sitting in a chair making notes. How do you carry on normally? I felt very foolish, like an overgrown schoolgirl. As a result I was both resentful and angry. Of course, part of Mrs R's job was to try and point out where I was going wrong or what opportunities I was missing. She was very successful in helping me to see that by stepping in early I could pre-empt Tommy's tantrums and so avoid all the verbal reinforcement he had been getting. As the programme progressed I found myself having to face some crucial issues. These issues had to be continually thought out and come to terms with. Poor Mrs R. had occasionally to endure some hostile and aggressive reactions from me. She did so with remarkable tolerance I thought.

Tommy's initial response to the programme was dramatic. His environment had changed from an inconsistent to a more predictable one; he knew that what his mother said as a threat would be carried out. Attention was valuable and therefore highly rewarding to Tommy. Time-out deprived him of this. His quick 'capitulation' belied the therapist's warning that Tommy's behaviour might deteriorate before it improved. It was, in fact, to do this later on.

With regard to the second goal, namely, increasing adaptive behaviours, four activities were chosen that spanned the whole day (e.g. dressing/undressing, together with any other behaviours that parents judged to be praiseworthy). It was worked out that there should be a chart for tokens (pictures called 'happy faces'). Happy faces denoted good behaviour and were to be exchanged for rewards in the form of outings and/or Smarties at the end of the day. Verbal praise and physical hugs were also to be given.

The reasons for a programme of positive reinforcement were explained to the parents in terms of time-out teaching Tommy what he could not do, and positive reinforcement providing guidance and encouragement with regard to what he should do (what is approved of). This was particularly the case with Tommy, a child who was manifesting so many maladaptive behaviours that the opportunities to gain rewards were few and far between. Sometimes, precisely because of the high frequency of target behaviours, his parents unwittingly forgot to provide him with those positive reinforcements. There seemed to be a need for a more systematically planned reward system, a matter to which Mrs M. agreed, but with some reluctance.

What followed underlines the necessity for frequent direct checks on the implementation of a programme. Complacency led to a slippage in criteria for parental action. Tommy's ingenuity at manipulating his parents and his verbal skills were also underrated. Thus two difficult periods arrived which held up the progress of the programme, and both parents, the mother in particular, became very despondent about its effectiveness. The first came eight days after the programme commenced. Tommy displayed a series of delaying strategies at the time that the parents tried to implement time-out, such as running away, endless arguments, refusals, dawdling on the way to his bedroom, appeals to go to the toilet, etc. The antecedent events to such 'subversive' tactics were situations where the parents felt some confusion about the application of the programme or disagreed about criteria. This transmitted itself as indecisiveness to Tommy. As a result of the child's delaying strategies—a variation of his non-compliance—Mrs M. responded by repeating a request, calling his name in a warning voice after she had given the initial warning, following him to see if he had obeyed her command to go to the room, and generally hovering over him when he had to carry out a request. Mr M. (if dealing with the situation) would repeat a request, followed by physical punishment used in conjunction with time-out. Tommy would then start screaming. Furthermore, Tommy's behaviour led to open disagreement between the parents in front of the child as to the application of the programme. This last consequence reflects a fundamental mistake that the therapists made, namely, the failure to include the father (who was not easily available) in the finer details of the working out of the programme. They left too much to Mrs M. to communicate to her husband. Tommy, a subtle child, soon took advantage of this situation 'to divide and rule'. He managed to create ambiguous situations in which it was difficult for the parents to be sure if they were being manipulated as part of Tommy's more immature repertoire (e.g. a babylike request for help) or whether he was expressing a legitimate request for parental help.

To counter this, the parents and therapist spent much more time going over again the theoretical principles operating in the programme. They worked out precisely what both parents were going to say when they issued commands to Tommy. What came through very forcibly was that both parents wanted to avoid forcing themselves in an 'authoritarian' manner on their son. So there tended to be an internal debate when action was required. They would silently argue with themselves 'should I?' or 'shouldn't I?' before they gave Tommy a command. They were often reluctant to carry through a threatened (i.e. promised) sanction, feeling 'sorry' for Tommy, or guilty afterwards. The author's ploy in cases like this is to ask the parents if they would break a promise to give their child a treat. The inevitable denial and explanation of the importance that a child should *trust* one's words, invites a discussion about breaking promises about punishment and the consequent debasement of the currency of words (and trust).

Precise cues were suggested to the mother so that she might avoid these agonizing dilemmas and so she could act at the right time in a decisive manner. Authoritative commands, it was hoped, would nip Tommy's target behaviours in the bud and prevent their unpleasant repercussions. On the consequential side, it was suggested that when Tommy tried his delaying strategies, at the point of implementing time-out, he was to be picked up, with no eye-contact and no verbal communication, and placed in his room, thus eliminating the attention he was gaining from his diversions. The response to this detailed plan was encouraging and the frequency of the target behaviours fell again to below baseline.

Another critical point came at the sixth/seventh week of the programme. Mrs M. again became very despondent about the programme, feeling that Tommy's target behaviour of aggression was not responding to her efforts. But despite the protestations, hostility and resentment that she expressed to the therapist, she persevered. Reinforcement (in the form of encouragement and praise) are as important to the mediators of change in the child (his parents) as to the problem child himself. After all, they are being asked to change addictive (reinforced) habits, and are in a learning situation too. Perhaps the acid test of the programme came during the eigth/ninth week when Tommy fell ill. This crisis was weathered. Following these two weeks, the frequency of the target behaviours decreased even further than they had already until they were a rare occurrence.

The record showed that from baseline frequency, non-compliance had reduced by 54 %. Aggression had fallen by 68 %; whining by 95 %; interfering by 94 %; and tantrums by 100 %. There was an increase of lunatic moods by 36 %. The reasons(s) for this increase are speculative. Possibly the mother was still finding it hard to prevent the onset of the mood. However, by the end of the programme (eleventh week), there was an average occurrence for both non-compliance and aggression of less than one per day. There were no occurrences of the other target behaviours. Mrs M. comments:

> Over a period of two months Tommy made amazing strides—from short visits to new friends where he would hardly leave my side, to attendance at a state nursery school for two and a half hours daily, where he showed no nervousness at being left at all. Now eight months on he attends nursery school all day and stays to dinner, has a large circle of friends, and happily attends parties and outings with me.
>
> Tommy's weaning from the house and my own successful 'jail-break' are victories of which I am particularly proud.

It should be noted that the introduction of the positive side of the programme (rewards) was not a smooth one. Mrs M. tended to verbalize the programme, talking about Tommy's opportunity to earn a happy face. As a result there arose a series of disputations between mother or father and Tommy. It was evident that we had planned a reward system which contained several loopholes as far as a perceptive and resourceful entrepreneur like Tommy was concerned. As so often happens in behavioural pro-grammes, we had to think again. A detailed plan was worked out with regard to the four behaviours that the parents wished to encourage. A more careful contract was designed, one which specified precisely how the parents were to respond to Tommy—determining (for example) a reasonable length of time to put toys away, deciding upon the parents' activities during this task, and determining when this task should take place. Happy faces were to be given to Tommy if he completed the task successfully without any prior cajoling or verbal warning of their delivery; the child himself was to be involved in sticking them on to the chart. As before, the tokens would be exchanged for sweets and/or trips, and praise and physical hugs were to be given as before.

Mrs M. objected not to social reinforcement but to tangible rewards which she felt constituted a form of bribery and, what is more, developed a 'sweet tooth' in Tommy. The therapists were of the opinion that the token system acted as a reminder to the mother to praise and smile at Tommy for his acceptable behaviour, and, in retrospect, the use of tangible rewards (Smarties) was probably redundant and ill-chosen. Tommy did in fact achieve all four tasks that his parents delineated for him. As Tommy's maladaptive behaviours decreased, there were more opportunities for the parents to 'enjoy' Tommy, which in themselves stimulated a high degree of mutual social reinforcement.

Termination

This phase came at the end of 12 weeks of treatment. Mrs M. faded out the token reinforcement programme but retained the use of positive social reinforcement (on an intermittent schedule consistent with real life) and the occasional use of time-out as a back-up to her now generally effective verbal control. The goals that were selected for treatment were achieved to the satisfaction of both parents. This expression of satisfaction which was confirmed by the monitoring of Tommy's behaviours constituted the main criteria for terminating the case. As a by-product of the programme, Tommy now gave the appearance of being a far happier child to the therapist (and more important) to his parents and their relatives. Mrs M. no longer looked the harrassed woman of 12 weeks previously; she now had a lightness in the presentation of her personality.

Follow-up

A series of checks by telephone and visits indicated that Tommy maintained his improvement for 12 months (our standard follow-up period). Mrs M. felt that she had successfully reintroduced the programme for short periods as and when it was necessary. Mrs M. experienced a setback when, as she said, she let her criteria slip and began to take the line of least resistance. A booster programme was contemplated, by the present author, but within a week of going back to recording Mrs M. found that she had the situation in hand, and the need for an intervention disappeared. Since then, several months have passed without any undue difficulties. During this period Tommy began school and settled in without any problems.

We leave the final words to Mrs M.:

It must be said that the programme was very successful in changing Tommy's and my behaviour and in the process turning him into a much happier individual. In achieving this, Mrs R. had to be adaptable and resourceful when Tommy altered his course or abruptly changed direction ...

Long before the programme was brought to an official close I was itching to take over the reins completely. As Tommy's behaviour improved I found myself more and more able to cope. I had learned when to intervene and how to. I had learned to act decisively when my instincts told me the time was right. Thanks to the therapists' careful explanations of the aims and methods of the programme, my husband was being fully supportive and so it was with considerable satisfaction that the programme could be terminated only three months after its start.... It appears obvious to me (eight months after the termination of treatment) that the mother is such an integral part of any management programme that her full cooperation is vital if there is to be any long-term success. The professionals can spend only a few hours each week with the child and so 'mum' must become the 'therapist in the field'. How vital the mother's role as therapist is has been proved to me in the months since the official termination of the programme. The daily reality of living with a difficult child is very hard to accept with equanimity and Tommy has three or four times threatened to return to his former behaviour. He is always dreaming up, with diabolical inventiveness, new and equally unacceptable variations. Without my 'training' it would be impossible to cope without frequent recourse to Dr H.

Case fragment 3: Joe, age 14

There were several behaviour problems mentioned when this case was first referred to the CTRU.* First, Joe was described as being wet by day and by night, as well as having unreliable control of his bowels. Secondly, there were complaints about his aggressiveness to other children and the mischief he wreaked through a variety of misbehaviours (as when he smashed milk bottles on the steps of other Community Homes in the vicinity). Thirdly, he was said to require an undue amount of supervision, since he was unable to wash and dress himself appropriately.

Joe was first identified formally as being of retarded ability at the age of three years four months by a school medical officer. Clearly, there had been several earlier observations of his relatively slow development. Subsequently, Joe was assessed on very many occasions and all test results indicated IQ levels within the range 37–44, i.e. very severe intellectual retardation. At the time of referral Joe attended a special school for the severely subnormal child; he had been to two previous special schools, and in addition he had attended the hospital school for a period of five years. As regards health and physical development, the most significant findings concerned his poor vision (myopia), occasional observations of mild spasticity (i.e. right thigh) and poor speech development (i.e. unclear diction). Also, Joe had had major oral surgery for dental abnormalities. He was considered to show bilateral neurological signs when given a neuro-psychiatric examination.

A series of interviews with all who cared for Joe formed the basis of the behavioural assessment of the problem; a behavioural checklist developed for the assessment of intellectually retarded patients was used in these interviews, which were designed to find out what Joe could or could not do. In addition, much information was gained from direct observations both in the Children's Home and at school. One difficulty in collating this information has been the marked variability of Joe's behaviour over time and the quite differing picture that might be given by different members of the child-care staff. The results of the assessment can be summarized as follows:

(1) *Sphincter control.* Joe had just been given some new clothes for his fourteenth birthday, and at the time of the initial assessment he had neither wet nor soiled his clothing for six weeks. As regards night wetting he had been occasionally dry (about twice per week), but it was clear that this was very rare. His house-mother was of the opinion that on occasions Joe did not completely empty his bladder, with the result that he dribbled. Also, he sometimes failed to use toilet paper, so that clothing was often badly stained.

*See Dean *et al.* (1976), Child Treatment Research Unit Reports.

(2) *Eating and drinking.* Joe used a knife and fork correctly and he needed little assistance at the table. Although he was said to be slovenly this reflected more a matter of manners (e.g. leaning across the table) rather than a distinctive lack of knowledge as to how to feed himself.

(3) *Locomotion.* It was apparent from the child's case files that Joe had always been considered to have poor balance. Perhaps, this was partly explicable in terms of his visual defect, which had been left uncorrected until about a year before the start of the behavioural programme. The possibility of mild spasticity has also been mentioned.

(4) *Personal hygiene.* This was the area where the views of the staff were sometimes in disagreement. Joe was able to wash his face, and staff said that he could bathe himself, so long as he was helped a little; it was, however, necessary for him to be watched by some staff member if he was to wash or bathe himself satisfactorily. His standard of care for his teeth and dental plate was considered to be very poor.

(5) *Dressing.* Joe could do up buttons and dress himself almost completely; the main exceptions being his inability to tie his shoe laces or knot his tie. Also, he required constant supervision if his dress was to be other than disordered.

(6) *Social development.* Joe's retardation along with his stay in hospital seemed to have resulted in poor social development. For example, when Joe had first arrived at the Home he was said to have had difficulty using the stairs and had little idea of danger. There had been some improvement but he was still unable to cross the road, had no idea of boundaries, and tended to get lost in the neighbourhood.

(7) *Conduct.* The child-care staff were most concerned about his disturbed behaviour when playing with the younger children, as he was disruptive and sometimes hurt them. This may have been in response to their teasing, but also arose from the fact that he was a solidly built 14-year-old and probably he did sometimes hurt younger children without realizing what he was doing. He had no-one to play with, other than much younger children, since he was rejected by children of his own age on account of his own intellectual retardation. Joe was fairly unpopular in the Home, both with the children and staff. In the latter case this was probably because he still needed much more supervision than the other children and often seemed to be deliberately naughty. Although he was said to have improved during the two years in his present Home, he still nevertheless caused a lot of extra work for an already busy staff.

The CTRU therapists also visited his school, to discuss his behaviour in the classroom, where they observed him with other children. He was described as not standing out as a problem child at school. He was said to get on well with other children and he was not particularly disruptive in class. Apart from having difficulty in tying his shoe laces, he was said to be reasonably independent and he did not require undue help with self-care at school. The school head teacher *was* concerned about his incoherent speech and the problem of persistent stealing.

Treatment plan

The results of the initial behavioural assessment indicated that Joe had areas of specific social and behavioural deficit, i.e. he could not tie his shoe laces or knot his tie, and he needed undue supervision over personal hygiene. As a result, he required extra supervision and help at the very time of day when there were relatively fewer staff available, and when those on duty were busy getting the children ready for school. It was hypothesized that teaching him some of these basic self-care skills would provide practical support for child-care staff, as well as improving Joe's acceptability to his peer group and perhaps also to some of the staff members. Clearly, to be successful, such a training programme would have to be shared with the residential care staff.

It seemed to be inappropriate to deal with his reported aggressiveness and destructiveness which were understandable in terms of the discrepancy between his age and that of the much younger children in the Home. It was apparent also that he was often blamed for misdemeanours of which he was either innocent or, at best, an unwitting perpetrator.

There was some improvement in bedwetting over the time Joe was being assessed; in view of this, and bearing in mind that Joe slept in a dormitory with five other children, and there was only one member of staff in residence over night, the house-mother was strongly of the opinion that it was not practical to use the 'bell and pad' method of treatment. Instead, a drug treatment was advised, and the family general practitioner prescribed Tofranil, a drug which is at least suppressive of enuresis. This is not normally as successful as the 'bell and pad' method, but it offered the advantage that it would not cause extra work for staff. Also, staff were advised to keep a daytime chart to reward Joe with a star on the chart for every day or night when dry. In sum, the problem of incontinence was found to have improved quite considerably during the phase of the initial behavioural assessment and it was not proposed to develop a more complex programme other than by combining drugs and reinforcement.

Procedure

Tying laces was the first skill tackled. The CTRU therapist initially demonstrated each step in the skill process on a large toy shoe. This skill was broken down into three stages—lacing the shoe, crossing the ends, and tying a bow. Joe was reinforced for every step initially with sweets, and later with picture cards. After about two months, Joe progressed to tying a real shoe on the table and finally to tying his shoes on his feet.

Washing was introduced about a week after the start of the lace tying. This skill was broken down into the following steps: (1) roll up sleeves, (2) take off glasses, (3) put plug in sink, (4) fill sink with water, (5) wash hands with soap, (6) put soap on flannel, (7) wash face with flannel especially around eyes, (8) rinse flannel, (9) rinse face, (10) dry face especially round eyes, (11) drain sink, (12) replace glasses. The steps were once again modelled and Joe was prompted when necessary and rewarded for the successful performance of each step. A cartoon chart was made giving precise instructions and illustrations of each step. This was placed on the wall over the sink and Joe received a star with sweets as back-up reinforcers when he successfully completed each step. Later, tokens were introduced—one for washing his hands, two each for round the face and round the eyes, and one for rinsing and drying. The tokens could then be exchanged for some picture cards which were used as back-up reinforcers.

When the washing was successfully learnt Joe was taught how to clean his teeth in a similar way. Knotting his tie was also introduced later and Joe learnt this particular skill very quickly.

The original aim with the teaching of these skills was that the CTRU staff would actually teach Joe in the evenings and the residential staff would reinforce him when he performed the skills in the morning. In the early stages of the training programme a CTRU therapist would arrive early in the morning to reinforce Joe for getting himself ready for school. But difficulties arose when, in the next phase, the purpose was to generalize the behaviour change so that Joe would continue to do this for the residential staff. They were asked to put stars on his washing chart and to give rewards for lace tying. This fading out of the CTRU therapist was not achieved and the reason for this seemed fairly obvious. There were only two staff present in the mornings to wake, dress and feed 15 children, most of whom were quite young. Thus the staff could not afford the time to supervise Joe's own efforts and, in fact, tended to do things for him as it was easier and quicker. Thus Joe was not practising his newly acquired skills in the normal daily routine, and the programme was altered so as to involve the staff more effectively in our work with Joe.

Two factors helped greatly in altering the situation. First, Joe's school bus was rerouted and this resulted in his being in the Home in the morning for half an hour after the other children had left for school. Thus the staff were more able to afford the time to leave him to get himself ready. The second factor was that a student social worker on placement at the CTRU was offered accommodation in one of the Homes in the vicinity and was thus able to supervise Joe two morning per week.

This system worked well and Joe carried out the full routine in the mornings when the student was present; he also learned to comb his hair, and the programme of self-care was extended to include teeth brushing. The next step was to encourage him to perform the skills without supervision; in order to do this the Home was visited just as Joe was ready for school and the student checked whether he had got himself ready and whether he had done so correctly.

In an attempt to involve the staff and to help reinforcement, we next introduced a token system. The student checked Joe before school, and if everything was correct he received one token. These were saved till the end of the week and could be exchanged in the following way: two picture cards for one token, one marble for one token, and one balloon for two tokens. The choice was arranged partly because Joe was tiring of cards, and also because it was felt desirable to introduce relative values as an introduction to later work with handling money. Initially the token system was operated for two weeks only on the days when the student was present, before approaching the staff for help. Then, the student asked the member of staff who took Joe to the school bus on the other three days to check him and distribute a token. In introducing this system, the student stressed the need for Joe to get himself ready, since this was a preparation for the time when he left to live in, say, a Hostel. Also, it was emphasized that the purpose was *not* for Joe to improve only when the student was present. Residential staff felt that Joe had improved generally within the Home and agreed to support the token system.

The token system was thus launched, not very successfully at first, as Joe always seemed to earn tokens from the student but not from the staff. This was because they were withheld even when Joe had earned them for self-care because he had been 'naughty'. The staff were asked to try to separate naughty behaviour from the self-care skills, and always to reward him for the latter if he fulfilled the requirements. They found this difficult to accept, but agreed to do so, and for the final three weeks Joe earned a token every morning.

There was a break for Christmas holidays, after which the token system was resumed with the staff now giving the material rewards as well as the tokens. However, this system had to be abandoned because of staff difficulties which arose in the Home, although these were quite unrelated to Joe.

The original plan had been to monitor Joe's progress by keeping diaries and by recording the frequency of behaviour problems. However, there were a number of reasons why this plan turned out to be impractical. First, the training programme spanned a period of three and a half years, during which time there were considerable staff problems in the Home. Secondly, it was found to be quite impossible to obtain even quite simple record charts. One feature of this and many similar Homes is that the part-time child-care and domestic staff tend to be on duty when the children are at school; thus, at times of maximum need for help and supervision there are fewer staff on duty. Consequently the available staff are too busy to keep a simple written record of events that have occurred.

As far as the present case was concerned the only solution was for members of the CTRU team themselves to keep as detailed and accurate a record as was possible; clearly, it was not feasible for someone from the CTRU to visit the Home every day of the week, and hence the records were, to put it charitably, patchy.

We can divide up the total involvement of the CTRU into broad phases as follows:

(1) assessment—1 month; Sessions 1–20;
(2) intensive behavioural training programme—10 months; Sessions 21–122;
(3) follow-up and intermittent training—28 months; Sessions 123–148.

During this long period of time there were changes of considerable significance, all of which had a definite bearing on the long-term planning of this case. This child had the same social worker from the time of his discharge from hospital until two years after the present treatment programme began. Thereafter, there was a period when no social worker was allocated, then Joe had four social workers in succession, and the Area Office responsible for the case was changed; the training programme was very seriously disrupted by staff difficulties in the Children's Home. For ease of presentation the results are presented by dealing with individual areas of behaviour modification separately. However, it should be emphasized that a session would encompass several areas at once; there was considerable variation as regards the duration of sessions, which lasted from 15 minutes to one and a half hours.

Tying shoe laces

In 17 sessions over a period of six weeks, Joe achieved the initial goal of being able to tie up the laces of a model wooden shoe into a bow. The skill was then transferred to tying up the laces of his own shoes, first while they were on a table in front of him, and then while wearing them. The transfer was, however, slow; for example, after 11 further sessions Joe was still taking six minutes to tie his shoe laces, and then he was successful only after the fourth attempt. It was not until nine sessions that he was able to tie up his laces within one minute. However, his performance was still not consistent enough and there was the additional difficulty that Joe tended to pull the lace ends so tightly that either the lace broke or the knot could not easily be undone. The reason for an emphasis on ensuring that Joe should be able to tie his laces with reasonable speed was simply that if the process took too long, he was likely to be distracted, leaving the original task incomplete. Also, there was the very practical problem that he got cramp when kneeling down tying his shoes for prolonged periods.

Joe had mastered the mechanics of tying shoes within some 37 sessions, spread over a period of three months, but it was not until after a further 58 sessions had elapsed that it was felt that Joe was competent enough to have mastered reliably this one skill component. The sessions devoted to this, in all, covered a period of six months.

Knotting a tie

This component in the treatment programme was not introduced until Joe had already acquired some skill in tying his shoe laces. It was hoped that there would be some generalization of skill from one task to the other.

The same basic procedure of breaking down the total task into small steps was used, and each time his success was reinforced immediately, either with a Smartie, or with a picture card and star token. Joe experienced some difficulty in knotting a tie; as with the tying of shoe laces he had problems in judging the degree of strength to use in pulling on the knot once it had been formed, and therefore in sliding the knot along the loose end of his tie.

Specific training in knotting his tie ceased after he was correct on each of three attempts and when he could do so within a reasonable time. This particular skill was acquired within 24 sessions.

Washing his face

As described above, Joe was encouraged to follow a particular sequence which emphasized such things as filling the bowl with a reasonable amount of water (as opposed to washing under a running tap); also he had to soap a flannel with not too much lather (this was emphasized since he otherwise tended to spend the whole session just rubbing the flannel on the tablet of soap). He also needed prompting to wash around his eyes.

It was always necessary to prompt Joe, even though he was able to follow the sequence of the chart on the wall of the washroom after 14 sessions. However, as his performance was very variable, the item of washing his face and hands was included for many more sessions. Even after 24 training sessions he was still requiring light prompts. Another difficulty was that Joe was very perseverative with the result that he would very readily spend the whole session just soaping his hands or flannel. By session 67 the student observed that he still required much prompting even though he was well able to wash, but at session 76 the same student observed that very few prompts were now necessary.

Cleaning his teeth

Initially, the therapist brushed Joe's teeth for him and used a mould of the lower jaw to show him the appropriate brush movements. In addition, Joe was shown how to clean his dental plate properly. Thereafter, teeth cleaning was incorporated into the general sequence of washing, and further training was mainly prompting. For example, in session 61, the therapist noted that Joe was having difficulty brushing his teeth on one side of his mouth. This difficulty was overcome quite simply by suggesting that Joe should hold his brush in the other hand when doing that side of his mouth. By session 67 he was observed to brush his teeth adequately within 45 seconds. However, his performance was inconsistent and prompts were needed, as in session 74 when he was observed to be brushing his teeth with his fingers. There were similar difficulties ensuring that he always remembered to clean his dental plate.

Bathing

Like so many other children in care, Joe was in a Home staffed exclusively by women; given that he was well into his teens, staff were somewhat reluctant to be too specific in instructing him about bathing. On session No. 51, the CTRU therapist supervised Joe's morning bath (this was after a night when he had wet his bed). There were three main problems apparent from this observation. First, Joe tended just to wallow in the water without any attempt to wash himself, and he perseverated by timelessly rubbing the soap on his flannel. Secondly, he found it difficult to wash any back part of his body; not only the back of his trunk but also the back of his arms and legs. Thirdly, he did not wash himself between the legs, and in particular, in his crutch.

The therapist told him how to wash himself, and emphasized the importance of washing less accessible parts of the body. His performance had improved by session No. 78, when he was observed again, but it was still necessary on that occasion to show him how to hold a flannel, to soap it, and to use it to wash under his arms and in the crutch area. As regards drying, it was more a matter of prompting him to dry his back (i.e. how to hold a towel in both hands so as to dry his back by a see-saw motion). also, he needed prompting to dry the back of his legs and between his toes.

Hair brushing

After a general review of Joe's progress (session No. 66), it was decided to incorporate specific training in how to comb and brush his hair. He was observed to find it difficult to comb the back of his hair and also to do a parting. The task was broken down into small steps and by session No. 77 he required only two prompts. There was a slight setback when his hair had been cut short and some alteration of technique was necessary. By session No. 84, the therapist considered that Joe's brushing and combing of his hair was entirely adequate.

Getting ready for school in the morning

It was clear by session No. 81 that Joe was able to perform with reasonable consistency all the above components. he could prepare himself for school, with a CTRU therapist prompting just now and again. But, the difficulty was that he still would do this only for the CTRU therapist—and there was little generalization to members of staff in the Home.

At that time staff were of the opinion that Joe's behaviour had improved very much; there was no more soiling, his self-care was acceptable, and within reasonable time limits, and he was beginning to help with minor household chores. In other words, it seemed that the hypothesis that provided the basis of the training programme was being confirmed; namely, that if Joe was better able to look after himself, then he would become more acceptable to other children and staff.

Consequently, the pattern of training was changed with the purpose of fading out the almost daily presence of a member of the CTRU staff and generalizing Joe's progress within the context of the Home in absence of outside support. It was arranged that a member of the CTRU team would call at the Home about half an hour before Joe was due to leave to catch the school bus. The purpose of the visit would be to check that Joe had got himself ready. The therapist encouraged him to check himself in the mirror and also checked more specifically to ensure that his teeth and dental plate were clean. He was then accompanied to meet the school bus. In order to ensure that Joe was reinforced for his apparent success in following instructions, a token system was used, whereby Joe was rewarded for each item which was completely correctly (e.g. brushed hair, clean face, tied tie and laces etc). The token cards were then exchanged for some small items such as a marble or balloon. These regular checks (about three times per week) continued up to session No. 92, and then the token system was transferred to members of the child-care staff. However, as mentioned above, there were immediate difficulties as Joe was being rewarded by the CTRU but not by the child-care staff who would withhold the rewards because of Joe's 'naughtiness' even if his self-care was adequate. After a further explanation and practice during 16 sessions when the token system was run jointly by CTRU and child-care staff it was decided to turn the whole system over to the staff at session No. 108. However, because of staff difficulties and shortage of time, the system broke down completely and was discontinued.

It would have been possible to continue further, as before, with the CTRU staff being once again actively involved; however, this was considered to be quite inappropriate on grounds of therapeutic priorities and the unlikelihood of further improvement in Joe's performance level, as well as the apparent pressures on the house-mother arising from shortage of staff.

APPENDIX II

Guide to the Application of Procedures

Method (Procedure No. on left)		Problems successfully dealt with
1	Graduated Reinforced Practice	Fears and avoidance behaviours Isolated behaviour
1/2	Incentive Systems (e.g. operant programmes—contingency management procedures, token economies, contingency contracts, self-reinforcement)	Language deficits Hyperactivity Bizarre behaviour Interpersonal conflict Non-compliance/negativism School phobia/truancy Various habit disorders (including toileting deficits: enuresis, encopresis, eating problems, etc.) Attentional deficits Academic skills/performance deficits Conduct disorders Delinquency Learning disabilities
3	Shaping	Skill/behavioural deficits
4/17	Modelling	Fears and avoidance behaviours Isolate behaviour Social skill deficits Conduct problems Learning disorders
	Symbolic Modelling	Preventive work: preparing children for dental and medical treatment
5/6/8	Stimulus Control and Change	Inappropriate behaviour Over-eating Non-compliance
	Provision of rules and response strategies	Attentional deficits

	Method (Procedure No on left)	Problems successfully dealt with
7	Extinction (withdrawal of reinforcement)	Inappropriate classroom behaviour Temper tantrums Attention-seeking disruptive behaviours Screaming Aggression Excessive crying
	Satiation	Fire-setting
9/12	Overcorrection	Disruptiveness
10	Time-out from Positive Reinforcement	Non-attending classroom behaviour Assaultive behaviour Disruptiveness Tantrums Aggression
11	Response Cost	Stealing Aggression Out of seat behaviour in the classroom Pestering Delinquency Intractable behaviour Disruptiveness Fire-setting
13	Promotion of Alternative Behaviour (Differential Reinforcement, DRO, RIB)	Inappropriate gender behaviour Disruptive behaviour Aggression Self-injurious behaviour Hyperactivity Norm-violating behaviour
14	Skill Training Interpersonal skill training (e.g. behaviour rehearsal, assertion training, social skills training)	Social skill deficits Interpersonal conflict Inappropriate gender behaviour Norm-violating behaviour
	Self-care/vocational/academic and other skill training Guided Rehearsal	Delinquency Learning disabilities Toileting skills deficits
15	Graded Exposure to Aversive Stimuli Desensitization	Fears and avoidance behaviours Hostility
18	Role-playing	Social skill deficits

	Method (Procedure No. on left)	Problems successfully dealt with
19	Cognitive Change Methods (e.g. problem-solving skill training)	Crisis interventions—problematic situations including separation, death and other upheavals Addictive behaviours Conflict situations Interpersonal functioning (conflict) Inhibitions Fears General coping situations Aggression
20	Self-control/Self-management/ Self-instruction	Interpersonal conflict Impulsivity Fear Academic performance deficits Hyperactivity
20/5	Self-management/Respondent/Operant Training (Bell and pad method)	Enuresis

APPENDIX III
Learning Theory and Choice of Methods

Those readers who are relative newcomers to learning theory (or in need of a 'refresher course') should study (with supplementary reading) the principles of learning and behaviour change described below. The procedures described in Section 4 are based on these principles.

The development of stimulus functions

To understand the development of stimulus control we must begin with the newborn child. Large aspects of his environment are essentially neutral in their effect on him, i.e. they exert little or no influence on his behaviour. As the infant grows older he acquires behaviours. He learns to crawl, walk, talk, sit at table, cooperate, read and so on and so forth.

Aspects of his environment begin to assume special properties for the child as a result of the quality of his experience of them. Some of them have pleasurable consequences, others have painful ones. He comes to associate his mother with warmth, comfort, stimulation and many other pleasant feelings. He tries to approach her or in some other way ensure her proximity. Some avoidance reactions to stimuli occur at an automatic level. If a child touches a hot stove the pain will cause him to withdraw it quickly. It won't take long for him to learn to associate pain and stoves and to avoid touching them. Brewer (1974) argues, with an impressive array of supportive evidence, that conditioning in adult human subjects is produced through the operation of higher mental processes, rather than vice versa. Conditioning theory refers to the hypothesis that events in conditioning come about in an automatic unconscious fashion. Cognitive theory refers to the hypothesis that events in conditioning result from the person becoming aware of the conditioned stimulus–unconditioned stimulus (CS–UCS) relationship in classical conditioning (see below) or aware of the reinforcement contingency in operant conditioning.

In any event, in the situation described above, it would be said that the child's behaviour has come to be regulated by 'antecedent stimulus events'; and they call such learning the acquisition of 'stimulus functions'. In other words he has learned to respond appropriately to particular situations. His survival would soon be in jeopardy if he didn't acquire these functions. Over time the person builds up complex habits of behaving and thinking.

Classical (respondent) conditioning

Some responses become functionally attached to stimuli by a process of association (or contiguity). This process, called 'classical conditioning', provides one explanation of how our behaviours come to be elicited by such a wide variety of stimuli. Some of them don't always have an obvious connection with the stimulus situation, nor do they always serve a useful purpose.

A conditioned response is formed when a neutral stimulus comes to evoke a response which is normally elicited by another stimulus.

In a typical experiment from Pavlov's laboratory (Pavlov, 1927) a dog would be given food (unconditioned stimulus) while viewing a stimulus of circular shape. After a few such combinations the presentation of the circle alone in the absence of the food would excite the feeding centres in the dog's brain, it would lick its chops, look into its bowl, and secrete saliva which could be measured. This salivary reaction to a visual stimulus (conditioned stimulus)—something which does not occur naturally—is an example of conditioning and is called a conditioned response (CR).

Conditioning Paradigm

Food (UCS)	— — — — — — — — — —	Salivation (UCR)
Circle	— — — — — — — — — —	?
Circle + Food	— — — — — — — — — —	Salivation
Circle + Food	— — — — — — — — — —	Salivation
Circle + Food	— — — — — — — — — —	Salivation
Circle (CS)	— — — — — — — — — —	Salivation (CR)

Pavlov was able to demonstrate that this new learning or conditioning could, in fact, be 'extinguished' by simply removing altogether the 'natural' stimulus associated with the situation. For example, the conditioned salivary response to seeing a circle would disappear unless the proper and appropriate stimulus (food, in this case) was also given in conjunction with the circle from time to time. In other words, if the dog has been trained to salivate to a circle alone, then repeated presentations of the circle without food will be accompanied by a progressively weaker response (less and less drooling) until eventually the reaction disappears altogether. Obviously the conditioned response needs some kind of intermittent 'reinforcement' (presentation of the food—the unconditioned stimulus) to sustain it over a long period of time.

Human beings also form conditioned responses. The mere thought of some event may produce an involuntary response. You may blush to think of some embarrassing incident.

Higher order conditioning

The effects of environmental events (stimuli) are even more far-reaching than those involved in simple classical conditioning. You have seen how conditioning can result in a neutral stimulus (CS) eliciting the same sort of reaction as an unconditioned stimulus (UCS).

Once stable conditioning has been achieved the CS itself can be used as an 'unconditioned stimulus' in conditioning the response to yet another and new stimulus. In other words, a response which has come to be elicited by one stimulus through conditioning can be transferred to a new stimulus.

Discrimination of stimuli

Let us return to that dog which drools when it sees a circle. It also secretes saliva, although generally a lesser amount to a stimulus such as an ellipse which approximates to a circle. If the dog was given food (reinforcement) only when a perfect circle was present, and if food was withheld when the ellipse was present, then eventually the dog would learn to *discriminate* between the circle and the ellipse, salivating in the presence of the former but not with the latter. This technique of training is called 'differential reinforcement'. Pavlov postulated that the disappearance of the salivary reflex was associated with the development of inhibition in certain nerve elements. This form of nervous inhibition is called 'internal inhibition'.

This internally acquired inhibition contributes to the delicacy and efficiency of the resolving power of the brain—its analytical power. Using these 'conditioning' techniques a dog can be made to make such fine distinctions as differentiating a circle to an ellipse with an 8·9 ratio of semi-axes, 100 metronome beats per minute from 96, and a tone of 500 vibrations per second from a tone of 498 vibrations.

Such a situation leading to normal discrimination learning can also lead to maladaptive learning, in other words, maladaptive psychological reactions.

Conflict

After the dog (mentioned above) had been trained to distinguish a circle from an ellipse the next stage was to make the ellipse resemble more closely the circle, thus making it more and more difficult for the dog to perceive whether or not this was a cue for food to follow.

At a certain critical stage in the proceedings when the dog found it impossible to discriminate between the stimuli being presented, the animal appeared to suffer a kind of breakdown in which it became intensely emotional, biting, struggling in its harness and howling. Thereafter a fear of the total situation seemed to develop and the animal would show neurotic-like behaviour whenever it was brought into the laboratory.

A point of interest was that not all dogs had such emotional reactions; only certain animals with a specific type of temperament seemed predisposed to display such behaviours. Other *conflict* situations have been used to induce neurotic-like behaviours in animals.

Adaptive and maladaptive responses

In everyday life children may be forced to make discriminations—such as where their loyalties lie in divorce situation—which are beyond their powers of resolution. Such conflicts may produce emotional problems.

Maladaptive responses

A large group of maladaptive behaviours is thought to arise from the fact that formerly innocuous and inappropriate stimuli can acquire the capacity to elicit highly intense emotional reactions. This category is referred to as 'inappropriate stimulus control'. The term 'defective stimulus control' is applied when the client appears to have an adequate behavioural repertoire but is unable (or unwilling) to respond to socially appropriate discriminative stimuli. An example would be the person who talks long and loud to his neighbour during a play. An example of inappropriate stimulus control is to be seen in an experiment by Watson and Rayner (1920). In this study Watson's aim was to investigate the acquisition of emotional responses, arguing that they are probably learned by the associative process referred to as conditioning. For this demonstration he chose 11-month-old Albert and set out to create a learned emotional reaction in this child. Having observed Albert's attraction to a tame white rat, he reversed this feeling by arranging for a loud noise to be made (by crashing two metal bars together behind Albert's head) whenever the child reached out for this pet. After just a few trials of this kind, Albert's fear, occasioned by the sudden loud noise, was transferred to the white rat so that every time this animal appeared Little Albert would whimper and crawl away. What is more, these pairings of the pet rat and a loud noise produced not only marked fear of the rat—which persisted—but (by a process of generalization) also other furry objects such as a white rabbit and even some cotton wool. What might have been adaptive learning to a really dangerous animal is here subverted so as to constitute maladaptive (dysfunctional) behaviour. It is essentially an irrational fear.

It has not always been possible to repeat this experiment. The fact is that the environment is not the only influence on learning. From Pavlov's work on, it has been observed that not all learning opportunities are realized or, if they are, there are individual differences in the quality and nature of the learning which is brought about. Experiments have shown that some animals appear to be susceptible to 'emotional' disturbance and others are more phlegmatic. These two types being labelled 'weak' and 'strong nervous system' types respectively. This differentiation has been repeatedly confirmed in the experimental work of other investigators and clearly shows that the *opportunity* to learn is not all that counts. A major influence is the basic temperament of the organism which is doing the learning.

A purely environmental view of human behaviour seems untenable in the light of what we know about potential for learning. The argument here (Seligman and Hager, 1972) is that all organisms appear to show a great readiness to acquire certain associations while other connections will be made only with difficulty if at all. They argue that the animal species have a biological bias for making particular learning connections. Has the evolutionary history of the human prepared him for this kind of learning?

It is not clear to what extent humans are affected by such 'preparedness'. Some connections appear to be 'natural' and occur quite readily; others do not. It has been suggested that a good example of preparedness is to be found in the prevalence of spider and snake phobias in our culture. Yet we are not at risk from these creatures. Could it be that somewhere in our evolutionary history, the human species has acquired a readiness to respond with fear to potential dangers, including spiders and snakes.

Temporary states of the organism can affect learning (see Vila and Beech, 1978). We know that symptoms of distress (e.g. an inability to go out of the house or to meet others socially without feeling anxious) may be preceded by a period of general tension and emotional upset. This kind of disturbance is quite commonly experienced by women who suffer in the few days prior to menstruation from pre-menstrual tension. If this condition is a good parallel to the situation in which abnormal fears can arise, then it should be possible to show a propensity for 'defensive' or 'adverse' learning in pre-menstrual days which is not present at other times in the cycle. This is, in fact, what has been found. The evidence indicates that the state of the organism at the time when some noxious event is present will not only determine the speed at which learning takes place but also any tendency for the learning to be preserved over time. It is as if such states prepare the ground for certain kinds of learning to take place—as if such states put the organism on a defensive footing, ready to react adversely to relatively minor provocation.

The adolescent may be vulnerable, because of the rapid physical changes taking place in his organism and the dramatic changes occurring in his psychosocial status, to the acquisition of emotional problems.

In summary, the explanations of maladaptive behaviour given so far are usually grouped under the formidable heading of 'inappropriate' or 'defective' stimulus control of behaviour. All this means is that faulty learning has taken place; irrelevant behavioural responses have become accidentally associated with consequences that are rewarding, or, as happens most frequently, learning has occurred in aversive (e.g. fear-provoking or conflictual) conditions and rituals and avoidance responses have been acquired because they prevent unpleasant outcomes.

Many of the problems that people have are not due to the individual learning *inappropriate* responses, but are the consequences of the failure to learn the *appropriate* behaviour. It has been noted by research workers that there is an important difference in the nature of many maladaptive behaviours in children and adults. Many behaviour problems in children (especially in the early years) are associated with inadequate skills or behaviour controls. These deficiencies are often connected with the activities of eating, sleeping, elimination, speaking and expressing aggression. In most instances the problem arises because the child had failed to develop an adequate way of responding, for example in bedwetting (enuresis), the inability to read (dyslexia) or certain disturbances of eating (anorexia). The over-aggressive child has failed to learn the socially desirable restraints over his hostile acts.

In adults, most problems seem to be concerned with maladaptive behaviours which arise because inappropriate responses have become attached to stimuli. Problems, such as chronic muscular tensions, intolerable anxiety reactions (and other forms of exaggerated activity of the autonomic nervous system), and symptoms of a wide variety of physical upsets such as chronic fatigue, insomnia, stomach and bowel disturbances may be at least partly understandable as conditioned emotional reactions. So may be many of the obsessions, compulsions and phobias of childhood.

Antecedent Stimulus Control

Involuntary reflexes and responses mediated by the autonomic nervous system (respondents), including those involved in emotional behaviour, are primarily under antecedent control.

Outcome Control

Voluntary responses (operants) mediated by the central nervous system, including speech and skeletal movement, are subject mainly to outcome (consequent) control.

Operants are voluntary responses which are conditioned to stimuli by their consequences. A response may be strengthened by arranging that it is followed by positive reinforcement; it may also be strengthened if it removes a negative reinforcement (e.g. punishment or the threat of it). Because an operant is instrumental in procuring a reward or avoiding a punishment it has also been termed an instrumental response.

Here then is another term (reinforcement) that you need to know for this manual: a *reinforcer* is any event, any stimulus in the environment, which affects the rate of a given operant. For Skinnerians the basic principle of change can be stated quite concisely; the consequences of any item of behaviour will affect the future of that behaviour. If the consequence is rewarding then the behaviour will be strengthened (i.e. rendered more likely to occur again); if it is punishing, then the same response will tend to be weakened. Using this basic proposition, it is argued, far-reaching changes can be made to occur.

Instrumental conditioning

The phenomenon called operant or instrumental conditioning can be illustrated by an experiment which is the basis for much educational and therapeutic work. The principle has been used, in fact, to aid the training of all sorts of humans and animals. Let us take a child experiment which illustrates the principle.

Yvonne Brackbill conducted an experiment on smiling in eight normal infants ranging in age from $3\frac{1}{2}$ to $4\frac{1}{2}$ months.

Brackbill (1958) studied her experimental subjects in two or three sessions a day for several days. After securing a base level of smiling in her infant subjects, i.e. after she had measured the amount of smiling normally shown by the infants, she carried out the conditioning sessions. During these sessions she stood motionless and expressionless 15 inches above the subject. As soon as the baby (S) smiled, the experimenter (E) smiled in return, began to speak softly and picked it up. After holding, jostling, patting, and talking to S for 30 seconds, E put it back in its crib. Brackbill put one group of four subjects on a schedule of regular reinforcement and the other group of four on intermittent reinforcement. Then she stopped the reinforcement altogether to extinguish the smiling response. The extinction interval was conducted in the same manner as the baseline period.

Brackbill measured the frequency of smiling throughout, plotting on a graph the child's acquisition of smiling response. The resultant cumulative curve showed a steep rate of acquisition for the infants subjected to conditioning. By contrast, a cumulative curve plotted for a control subject, who was run, but *without reinforcement*, for 19 conditioning periods or three times longer than the experimental subjects, showed no acquisition. In other words, the smiling response of eight normal infants between $3\frac{1}{2}$ to $4\frac{1}{2}$ months was brought under *control*. Infants 'can be taught' to increase the frequency of their smiling; smiling can be brought to some extent under stimulus control.

To be more technical: stimulus control refers to the extent to which the value of an antecedent stimulus determines the probability of occurrence of a conditioned response; a response that is repeatedly reinforced in the presence of one stimulus but not another will occur more often on future occasions when the stimulus is presented. The stimulus with which reinforcement is to be connected—the discriminative stimulus—is referred to as S^D. The stimulus with which reinforcement is not associated is referred to as S^Δ (ess-delta). When a desired response is more likely to occur in the presence of the S^D than in the presence of the S^Δ it is said that *stimulus control* has been established.

Let's translate this situation (or, rather its opposite) into down-to-earth terms: disruptive classroom behaviour. A child who is frequently out of his seat, flitting from one thing to the other, pestering, and making a noise, usually derives less from his education than those of his classmates who are able to behave more acceptably. He is likely to fall behind with his studies. In addition he may be rejected with his peers as he disturbs their concentration and interferes with their games. In a busy classroom, such a child is likely to be reprimanded frequently by the teacher when he is being difficult. He receives very little attention for being reasonably behaved since this occurs infrequently and he rarely produces work of a high enough standard to merit approval. Relatively mild scoldings from the teacher may be more rewarding for the child (being preferred to no attention at all) so the child is rewarded for being disruptive and ignored for practically everything else. This pattern of reinforcement encourages the very behaviour the teacher deprecates. There is no stimulus control here!

Cognitive learning

Instrumental Conceptualism is the term used by Jerome Bruner to define his own attempt at a consistent description of learning. Bruner's approach is very much in the cognitive tradition; it sees learning not merely as passive behaviour elicited by a stimulus and strengthened or weakened by reinforcement but as an active process in which the learner infers principles and rules and tests them out. By contrast, the description of the behavioural approaches given so far suggests a rather mechanistic conception of learning. Insight, reasoning, explanation, logical argument and other ways in which we come to modify or correct our view of things appear to count for little; the assumption is that the therapist simply can't talk anyone out of being phobic or antisocial; the patient must be taught to do so by a painstaking and carefully conceived programme of training which avoids any appeal to 'mental' phenomena. Yet there is no doubt that cognitive learning does occur since people can be encouraged to behave differently as a result of being told that this or that is the case, or by receiving instructions to do something in a particular way.

In other words learning is not simply something that happens to the individual, as in the operant conditioning model, but something which *he himself* makes happen by the manner in which he handles incoming information and puts it to use. For the therapist the main difference between Bruner's model and that of Skinner is that, while not denying the potential importance of the stimulus and the reinforcement in the S–R paradigm, Bruner considers that operant theorists pay insufficient attention to the element that comes in between, namely the learner's own behaviour (B). This behaviour is not simply something 'elicited' by a stimulus and strengthened or otherwise by the nature of the reinforcement that follows; it is in fact a highly complex activity which involves three major processes, namely (1) the acquisition of information, (2) the manipulation or transformation of this information into a form suitable for dealing with the task in hand, (3) testing and checking the adequacy of this transformation (Bruner, 1975).

A cognitive approach having features which are 'behavioural' in character is Rational Emotive Therapy. For example, the main thrust of the technique (Ellis, 1962) derives from the assumption that faulty thinking is revealed in what people say to themselves; such 'self-talk' influences overt behaviours. Changing the cognitions in therapy can influence the way the client acts and feels.

Observational learning (imitation)

Most complex and novel behaviour (be it adaptive or maladaptive) is acquired by watching the behaviour of exemplary models. These may be people the child observes in his everyday life or they may be symbolic models that he reads about or sees on television. This process is called 'observational learning'; it is considered by social learning theorists to be the cornerstone of learning for socialization, and a significant basis for therapeutic interventions.

A basic distinction is made between the acquisition and the performance of the imitative response. Acquisition is thought to result mainly from the contiguity of sensory events. When the observer performs no overt imitative response at the time of observing the model, he can acquire the behaviour only in cognitive representational form. During the *acquisition* phase the child observes a model and the stimuli are coded into images or words which are stored in memory; they now function as mediators for subsequent retrieval and reproduction of the observed behaviours. The *performance* of observed acts is thought to be influenced by the observed consequences of responses, that is to say, operant conditioning (see Bandura, 1977).

Observational learning involves two representational systems—an imaginal one and a verbal one. After modelling stimuli have been coded into images or words for memory representation, they function as mediators for response retrieval and reproduction. Imagery formation is assumed to occur through a process of sensory conditioning ... modelling stimuli elicit in observers perceptual responses that become sequentially associated and centrally integrated on the basis of temporal contiguity of stimulation.

Summary. The charge often levelled at the behavioural approach is that it ignores the conceptual thinking that is so peculiarly and significantly human. This is a misunderstanding of the current situation in behaviour modification. It is apparent that the kind of learning process required to effect change depends upon what aspects of a client's behaviour we are trying to modify. Furthermore, it is argued that mental events (cognitions, thoughts) are also behaviours and amenable to the same laws and, to an extent, to similar training methods.

Most problem situations can be analysed (and a therapeutic intervention planned) in terms of antecedent events, consequent events, organismic and self variables.

(a) *Antecedent events and classical conditioning.* The focus of intervention in the classical or Pavlovian model is the relationship between certain *antecedent conditions* and the problem behaviour they elicit. Current antecedent events can be altered for therapeutic purposes by removing stimulus events that *elicit* deviant behaviours, while encouraging those that are associated with prosocial activities. Another approach is to remove stimulus events that reinforce problematic behaviour while strengthening those that reinforce acceptable actions. The clinical practitioner has an essentially simple and empirical definition of stimulus control: it exists to the extent that the presence or absence of a stimulus controls the probability of a response.

(b) *Consequent events and operant conditioning.* This is the process by which the strength or probability of repetition of responses increases or decreases according to their consequences. Actions followed by pleasant consequences tend to be repeated frequently, while those followed by punishing consequences tend to reduce in strength or frequency. The focus of intervention in the operant conditioning model, therefore, is the relationship between the problem behaviour and its consequences for the child.

There are three basic outcome control procedures based on operant principles:

(1) *reinforcement* procedures which increase the future probability of a desirable response they follow;
(2) *punishment* procedures which decrease the future likelihood of an unacceptable response they follow;
(3) *extinction* procedures which decrease the probability of undesirable responses to which they are applied.

Use of these essentially simple principles, if consistent and systematic, can produce marked changes in a child's behaviour, even when apparently intractible and deviant.

(c) *Organismic factors.* These are discussed on p. 58.

(d) *Self variables.* These, too, are touched upon on p. 146.

For excellent guides to the literature on general principles see Kazdin (1980), Rimm and Masters (1979), Wilson and O'Leary (1980). Hintzman (1978) provides a useful text on learning theory.

APPENDIX IV

Handout for Parents attending the Child Treatment Research Unit

Ways to help you change your child's behaviour

You have decided that you need help in coping with your child whose behaviour you find a problem. This leaflet I hope will give you information which you can use to help you understand your child's behaviour yourself.

The nature of children's emotional and behaviour problems

Children are usually a source of great pleasure and endless wonder to their parents. These joys are sometimes tempered by the concern and heavy sense of responsibility that also accompany parenthood; the pleasure may be transformed into anxiety and the wonder into puzzlement when the child begins to behave in a peculiar or erratic manner. The youngster who has *not*, at some stage of his development, been the cause of quite serious worry to his mother and father is unique.

Most parents and teachers refuse to be deterred by the frustrations caused by these problems. But they might find life a lot easier if more were generally known about the nature of problem behaviours in childhood, why and how these come about and what can be done about them. We do not, unfortunately, have anything like complete answers to these vital questions; but an endeavour will be made to provide some of the available information during your attendance at the Unit.

Emotional upsets and behaviour disturbances can best be thought of as problems which arise—as by-products—from coping with the difficulties of life. The point about these emotions and behaviours is that they have unfavourable consequences for the child. They are ineffectual, inappropriate, or in some other way self-defeating.

Psychologists are aware that there are 'crises' associated with different periods of development. This highlights yet another complication in our quest for the 'problem child'—so mercurial are changes of behaviour during the rapid growth of childhood, that it is difficult to pinpoint the beginnings of serious troubles. What is normal at one age may not be so at another. The girl who displays temper tantrums at two is not a problem child; the girl who frequently does so at 11 may well be.

Children vary greatly in temperament; some are very extraverted and outgoing, and what is normal social behaviour for them may differ widely from what is normal for children who by nature are introverted and inward-looking. Other youngsters are highly individualistic, and rebel against some of the standards that are imposed upon them. And we mustn't forget that they *may* do this with justification; not all our standards and demands are reasonable ones. Nevertheless, there are some personality traits, such as aggressiveness and rudeness, which can be very irritating.

Problem behaviour tends to be very annoying behaviour, but this does not necessarily mean that all behaviours which annoy and create problems for parents are to be equated with maladjustment. Parents vary in what they can tolerate in the way of 'bad' behaviour.

The term 'problem child' is rather unfortunate, as it seems to suggest that the child, as a person and in a general sense, is abnormal. In fact, the problem child is not all 'problem'! He is simply a child with some handicapping problems.

Ultimately, the professional judgement of a child's mental well-being must be made in individual terms, taking into account the child's unique personality, his particular circumstances and all the opportunities, disappointments and stresses associated with them. It is the task of the clinician to ascertain where a child stands on the developmental scale, whether his progress and status—mental and physical—are appropriate to his age, retarded or advanced. In the light of this background information, the psychologist or psychiatrist has to decide whether or not the child requires help. He may do this by applying *several* criteria to the facts he has gleaned about the child and his circumstances. This involves asking a series of questions.:

(1) Is the child's behaviour appropriate to his age, intelligence and social situation?
(2) Is the environment making reasonable *demands* of the child?
(3) Is the environment satisfying the crucial *needs* of the child—that is to say, the needs that are vital at his particular stage of development?

Finally, the clinician needs to ask the question:

(4) What are the consequences—favourable or unfavourable—of this child's pattern of traits and ways of behaving? Does his style of life in general, or do his conflicts and tensions in particular, prevent him from leading a happy life in which he is able to grow, enjoy social relationships, and work and play effectively?

More specifically he will ask whether the child's adjustments are such as to make him unhappy and depressed, excessively anxious, morbidly guilty, inflexible in the face of failure, or unable to establish affectionate, loving and lasting relationships. These are but a few of the evaluative criteria which are used by clinicians. All must be applied with caution; *no one of them taken alone* can be used with confidence.

(This account may have to be explained, elaborated or summarized for some parents. It may be too abstract for others and entirely dispensed with, in favour of a simple and different introduction.)

How does a child develop problems?

Psychologists define learning as *any enduring change in behaviour which results from experience.* Memorizing a formula, recognizing a face and reading music are all examples of learning.

The vast majority of the child's behaviours are learned, and this includes his problem behaviours.

Suppose a child cries when he is made to go to bed, and his mother, who cannot bear to see his tears, gives in and lets him stay up late. After several similar scenes with the same outcome—mum giving in—she finally appreciates that she has been encouraging or teaching an undesirable habit. The child has also discovered, of course, that crying is instrumental in obtaining has reward—staying up late. The mother decides to stand firm and prove herself impervious to his tears. So she makes the child go upstairs to bed no matter how long or heartrendingly he cries. How long will it take to extinguish his crying habit? This will depend in large part on how often the mother has previously let him have his own way. We can see from this example how 'bad habits' may be learned (reinforced).

Of course, we can also reinforce 'good habits'; when they are present, with social approval and encouragement. And by reinforcement-training, we can instil those habits that are still absent from the child's repertoire of behaviour.

A clinical illustration of the *positive reinforcement of problem behaviour* is provided by the case of a four-year-old boy, Peter S. Peter had been brought to a university clinic because he was extremely difficult to manage. His mother told the staff that she was helpless in dealing with his frequent tantrums and disobedience. Peter often kicked objects or other people, removed or tore his clothing, called people rude names, annoyed his younger sister, made a variety of threats, hit himself and became very angry at the slightest frustration. He demanded attention almost constantly, and seldom cooperated with his mother. He was found, on examination, to be overactive.

After observing the mother and child in the home, the psychologists noted that many of Peter's undesirable behaviours appeared to be maintained by *attention* from his mother. When the boy behaved objectionably, she would often try to explain why he should not act in such a way; or she would try to interest him in some new activity by offering toys or food. Peter was occasionally punished by having a misused toy or other object taken away, but he was often able to persuade his mother to return the item almost immediately. He was also punished by being placed on a high chair and forced to remain there for short periods. However, such disciplinary measures were usually followed by tantrums which were quite effective in maintaining the mother's attention.

What the clinicians are looking for in this type of problem is the relationship between the individual's own activity and the rewarding results it produces; those behaviours (i.e. Peter's attention-seeking disruptive behaviour) that lead to satisfying consequences tend to be repeated under similar circumstances.

This is only one example, and a rather simple one at that. Imagine though that a child (like a learner driver) wore an L plate. How much more understanding and calm we would remain about the difficulties he's having with life!

Many of the problems of childhood are not due to the child learning *inappropriate* responses, but are the consequence of the child's *failure* to learn the *appropriate* behaviour. Here is an important difference in the nature of behaviour disturbances in children and adults. Many behaviour problems in children (especially in the early years) are associated with inadequate skills of behaviour control. These deficiencies are often connected with the activities of eating, sleeping, elimination, speaking and expressing aggression. In most instances the problem arises because the child has failed to develop an adequate way of responding—for example, in controlling anger (tantrums), in learning to control wetting (enuresis), and in learning to articulate speech smoothly (stammering).

The over-aggressive child has failed to learn the socially desirable restraints over his hostile acts.

Learning theory

The basic idea which you need to know is that your child will tend to repeat any behaviours which bring him some beneficial outcome or 'pay-off' and tend to avoid those behaviours that fail to produce rewards. In other words, your child will only continue to perform those behaviours which are worthwhile and rewarding to him, and he will stop performing behaviours which do not give him any rewards.

You have used this idea to teach your child many things without knowing it. Some of the things you have taught him will be the things you want him to do, but unfortunately it is also easy to teach a child to do things you do not want him to do. Of course you teach your child to do socially desirable things in many different ways: you set an example, you give explanations, you instruct, praise and encourage. All these methods are used in behaviour therapy in order to provide the youngster with alternative (and happier) ways of solving his problems and difficulties. This is but one way of looking at treatment. It may be the parents, as much as the child, who need some assistance in re-thinking their management of the child. There is no more reason to be embarrassed about this than going to the doctor for advice about his health and physical well-being.

Behaviour therapy

Most parents attempt to change and control the behaviour of their children. They do it by reasoning and instruction; they also use punishments and rewards, or the threat of them, although of course the punishments and rewards may be symbolic rather than actual. Only the most pessimistic of parents would deny that it is possible to modify behaviour considerably in such ways.

Psychologists have made it their business to study, among other things, the processes of learning, of social influence and attitude formation; and it would be only the most sceptical who would deny that it is possible to modify, not only 'normal' (acceptable, prosocial) behaviour and attitudes but also 'abnormal' (unacceptable, antisocial) phenomena. The methods they have devised will be familiar to you; in any event they will be described to you in due course. But here is another down-to-earth illustration.

Many young children go through 'phases' which are both annoying or upsetting to their parents. An example of this would be the 'terrible two's' and the temper tantrums frequently associated with toddlerhood. In nearly all cases such episodes are transitory. In a few cases they persist much longer, or with greater severity, and perhaps begin to disturb the family's equanimity. Providing medical causes are excluded, the therapist may attempt to modify the behaviour by applying (in this case) appropriate operant methods.* Very often it is found that the child has an audience, i.e. attracts a great deal of attention, when he throws a tantrum, usually because it is distressing to his parents. On the other hand, when he is occupied and behaving well, his parents, grateful for some peace and

*Operant methods are training procedures using rewards (reinforcers) and punishments.

quiet, turn their attention to other things. In effect they are ignoring good behaviour. You might say that the child is being rewarded for having a tantrum but is punished (as being ignored can seem punitive) for being well-behaved. Small wonder that bad behaviour becomes a feature of the child's life-style, and good behaviour becomes a rarity. Tantrums may be modified simply by reversing reward and punishment; his parents leave him to his own devices or send him to his room briefly when he has a tantrum, but take great care to pay attention to him (e.g. play with him and talk to him) when he is being good. Applied systematically such a straightforward alteration of reinforcements can have a gratifyingly speedy and beneficial outcome.

APPENDIX V

An Explanation of Treatment Principles for Enuresis*

A very high level of skill is needed before the bladder can be properly controlled during sleep. Some children find this is a difficult skill to learn, just as some children find it difficult to learn to swim or to ride a bicycle. It is perhaps not surprising that some children do not learn bladder control as infants, or easily lose their ability to control the bladder at night—we should perhaps be more surprised that so many do manage to learn such a complicated skill.

Some children who wet the bed have other problems, while others have few difficulties apart from their bedwetting. In either case it is usually possible to help the child to overcome the bedwetting problem.

It is likely that unpleasant experiences make the learning of bladder control more difficult, and often a child who has already become dry may begin to wet again after some disturbing event. Whether a child has been wet all his life, or has more recently lost control over his bladder, he needs special help in the difficult task of learning bladder control. The child will usually be examined first by a doctor in case there is a physical cause for his bedwetting, although this is rare. A sample of his urine will also be taken for examination.

When a child wets the bed, it seems that his brain is not properly aware of the amount of urine in his bladder, allowing it to empty automatically while he is asleep. The child cannot help this.

A device known as the 'enuresis alarm' has been developed to help children to overcome the problem of bedwetting. Basically, the alarm is made up of a pair of detector mats on the bed, connected to a buzzer next to the child's bed. As soon as the child begins to wet in his sleep, the buzzer sounds. The sound of the buzzer normally has two effects. First, the muscles that have relaxed to allow urine to pass contract once more, stopping the stream of urine that has already started (it may have been noticed that loud noises will often interrupt the stream of urine). Secondly, the sound of the buzzer awakes the child.

The use of the alarm produces these two actions—stopping the stream and waking—whenever the child's bladder begins to empty automatically during sleep. Gradually the child's brain learns to connect these two actions with the feeling of a full bladder. After a time, the brain becomes more aware of the amount of urine in the child's bladder—and itself begins to take the two actions of contracting the muscles and waking the child when

*Based on Morgan (1975).

the bladder is full. As the brain's control over the bladder becomes stronger, one can see how the actions learned from the alarm are used; the wet patches become smaller as the child's muscles are contracted more quickly, and when the bladder is really full he begins to awaken on his own before passing any urine at all. Eventually, the child is able to sleep without wetting, waking up on his own if he needs to use the toilet at night.

References

Albino, R. (1980). *Psychotherapy: Is it more than Persuasion and Teaching?* Paper presented at the South African Society of Clinical Psychologists Conference—Durban, July 1980 (22 pages).

Ayllon, T. and Azrin, N. H. (1968). *The Token Economy: A Motivational System for Therapy and Rehabilitation*. Appleton-Century-Crofts, New York.

Baker, B. L. (1969). Symptom Treatment and Symptom Substitution in Enuresis. *Journal of Abnormal Psychology*, **74**, 1, 42–49.

Bandura, A. (1969). *Principles of Behaviour Modification*. Holt, Rinehart and Winston, New York.

Bandura, A. (1973). *Aggression: A Social Learning Analysis*. Prentice-Hall, Englewood Cliffs, N. J.

Bandura, A. (1977). *Social Learning Theory*. Prentice-Hall, Englewood Cliffs, N. J.

Bandura, A. (1977). Self-efficacy: Toward a unifying theory of behavioural change? *Psychological Review*, **84**, 191–215.

Beck, A. T., Rush, A. J., Shaw, B. F. and Emery, G. (1979). *Cognitive Therapy of Depression*. John Wiley, London.

Becker, W. (1971). *Parents are Teachers: A Child Management Program*. Research Press, Champaign, Illinois.

Bell, R. Q. (1971). Stimulus Control of Parent or Caretaker Behavior by Offspring. *Developmental Psychology*, **4**, 63–72.

Blackham, G. J. and Silberman, A. (1975). *Modification of Child and Adolescent Behaviour*. Wadsworth, Belmont, California.

Bornstein, M. R., Bellack, A. S. and Hersen, M. (1977). Social Skills Training for Unassertive Children: A Multiple Baseline Analysis. *Journal of Applied Behaviour Analysis*, **10**, 183–195.

Bornstein, P. H. and Quevillon, R. P. (1976). The Effects of a Self-Instructional Package on Overactive Preschool Boys. *Journal of Applied Behaviour Analysis*, **9**, 179–188.

Bowers, K. S. (1973). Situationism in Psychology: An Analysis and a Critique. *Psychological Review*, **80**, 307–336.

Brackbill, Y. (1958). Extinction of the Smiling Response in Infants as a Function of Reinforcement. *Child Development*, **29**, 115–124.

Brewer, W. F. (1974). There is no Convincing Evidence for Operant or Classical Conditioning in Adult Humans. *In* W. B. Wilken and D. S. Palermo (Eds.), *Cognition and the Symbolic Processes*. Lawrence Erlbaum Associates, Hillsdale, N. J.

Bromley, D. G. (1977). *Personality Description in Ordinary Language*. John Wiley, Chichester.

Bruner, J. S. (1975). *Beyond the Information Given*. Allen and Unwin, London.

Cameron, K. (1975). Diagnostic Categories in Child Psychiatry. *British Journal of Medical Psychology*, **28**, 67–71.

Carlson, C. S., Arnold, C. R., Becker, W. C. and Madsen, C. H. (1968). The Elimination of Tantrum Behaviour of a Child in an Elementary Classroom. *Behaviour Research and Therapy*, **6**, 117–119.

Carter, quoted in Gambrill (1977).

Cautela, J. R. (1965). Desensitization and Insight. *Behaviour Research and Therapy*, **3**, 59–64.

Chandler, M. (1973). Egocentrism and Antisocial Behaviour: The assessment and training of social perspective-taking skills. *Developmental Psychology*, **9**, 326–332.

Clarke, R. G. V. (1977). Psychology and Crime. *Bulletin of the British Psychological Society*, **30**, 280–283.

Cobb, J. A. and Ray, R. S. (1970) *Manual for Coding Discrete Behaviour in the School Setting.* Oregon Research Institute Learning Project Public.

Combs, M. L. and Slaby, D. A. (1978). Social Skills Training with Children. *In* B. Lahey and A. Kazdin (Eds.), *Advances in Child Clinical Psychology*, Vol. 1, Plenum, New York.

Coopersmith, S. (1967). *The Antecedents of Self-Esteem.* W. H. Freeman, London.

Cotler, S. B. and Guerra, J. J. (1976). *Assertion Training: A Humanistic-Behavioural Guide to Self Dignity.* Research Press, Champaign, Illinois.

Danziger, K. (1971). *Socialization.* Penguin Books, Harmondsworth.

Dean, G., Gannoway, K., Jagger, D., Jehu, D., Morgan, R. T. T., and Turner, R. K. (1976). *Teaching Self Care Skills to the Mentally Handicapped in Children's Homes.* CTRU Paper No. 6; School of Social Work, Leicester University.

De Risi, W. J. and Butz, G. (1975). *Writing Behavioural Contracts.* Research Press, Champaign, Illinois.

Drabman, R. J. and Tucker, R. D. (1974). Why Classroom Token Economies fail. *Journal of School Psychology*, **12**, **3**, 178–188.

Durlak, J. A. (1979). Comparative Effectiveness of Paraprofessional and Professional Helpers. *Psychological Bulletin*, **86**, (1) 80–92.

D'Zurilla, T. J. and Goldfried, M. R. (1971). Problem Solving and Behaviour Modification. *Journal of Abnormal Psychology*, **78**, 107–126.

Ellis, A. (1962). *Reason and Emotion in Psychotherapy.* Lyle Stuart, New York.

Erikson, E. (1965). *Childhood and Society.* (Rev. Ed.). Penguin Books, Harmondsworth.

Erwin, E. (1979). *Behaviour Therapy: Scientific, Philosophical and Moral Foundations.* Cambridge University Press, Cambridge.

Estes, W. K. (1971). Reward in Human Learning: Theoretical Issues and Strategic Choice Points. *In* R. Glaser (Ed.), *The Nature of Reinforcement.* Academic Press, New York and London.

Fischer, J. (1978). *Effective Casework Practice: An Eclectic Approach.* McGraw-Hill, New York.

Flowers, J. V. and Booraem, C. D. (1980). Simulation and Role-playing. *In* F. H. Kanfer and A. P. Goldstein, *Helping People Change* (2nd Ed.). Pergamon, Oxford.

Foster, S. L. and Ritchey, W. L. (1979). Issues in the Assessment of Social Competence in Children. *Journal of Applied Behaviour Analysis*, **12**, 625–638.

Friedman, E. (1980). *An Investigation into the Effects of Praise, Tangible Reinforcement and a Spelling Programme on the Spelling Performance and Non-Attending Behaviour of a First Form Remedial Class in an Upper School.* Unpublished Ph.D. Thesis. School of Education, University of Leeds. March, 1980.

Furness, P. (1976). *Role Play in the Elementary School: A Handbook for Teachers.* Hart Publishing Co., New York.

Gambrill, E. D. (1977). *Behaviour Modification: A Handbook of Assessment, Intervention and Evaluation.* Jossey-Bass, London.

Gardner, J. M. (1976). Training Parents as Behaviour Modifiers. *In* S. Yen and R. McIntire (Eds.), *Teaching Behaviour Modification.* Behaviordelia, Kalamazoo, Michigan.

Gelfand, D. M. and Hartman, D. P. (1975). *Child Behaviour: Analysis and Therapy.* Pergamon Press, Oxford.

Giffin, M. and Hudson, A. (1978). *Parents as Therapists: The Behavioural Approach.* P.I.T. Press, Victoria, Australia.

Glass, G. V., Willson, V. L. and Gottman, J. M. (1973). *Design and Analysis of Time-Series Experiments.* Laboratory of Educational Research Press; Boulder, Colorado.

Goldfried, M. R. (1971). Systematic Desensitization as Training in Self-centrol. *Journal of Consulting and Clinical Psychology*, **37**, 228–234.

Goldfried, M. R. and Davison, G. C. (1976). *Clinical Behaviour Therapy.* Holt, Rinehart and Winston, London.

Goldstein, A. P. (1980). Relationship-Enhancement Methods. *In* F. H. Kanfer and A. P. Goldstein

(Eds.), *Helping People Change* (2nd Ed.). Pergamon Press, Oxford.

Goldstein, A. P., Sherman, M., Gershaw, N. J., Sprafkin, R. P. and Glick, B. (1978). Training Aggressive Adolescents in Pro-social Behaviour. *Journal of Youth and Adolescence*, **7**, 73–92.

Gordon, S. B. (1975). Multiple Assessment of Behaviour Modification with Families. *Consulting and Clinical Psychology*, **43**, 6, 917.

Gottman, J. M. and Leiblum, S. R. (1974). *How to Do Psychotherapy and How to Evaluate it: A Manual for Beginners*. Holt, Rinehart and Winston, New York.

Gottman, J. M., McFall, R. M. and Barnett, J. T. (1969). Design and Analysis of Research Using Time Series. *Psychological Bulletin*, **72**, No. 4, 299–306.

Graziano, A. M., De Giovanni, I. S. and Garcia, K. A. (1979). Behavioural Treatment of Children's Fears: A Review. *Psychological Bulletin*, **86**, (4) 804–830.

Greenwald, A. G. (1976). Within-subjects Designs: to use or not to use? *Psychological Bulletin*, **83**, 2, 314–320.

Guthrie, E. R. (1935). *The Psychology of Learning*. Harper, New York.

Gurman, A. B. and Razin, A. M. (1977). *Effective Psychotherapy: A Handbook of Research*. Pergamon Press, Oxford.

Hall, R. V. and Fox, R. G. (1977). Changing-criterion Designs: An alternative applied analysis procedure. In B. C. Etzel, J. M. LeBlanc and D. M. Baer (Eds.), *New Developments in Behavioural Research Theory, Methods and Applications*. Lawrence Erlbaum Associates Inc, Hillsdale, N. J.

Hartmann, D. P. and Atkinson, C. (1973). Having your Cake and Eating it too: A note on some apparent contradictions between therapeutic achievements and design requirements in $N = 1$ studies. *Behaviour Therapy*, **4**, 589–591.

Hatzenbuehler, L. C. and Schroeder, R. (1978). Desensitization Procedures in the Treatment of Childhood Disorders. *Psychological Bulletin*, **85**, (No. 4), 831–844.

Haynes, S. N. (1978). *Principles of Behavioural Assessment*. Gardner Press, New York.

Herbert, M. (1974). *Emotional Problems of Development in Children*. Academic Press, London and New York.

Herbert, M. (1975). *Problems of Childhood*. Pan Books, London.

Herbert, M. (1978). *Conduct Disorders of Childhood and Adolescence: A Behavioural Approach to Assessment and Treatment*. John Wiley, Chichester.

Herbert, M. (1980). Socialization for Problem Resistance. *In* P. Feldman and J. Orford (Eds.), *The Social Psychology of Psychological Problems*. John Wiley, Chichester.

Herbert, M. and Iwaniec, D. (1980). Behavioural Casework and Failure to Thrive. *Journal of Australian Child and Family Welfare*, **5**, (1, 2), 29–31.

Herbert, M. and O'Driscoll, B. (1978). Behavioural Casework—A Social Work Method for Family Settings. *Journal of Australian Child and Family Welfare*, **3**, No. 2, 14–25.

Herbert, M., Holmes, A., Jehu, D., Morgan, R. and Turner, K. (1981). Behavioural Interventions in the Natural Environment. *Behaviour Research and Therapy Monographs*, Pergamon Press, Oxford (in press).

Hintzman, D. L. (1958). *The Psychology of Learning and Memory*. San Francisco, W. H. Freeman.

Hobbs, N. (1962). Sources of Gain in Psychotherapy. *American Psychologist*, **17**, 741–747.

Jacobson, E. (1938). *Progressive Relaxation*. University of Chicago Press, Chicago.

Jackson, D., Della-Piana, G. and Sloan, H. (1973). *How to Establish a Behaviour Observation System: A Self-Instruction Programme*.

Jehu, D. (1975). *A Behavioural Approach in the Treatment of Childhood Aggression*. Unpublished Child Treatment Research Unit paper, School of Social Work, Leicester University.

Jehu, D., Hardiker, P., Yelloly, M. and Shaw, M. (1972). *Behaviour Modification in Social Work*. John Wiley, Chichester.

Johnson, D. W. (1980). Attitude Modification Methods. *In* F. H. Kanfer and A. P. Goldstein (Eds.), *Helping People Change*. (2nd Ed.), pp. 58–96. Pergamon Press, Oxford.

Johnson, S. M. (1970). Self Reinforcement versus External Reinforcement in Behaviour Modification with Children. *Developmental Psychology*, **3**, 147–148.

Jones, R. T. and Kazdin, A. E. (1975). Programming Response Maintenance After Withdrawing Token Reinforcement. *Behavior Therapy* **6**, 153–164.

Jones, R. R., Weinrott, M. R. and Vaught, R. S. (1975). *Visual vs. Statistical Inference in Operant Research*. Paper presented at the A. P. A. Convention, 'Symposium on the Use of Statistics in $N = 1$ Research'. Alan E. Kazdin, Chairman, Chicago, Illinois, Sept. 1975.

Karoly, P. (1977). Behavioural Self-Management in Children: Concepts, Methods, Issues and Directions. *In* M. Hersen, R. M. Eisler and P. M. Miller (Eds.), *Progress in Behaviour Modification*, pp. 197–213. Academic Press, New York and London.

Kazdin, A. E. (1980). *Behaviour Modification in Applied Settings* (Rev. Ed.). The Dorsey Press, Homewood, Ill.

Kazdin, A. E. and Bootzin, R. R. (1972). The Token Economy: An Evaluation Review. *Journal of Applied Behaviour Analysis* **5**, 343–372.

Kelly, G. A. (1955). *The Psychology of Personal Constructs*. Norton, New York.

Kendall, P. C. (1981). Cognitive-Behavioural Interventions with Children. *In* B. Lahey and A. E. Kazdin (Eds.), *Advances in Child Clinical Psychology*, Vol. 4, Plenum Press, New York.

Kent, R. N. and Foster, S. L. (1977). Direct Observational Procedures: Methodological Issues in Naturalistic Settings. *In* A. R. Cimenero, K. S. Calhoun and H. E. Adams (Eds.) *Handbook of Behavioural Assessment*, pp. 279–328. John Wiley, London.

Kifer, R. E., Lewis, M. A., Green, D. R. and Phillips, E. L. (1974). Training Predelinquent Youths and Their Parents to Negotiate Conflict Situations. 7, 357–364.

Kubany, E., Bloch, L. and Sloggett, B. (1971). The Good Behavior Clock: Reinforcement–Timeout Procedure for Reducing Disruptive Classroom Behavior. *Journal of Behaviour Therapy and Experimental Psychiatry*, **2**, 173–174.

Kuypers, D. S., Becker, W. C. and O'Leary, K. D. (1968). How to Make a Token System Fail. *Exceptional Children*, **35**, 101–109.

Lange, A. J. and Jakubowski, P. (1976). *Responsible Assertive Behaviour: Cognitive/Behavioural Procedures for Trainers*. Research Press, Champaign, Illinois.

Lee, S. G. M. and Herbert, M. (Eds.) (1970). *Freud and Psychology*. Penguin Books, Harmondsworth.

Lesoff, R. (1977). What to Say When. *Clinical Social Work Journal*, **5**, No. 1.

Lovitt, T. C. and Curtiss, K. (1969). Academic Response Rate as a Function of Teacher and Self-imposed Contingencies. *Journal of Applied Behavior Analysis*, **2**, 49–53.

Macfarlane. J. W., Allen, L. and Honzik, M. (1954). *A Developmental Study of the Behaviour Problems of Normal Children*. University of California Press, Berkeley.

Mahoney, D. M., Harper, T. M., Braukmann, C. J. and Fixsen, D. L. (1978). The Teaching of Conversation-Related Skills to Predelinquent Girls by Teaching Parents and Juvenile Peers. *Journal of Applied Behaviour Analysis*.

Mahoney, M. J. (1974). *Cognition and Behaviour Modification*. Ballinger, Cambridge, Mass.

Mahoney, M. J. (1977). Personal Science: A Cognitive Learning Therapy. *In* A. Ellis and R. Grieger (Eds.), *Handbook of Rational Psychotherapy*. Springer, New York.

Mahoney, M. J. and Arnkoff, D. B. (1978). Cognitive and Self-control Therapies. *In* S. L. Garfield and A. E. Bergin (Eds.), *Handbook of Psychotherapy and Behaviour Change* (2nd. Ed.), pp. 689–722. John Wiley, Chichester.

McAuley, R. and McAuley, P. (1980). The Effectiveness of Behaviour Modification with Families. *British Journal of Social Work* **10**, 43–54.

McCandless, B. (1969). *Children: Behaviour and Development* (2nd. Ed.). Holt, Rinehart and Winston, London.

McIntyre, R. W., Jensen, J. and Davis, G. (1968). *Control of Disruptive Behaviour with a Token Economy*. Paper presented to Eastern Psychological Assoc., Philadelphia.

McLaughlin, T. and Malaby, J. (1972). Reducing and Measuring Inappropriate Verbalizations in a Token Classroom. *Journal of Applied Behaviour and Analysis*, **5**, 329–333.

McWhirter, E. P. (1980). The Social Work Context. *In* J. Radford and D. Rose (Eds.), *The Teaching of Psychology*, pp. 271–286. John Wiley, Chichester.

Meacham, M. L. and Wiesen, A. E. (1969). *Changing Classroom Behaviour: A Manual for Precision Teaching*. International Textbook Co., Scranton, Pennsylvania.

Meichenbaum, D. H. (1977). *Cognitive Behaviour Modification: An Integrative Approach*. Plenum, New York.

Meichenbaum, D. H. and Goodman, J. (1971). Training Impulsive Children to talk to Themselves: A Means for Developing Self-Control. *Journal of Abnormal Psychology*, **77**, 115–126.

Melamed, B. G. and Siegel, L. J. (1975). Reduction of Anxiety in Children Facing Surgery by Modelling. *Journal of Consulting and Clinical Psychology*, **43**, 511–521.

Miller, N. B. and Cantwell, D. P. (1976). Siblings as therapists: a behavioural approach. *American Journal of Psychiatry*, **133**, 4, 447.

Mischel, W. (1968). *Personality and Assessment*. John Wiley, New York.

Morgan, R. T. T. (1975a). *Behaviour Therapy Techniques*. Unpublished CTRU Paper, School of Social Work, Leicester University.

Morgan, R. T. T. (1975b). *Enuresis and the Enuresis Alarm*. Unpublished CTR Unit Manual, School of Social Work, Leicester University.

Murray, H. A. (1938). *Explorations in Personality*. Oxford University Press, New York.

Notcutt, B. (1953). *The Psychology of Personality*. Philosophical Library, New York.

O'Leary, K. D. and Drabman, R. S. (1971). Token Reinforcement Programme in the Classroom: A Review. *Psychological Bulletin*, **75**, 379–398.

O'Leary, K. D. and O'Leary, S. G. (1972). *Classroom Management: The Successful Use of Behaviour Modification*. Pergamon Press, Oxford (Rev. Ed., 1977).

O'Leary, S. G. and Dubey, D. R. (1979). Applications of self-control procedures by children. A Review. *Journal of Applied Behaviour Analysis*, **12**, 449–465.

Patterson, G. R. and Reid, J. B. (1970). Reciprocity and Coercion: Two Facets of Social Systems. *In* C. Neuringer and J. Michael (Eds.), *Behaviour Modification in Clinical Psychology*, pp. 133–177. Appleton Century Crofts, New York.

Patterson, G. R., Ray, R. S., Shaw, D. A. and Cobb, J. A. (1969). *Manual for Coding Family Interactions*, Sixth Revision. Available from ASIS National Auxiliary Publications Service, in care of CCM Information Service Inc., 909 Third Avenue, N. Y. 10022. Document 01234.

Patterson, G. R., Reid, J. B., Jones, J. J. and Conger, R. E. (1975). *A Social Learning Approach to Family Intervention: Vol. 1. Families with Aggressive Children*. Castalix Publishing Col, Eugene.

Pavlov, I. P. (1927). *Conditioned Reflexes*. (Transl. G. V. Anrep). Clarendon Press, Oxford.

Piaget, J. (1932). *The Moral Judgement of the Child*. Harcourt Brace, New York.

Ray, R. S., Shaw, D. A. and Cobb, J. A. (1970). The Workbox: An Innovation in Teaching Attentional Behavior. *The School Counselor*, **18**, 15–35.

Rimm, D. C. and Masters, J. C. (1979). *Behaviour Therapy: Techniques and Empirical Findings* (2nd Ed.). Academic Press, New York and London.

Robins, L. N. (1966). *Deviant Children Grow Up*. Williams and Wilkins, Baltimore.

Rose, S. D. (1972). *Treating Children in Groups: A Behavioural Approach*. Jossey-Bass, San Francisco.

Rotter, J. B. (1966). Generalized expectancies for internal versus external control of reinforcement. *Psychological Monographs*, **80**, 1, Whole No. 609.

Rutter, M., Tizard, J. and Whitmore, K. (Eds.) (1970). *Education, Health and Behaviour*. Longmans Green, London.

Rutter, M., Maughan, B., Mortimore, P. and Ouston, J. (1979). *Fifteen Thousand Hours: Secondary Schools and their Effects on Children*. Open Books, London.

Ryall, R. (1974). Delinquency: The Problem for Treatment. *Social Work Today*, **15**, No. 4, 98–104.

Sadler, O. W. and Seyden, T. (1976). Groups for Parents: A guide for Teaching Self Management to Parents. Special Monograph Supplement: *Journal of Community Psychology*. Clinical Psychology Publishing Co. Inc. (4 Conant Square, Brandon, VT05733).

Sandler, J. (1980). Aversion Methods. *In* F. H. Kanfer and A. P. Goldstein (Eds.), *Helping People Change* (2nd Ed.), pp. 294–333. Pergamon, Oxford.

Schaffer, R. (1977). *Mothering*. Penguin Books, Harmondsworth.

Schneider, M. (1974). *Turtle Technique in the Classroom*. Teaching Exceptional Children, Fall 22–24.

Schneider, M. and Robin, A. (1975). *A Turtle Manual.* State University of New York at Stony Brook.

Schneider, M. and Robin, A. (1976). The Turtle Technique: A Method for the Self-Control of Impulsive Behaviour. *In* J. D. Krumboltz and C. E. Thoreson (Eds.), *Counselling Methods,* pp. 157–163. Holt, New York.

Seligman, M. E. P. (1975). *Helplessness.* Freeman, San Francisco.

Seligman, M. E. P. and Hager, J. L. (1972). *Biological Foundations of Learning.* Appleton Century Crofts, New York.

Senn, M. J. E. (1959). Conduct Disorders. *In* W. E. Nelson (Ed.) *Textbook of Pediatrics.* W. B. Saunders, Philadelphia.

Shepherd, M., Oppenheim, B. and Mitchell, S. (1971). *Childhood Behaviour and Mental Health.* University of London Press, London.

Sidman, M. (1960). *Tactics of Scientific Research: Evaluating Experimental Data in Psychology.* Basic Books, New York.

Spivack, G. and Shure, M. B. (1973). *Social Adjustment of Young Children: Cognitive Approach to Solving Real-life Problems.* Jossey-Bass, San Francisco.

Staats, A. and Staats, C. (1963). *Complex Human Behaviour.* Holt, Rinehart and Winston, New York.

Stolz, S. B., Wienckowski, L. A. and Brown, B. S. (1975). Behaviour modification: A perspective on critical issues. *American Psychologist,* **30**, 1027–1048.

Strupp, H. H. (1977). A Reformulation of the Dynamics of the Therapist's Contribution. *In* A. S. Gurman and A. M. Razin (Eds.), *Effective Psychotherapy: A Handbook of Research,* pp. 1–22. Pergamon Press, Oxford.

Stuart, R. B. (1971). Behavioral Contracting within the Families of Delinquents. *Journal of Behavior Therapy and Experimental Psychiatry,* **2**, 1–11.

Thelen, M. H., Fry, R. A., Dollinger, S. J. and Paul, S. C. (1976). The use of videotaped models to improve the interpersonal adjustment of delinquents. *Journal of Consulting and Clinical Psychology* **44**, 492.

Thomas, A., Chess, S. and Birch, H. G. (1968). *Temperament and Behaviour Disorders in Children.* University of London Press, London.

Toone, R. (1981). *Unpublished Case Study,* Child Treatment Research Unit, School of Social Work, Leicester University.

Trower, P., Bryant, B. and Argyle, M. (1978). *Social Skills and Mental Health.* Methuen, London.

Turner, R. K. (1973). Conditioning treatment of nocturnal enuresis: Present status. *In* I. Kolvin, R. C. MacKeith and S. R. Meadow (Eds.), *Bladder Control and Enuresis.* Heinemann, London.

Ulman, J. D. and Sulzer-Azaroff, B. (1975). Multielement baseline design in educational research. *In* E. Ramp and G. Semb (Eds.), *Behaviour Analysis: Areas of Research and Application.* University of Kansas Press, Kansas.

Urbain, E. S. and Kendall, P. C. (1980). Review of social-cognitive problem-solving interventions with children. *Psychological Bulletin,* **88**, (No. 1), 109–143.

Van Hasselt, V. B., Hersen, M., Whitehill, M. B. and Bellack, A. S. (1978). Social skills assessment and training for children: An evaluative review. *Behaviour Research and Therapy,* **17**, 413–437.

Van Lieshout, C., Leckie, G. and Van-Sonsbeck, B. (1976). Social perspective-taking training: empathy and role-taking ability of preschool children. *In* K. F. Riegel and J. A. Meachem (Eds.), *The Developing Individual in a Changing World.* Aldine, Chicago.

Vila, J. and Beech, H. R. (1978). Vulnerability and defensive reactions in relation to the human menstrual cycle. *British Journal of Social and Clinical Psychology,* **17**, 93–100.

Wahler, R. G., Winkel, G. H., Peterson, R. F. and Morrison, D. C., (1965). Mothers as behaviour therapists for their own children. *Behaviour Research and Therapy,* **3**, 113–124.

Walker, H. M. and Buckley, N. K. (1974). *Token Reinforcement Techniques.* Engelmann-Becker, Oregon.

Watson, J. B. and Rayner, R. (1920). Conditioned emotional reactions. *Journal of Experimental Psychology,* **3**, 1–14.

Welsh, R. S. (1968). *The use of stimulus satiation in the elimination of juvenile fire-setting behaviour.*

Paper read at the Eastern Psychological Association, Washington, D. C., April.

West, D. J. and Farrington, D. P. (1973). *Who Becomes Delinquent?* Heinemann, London.

White, R. W. (1959). Motivation Reconsidered—The Concept of Competence. *Psychological Review*, **66**, 297–333.

Wildman, R. W., II, and Wildman, R. W. (1975). The generalization of behaviour modification procedures: a review—with special emphasis on classroom applications. *Psychology in the Schools*, **12**, 432–448.

Wilson, G. T. and O'Leary, K. D. (1980). *Principles of Behaviour Therapy*. Prentice-Hall, Englewood Cliffs, N. J.

Yelloly, M. (1972). The Concept of Insight. *In* D. Jehu (Ed.), *Behaviour Modification in Social Work*. John Wiley, Chichester.

Zeilberger, J., Sampen, S. and Sloane, H. (1968). Modification of a child's problem behaviours in the home with the mother as therapist. *Journal of Applied Behaviour Analysis* **1**, 47–53.

Zimbardo, P. G. (1977). *Shyness*. Addison-Wesley, Reading, Mass.

Index

Page numbers in **bold type** indicate that more than a few lines are devoted to the subject in the text.
References in *italics* indicate diagrams or charts.